MATTIE P. WILSON

FROM DARKNESS TO LIGHT

Preparing for a Glorious Future

Gotham Books

30 N Gould St.
Ste. 20820, Sheridan, WY 82801
https://gothambooksinc.com/

Phone: 1 (307) 464-7800

© 2024 *Mattie P. Wilson*. All rights reserved.

No part of this book may be reproduced, stored in a retrieval system, or transmitted by any means without the written permission of the author.

Published by Gotham Books (June 18, 2024)

ISBN: 979-8-88775-875-6 (H)
ISBN: 979-8-88775-873-2 (P)
ISBN: 979-8-88775-874-9 (E)

Because of the dynamic nature of the Internet, any web addresses or links contained in this book may have changed since publication and may no longer be valid.

The views expressed in this work are solely those of the author and do not necessarily reflect the views of the publisher, and the publisher hereby disclaims any responsibility for them.

Table of Contents

Acknowledgement vii
Dedication viii
Preface ix
Chapter 1   **God is…** 1
    God's Creation 1
    Man Versus Animals 2
    Man and Woman 3
    The Flood: A Warning to All People 8

The Light that Preceded the Illuminated Present

Chapter 2   **The Love of God, The Word was Made Flesh** 15
    The Wisdom of Jesus 18
    What The Team Did to Our Lord: 21
Chapter 3   **Prophecy Fulfilled** 23
    Death 25
    Burial 27
    Resurrection 28
    Ascension 28

Dark Past Chained: Inhumane Treatment

Chapter 4   **The Life of the Black Man** 34
    The Long Battle for Freedom & Justice 35

The Illuminated Present

Chains have been removed: Freedom, Opportunities, Choices are ours

Chapter 5   **Going Forward** 56
    Gifts From God: Children 56

Children's First Example	56
Chapter 6 **Respect for God's House**	59
Where Should You Go?	61
Changes/Decisions	64
Spring Season of Life	69
Chapter 7 **Systemic Racism in America, the Beautiful**	71
USA-Leader of the Free World	71
Can we Co-exist Peacefully?	76
Hate Crimes in America	79
Light has Come, Yet it is Dark in America	81
Chapter 8 **Skin Color, the Barrier**	86
Discrimination	86
The Rule of the People	87
The War of Change	88
Chapter 9 **Partners in Love**	90
Consult God: Choose Your Mate	90
The Second Season of Life: Summer	91
Abortion/Pro-life	97
Chapter 10 **Church of Yester-Years**	102
In the Country	102
A Man of God	106
Christian Duties	109
Chapter 11 **Quiet Time/Before Work**	112
Morning Devotion	112
Right Mind-Set	117
Reflect on Paul's Experience	122
Chapter 12 **In Times of Loneliness**	125
Look-Up and Live	126
Chapter 13 **The Power of Prayer**	131
Third Season of Life: Fall or Autumn	131
The Christian's Daily Walk	132

Chapter 14	**Remembering the Clarkson Legacy**	137
	God Has Plans for Our Lives	138
Chapter 15	**Those Who Serve/Served Our Country**	146
	Brave Heroes	146
	An On-going War	150
Chapter 16	**Opportunities of Today**	152
	Making a Difference	152
	A Need for Change	164
Chapter 17	**The Dutiful Housewife**	173
	Her Job	173
	Her Husband's Job	175
Chapter 18	**Marriage/Divorce**	177
	Prestigious Wedding	177
	Disappointments	180
	The Modest Wedding	183
Chapter 19	**A Mind-Blowing Experience**	185
	Facing Adversity	185
	180 Degree Turn	190
	Deception or Betrayal	197
	The Dawning of a New Day	198
Chapter 20	**Church of Today**	202
	A Commandment to Evangelize	207
	Obey God	211
Chapter 21	**Giving According to God's Word**	224
	Be Faithful	224
	Know God's Word by Studying	226
Chapter 22	**Serving During Challenging Times**	233
	Anticipating the Winter Season	233
Chapter 23	**History Made in the USA**	238
	The Light of Day	238
Chapter 24	**Sickness and Medical Care**	246

Ups and Downs 247
Chapter 25 **Sickness and Death** 250
    Miraculous Improvement 250
    Dealing with Death 251
Chapter 26 **Nurses Support Group** 257
    Fourth Season of Life: Winter 257
    When the Patient Becomes Depressed 259
Chapter 27 **Perilous Times** 261
    Coronavirus Disesase 261
    Have We Forgotten Sodom & Gomorrah? 264

Glorious, Victorious Future For Prepared People

Chapter 28 **When All is Well** 266
    Confession of Sin to God 266
    The Fifth Season: On the Other Side Through 269
    Relevant Information 272
Chapter 29 **Rapture/Judgement** 277
    Tribulation Period 278
    The Devil is Bound 278
    The 2nd Coming of Jesus 280
    The Loosing of Satan 281
    Great White Throne Judgement 281
Chapter 30 **Joint Heirs with Christ** 285

JESUS IS LORD

Today is the day of salvation!
Accept Christ and form a relationship with him. He is King of Kings, Lord of Lords; the Great I Am! We must study the Word of God to avoid living in ignorance. In Him we will have shelter during the storms of life which are imminent and strength in weaknesses. He is our "Strong Tower." We may have peace with God knowing He is a Mighty God who is with us always, even until the end of the world. God is our Protector; our Source! **Choose life.**

God brought our forefathers through dark days of slavery, atrocities (wicked acts), doom and gloom. In spite of all, they still had hope. We, their offspring entered an illuminated era of hope and opportunities. To God be the glory for the things He has done. He sent his Son, Jesus, the **Light of the world, the Light of life;** He paid our sin debt in full. He did it all! GLORY to GOD!

Mattie P. Wilson

This narrative: FROM DARKNESS TO LIGHT
Subtitle: PREPARING FOR A GLORIOUS FUTURE
is
A Sequel to: THE JOURNEY FROM EARTH TO GLORY

Cover Photo:
Possibly, members from various churches congregated at the Old Galilee Baptist Church located on the corner of Williamson and Snow Streets in Shreveport, LA. The church was built in 1877 by **freed slaves**. Dr. Martin Luther King, Jr. spoke twice at the historic church. Its doors were closed in 1975.

The exact date the photo was taken is not known. We do know it was made prior to 1975.

Photographer: Unknown

Review of: The Journey From Earth to Glory
by James J.

The Journey touches on a plethora of topics. Firstly, the author wrote about the creation of man and the bias that exists in today's world between black and white races. She further discussed the four seasons of life, which are spring, summer, fall and winter, and gave the insightful significance of these seasons when applied to how we live as humans. They represent different stages of life and activities as well as character traits incidental to those stages.

The author wrote about the birth of Jesus and the love of God toward us. She also talked about mate selection, parenting, the benefits of quiet time and prayer, etc. She gave tips on how to get through loneliness. Read **The Journey from Earth to Glory** to get Mattie P. Wilson's perspective on life.

I love the simplicity of the book. This allows the reader a chance to understand her words without difficulty. I also love the use of illustrations and stories to explain certain topics in the book. The stories and illustrations made for easy assimilation of the message the author was passing across to the readers. I love the use of seasons to explain the different stages of life because that is something everybody can relate to. Loneliness is a feeling I am very conversant with in my personal life; her tips on how to deal with such feelings changed my life for the better.

This book is recommended to believers and new converts because it will enable them to grow in Christ and know what to do when they face certain challenges. I also recommend this book to parents who desire to learn a few things about godly parenting. This will also be a great read for you if you are hoping to learn how to navigate through the different stages of life.

May 23, 2022

From Darkness:
Chained, Inhumane Treatment

To Light:
Unchained, Freedom, Opportunities; Choices

Preparing for a Glorious Future

INTRODUCTORY SONG

"Because He Lives"

Written
By
Bill and Gloria Gaither

Portrays the Accounts...

ACKNOWLEDGEMENT

Father God, <u>I thank you</u> for bringing our forefathers through the Dark Ages of Slavery. The era was wrapped with death and defined by atrocities. We entered an Illuminated Present; a time of opportunities and choices. The chains have been broken; You are blessing us to excel. We are free to study Your word, achieve our dreams and prepare for a glorious future.

To you Lord God be the glory for the things You have done! With Your love, You have saved us. With Your power, You have kept us. With Your strength, You have been and is our guide.

All to Thee we owe.
Thank You Father!

DEDICATION
to
"My Girls"

Kashundra L. Wilson-Lynch, MBA, BS-CIS
Director of Child Nutrition for Caddo Parish Schools
&
Cheryl C. Wilson-Cuningham, RN-ADN, LVN, ORT, USNC
Dallas Regional Hospital

Work hard and cheerfully at all you do, just as though you were working for the Lord and not merely for your masters, remembering that it is the Lord Christ who is going to pay you, giving you your full portion of all he owns. He is the one you are really working for.
                                                              Colossians 3: 23-24 TLB

PREFACE

Non-Fiction Narrative: From Darkness to Light is a sequel to "The Journey from Earth to Glory."

From Darkness to Light demonstrates how God in his infinite wisdom caused the division of darkness and light. He created man and placed him in a perfect environment.

The narrative paints a vivid picture of yester-years and its atrocities; it mirrors specific sections of "The Journey." Recorded notable historical events will grasp one's undivided attention. Photos tell the story better than anyone can explain the heartache. Some happenings are almost too much for the human mind to comprehend. This generation may be totally astonished! They cannot identify with such occurrences.

God did that which man could not do for himself. Progress began after the removal of the chains of bondage (slavery or Involuntary Servitude). Therefore, blinders have been removed, light can be seen shinning clearly and illuminates safe passage. Thereby, progress has become a reality and is unstoppable. The narrative assures the future is bright for those who prepare for it.

We must choose Christ for everlasting life; come out of darkness (the world) and walk in the light. Forsake the ways of the heathens. The narrative sets a precedence and illustrations magnify most chapters.

Let me be clear: We must acknowledge All-Mighty God. His word says: Trust in the Lord with all thine heart and lean not to thine own understanding. In all thy ways acknowledge him (God) and he shall direct thy path. Sometimes we think we know what we want in life, which path to take, but our desires may not be best. God knows what we are best suited for because he knows our ability or several abilities.

Moses penned: If you will only listen and obey the commandments of the Lord your God that I am giving you today, he will make you the head and not the tail, and you shall always have the upper hand.
Deuteronomy 28:13 TLB

Moses wrote concerning obedience to God.

The narrative outlines achievements and it is my desire to encourage our young people to reach for the stars. Many who are not so young may also be encouraged to finish what was started before disaster interrupted their lives, or their goals were derailed. It is a true saying: You can begin again.

We, the Ambassadors for Christ must work while it is day, when night comes, no man can work (when we close our eyes in death). We have been called out of darkness into God's <u>marvelous light</u> and must work to reach the loss (the unsaved). We must work courageously to reclaim backsliders; strive to be a living example, wholly and acceptable unto God. Note: Right living makes righteous and prepares one for a glorious future in that land where we will never grow old.

CHAPTER 1
GOD is

God is Holy, All-Mighty, our Creator, Maker, Merciful and Everlasting Father. God is omnipotent, omnipresent and no one can compare to Him. In Him is life and there is no <u>darkness</u>. He is the way, the truth and the <u>Light</u>. God is and always will be! Soloman was wise and his wisdom was from God who is All-Wise. Augusta Rodin designed the "thinker," a male clay figurine of heroic. It conveys the impression of a man in deep thought while using his <u>right hand to supports his head</u>. Let's say, his thoughts were directed "upward." We must look upward to God, Our Father who has all knowledge. He holds the <u>world in His hand</u> and there is no failure in Him. He has all the answers. Consult God today! Christ is our "hero."

GOD'S CREATION
<u>Darkness</u> was upon the face of the deep...

In the beginning was the Word (Christ), *and the Word was with God, and the Word was God. He was with God in the beginning. Through him all things were made; without him nothing was made that has been made.*

John 1 NIV

<u>God created everything</u>, the heaven and the earth, which was without form and void; **<u>darkness</u>** was upon the face of the deep.

God said, "Let there be light; there was light. God saw the light and it was good. He divided the **light from the darkness**. God called the light day; he called the darkness night. He made the firmament (the heaven). He divided the waters which were under the heaven from the waters which were above the heaven. And God said, Let the waters under the heaven be gathered together unto one place, and let the dry land appear: and it was. And God called the dry land Earth. He called the gathered together waters seas. Everything God did was good. God spoke and the Earth brought forth grass, the herb yielding seed, and the fruit tree yielding fruit after his kind, whose seed is in itself, upon the earth. All was good. God said, Let there be lights in the firmament of the heaven to divide the day from the night; and let them be for signs, and for seasons, and for days, and years. God is awesome! He made two great lights; the greater light (sun) to rule the day and the lesser light (moon) to rule the night; He made the stars also. They give light upon the Earth and divide the light from the darkness. And God said, Let the waters bring forth abundantly the moving creature that hath life, and fowl that may fly above the earth in the open firmament of heaven. And God created great whales, and every living creature that moveth, which the waters brought forth abundantly, after their kind, and every winged fowl after his kind: and God saw that it was good. And God said, Let the earth bring forth the living creature after his kind, cattle, and creeping thing, and beast of the earth after his kind: and it was so. God has a purpose for everything which he spoke into being. No one could do this but God and there was no one before him. He is the first and the last. O' the power of Almighty God!

MAN VERSUS ANIMALS

*And God said, Let us make man in our image, after our likeness...*God, our Creator refers to Himself. He uses the plural pronouns "us" and "our." He said, let us ***make man*** *-someone like ourselves to be master of all life upon the earth and in the skies and in the sea."* (Genesis 1:26 TLB). We refer to "us" as God the Father, God the Son and God the Holy Spirit. Only God is our Creator.

After God's creation was finished, He ceased from his work. He blessed the seventh day and declared it holy.

God supplied man with everything that he needed to survive. Life began in the Garden of Eden also called Paradise. Africa is where the Garden of Eden is located. Many refer to it as the mother land. There God created man (formed him from the dust of the ground) in his own image. He breathed into his nostrils the breadth of life. And so, it is written, **The first man, Adam was made a living soul.** The Lord God placed man in the Garden of Eden as its gardener to tend and care for it. A river ran from Eden and separated into four rivers: Pishon, Gihon, Tigris and Euphrates. Rivers/Water= One of the most essentials for the survival of man. It is sometimes referred to as H (hydrogen) 2 (Oxygen). Man had everything he needs for survival.

MAN AND WOMAN

God is all-knowing; he knew that man was lonely. And the Lord said, *"It is not good for man to be alone; I will make a companion for him, a helper suited to his needs."* God created Woman. He did NOT create another man to be Adam's helpmate. He took a rib from Adam's side and he made woman (woman from man). She was created to be by man's side. Her name is Eve which means life-giving. Eve is the mother of all living. Since the creation of Eve all living have been born of **woman**. No male can take credit for the birth of a child except to be a sperm donor. If there were no women, there would be no "births." All living are off-springs of Adam and Eve. A man needs a woman in order to reproduce. God said unto them (Adam and Eve), *be fruitful and multiply, and fill the earth*. We must recognize God's order: Man + Woman+ Children = Family. God ordained the family. **Let's be clear**, there is no other way to fill the earth, not by woman and woman, not by man and man. A woman cannot be a father and neither can a man be a mother. Only a woman is suited to meet the needs of man. Regardless of what the courts may rule, God set the standards; any time man deviates from what God says there will be problems.

Adam and Eve were the first husband and wife (male and female). They had three sons: Cain, Abel and lastly Seth. Cain was a farmer; Abel became a shepherd. Seth was the father of Enosh; Eve became the mother of all mankind.

Bobby R. Taylor & wife, Thelma Taylor
Bobby is the Grandson of Willie Clarkson

Marriage is a God-ordained, covenant relationship between a <u>man and a woman</u>.

Bobby and Thelma have three sons: Reginald is a Fire-Fighter, protector of lives and property. Kelvin is a Barber and Omarsa is an Autonomous Vehicle Specialist.

Man has intellectual faculties or one may say man's brain dictates to him how to respond. He also has spiritual qualities and he was <u>made in the image of God.</u> Notice the contrast: Animals were <u>spoken into being.</u> They are not on the same level as human beings and when they are dead, <u>they are done</u>! It's over for them!

Fast-forward: Not so for Man, he has to go before God for judgement. GOD is the JUST JUDGE. One may appear before many judges while on this journey called LIFE and <u>many</u> are not just! May I serve notice to them: You must also stand before the Judge, God Almighty.

So, then every one of us shall give account of himself to God.
Romans 14:12 KJV

God spoke to a man and a woman. He is a God of order and His word says in I Cor. 14:40 KJV

*Let **all** things be done decently and in order.*

There is a right way to do all things. Although man tends to do what he will when he chooses to. We must be cognizant of the fact: Consequences for our actions.

Adam had everything that he needed; like disobedient man of this generation, he messed up. Paradise was lost because of sinful man. As previously stated, Adam and Eve had two sons, Cain and Abel. Cain slaughtered his brother Abel and the first murder was committed. *Cain was banished from the ground which he defiled with his brother's blood. He became a fugitive and a tramp upon the earth, wandering from place to place.* Adam and Eve had another son, Seth meaning "Granted" after Cain slew Abel.

Today, the murder rate is at an all-time high. Jealousy, hatred, sinful acts; all manner of evil continues. Fathers are against sons and mothers are against daughters. These are perilous times and the world is filled with chaos! Because of chaos and evil deeds, the world is dark.

Cain went out from the presence of the Lord and settled in the land of Nod. His wife conceived and presented him with a baby son named Enoch. The Bible does not state that Adam and Eve had other children, but since they were the first husband and wife, there were other children. Cain's wife was possibly his niece or maybe his cousin. The Bible does not say who she was. In those days, men married their relatives. How do I know this?

So, Isaac called for Jacob and blessed him and said to him, "Don't marry one of these Canaanite girls. Instead, go at once to Padanaram, to the house of your grandfather Bethel, and marry one of your cousins---your Uncle Laban's daughters. God Almighty bless you and

give you many children; may you become a great nation of many tribes!

Genesis 28: 1-4 TLB

Know this:
By the first man (Adam) came death. For as in Adam all die. *Everyone dies because all of us are related to Adam, being members of his sinful race, and wherever there is sin, death results. But all who are related to Christ will rise again.*

1 Corinthians 15:22 KJV

The earth has been filled. *And God hath made of one blood all nations of men for to dwell on all the face of the earth, and hath determined the times before appointed, and the bounds of their habitation;*

Acts 17: 26 KJV

Habitation means living in a particular place (on planet earth) This was established by God. He did not say that man is to dwell on either of the other planets. We must remember God is all-knowing (omnipotent); an all-wise God. His thoughts are not our thoughts and His ways are past finding out.

Isaiah penned, *Who else has held the oceans in his hands and measured off the heavens with his ruler? Who else knows the weight of all the earth and weighs the mountains and the hills? Who can advise the Spirit of the Lord or be his teacher or give him counsel? Has he ever needed anyone's advice?* Glory!!

Isaiah 40: 12-14 TLB

The Way of Man
Man has become so adventurous, wise yet weaker. He chooses to do his own thing his own way. He thinks he can go to the moon! God is in control of everything. He placed man where he wants him to dwell and He told him to subdue (conquer) the earth, no other planets. Man will eventually destroy or out-smart himself. If God wanted man on Planet Mars, He would have formed him there. Man cannot change God's plan! Things happen by His permissive will or His divine will! We must remember: Satan disrupts peace by going to and fro seeking whom he may devour or destroy. We must be vigilant; seek God's will. Sometimes man does things which are contrary to the will of

God. I recall, there is a way that seems right to a man, but the end thereof are the ways of death.

Attention:
Satan is a dirty fighter and the father of all lies! We remember, God asked Satan, *Have you considered My servant Job*? Job was a good man who stayed away from evil and he feared God. Satan wanted him to turn away from God and fall into disbelief. After Satan went out from the presence of the Lord, he struck Job with boils. In all this, Job did not sin or charge God with wrong.

He asked God three questions:

      1. Wherefore was I born?
      2. How can man be just with God?
      3. If a man die shall he live again?

God asked Job: *Where were you when I laid the foundations of the earth?* (Job 38:4) *Have you ever in your days commanded the morning light?*

Job 38:12

The point is: God is in control; He has the last word. God can do whatever he chooses to do.

The Narrative Continues...
Noah, the son of Lamech (a wicked descendant of Cain) was 500 years old and had three sons: Shem, Ham and Japheth. A population explosion took place upon the earth. *Beings from the spirit world looked upon the beautiful earth women and took any they desired to be their wives. In those days, and even afterwards, when the evil beings from the spirit world were sexually involved with human women, their children became giants.*

Genesis 6:4

The Lord saw that man had become wicked and it broke his heart. He was sorry he had made them. And he said, "I will blot out from the face of the earth all mankind that I created. Yes, and the animals too, and the reptiles and the birds. For I am sorry I made them."

Genesis 6:7 (TLB)

Noah was the only truly righteous man living on the earth <u>at that time</u>. He found grace in the eyes of the Lord. God decided to destroy all mankind, for the earth is filled with crime <u>because of man.</u> God told Noah to make a boat. He was given all the instructions to complete it. The boat was built with three decks and a door in the side. <u>Noah</u> warned the people that it was going to rain, but they ignored him. Within the time frame of 120 years the people could have repented and changed their ways. However, they kept doing as they desired. After the boat was finished, Noah and his family (his wife, sons and their wives) entered into the Ark. The animals went into the Ark two by two. Please note: Two of every animal (male and female) of sheep, goats, cattle and so forth. The reason was for each pair of animals to reproduce its own kind. Noah was 600 years old when the flood came.

The Flood: A Warning to All People

God brought judgement upon the people...
It rained forty days and forty nights without stopping. Didn't it rain; rain?

For forty days the roaring floods prevailed, covering the ground and lifting the boat high above the earth. As the water rose higher and higher above the ground, the boat floated safely upon it; until finally the water covered all the high mountains under the whole heaven, standing twenty-two feet and more above the highest peaks. It rained!!!

Geneses 8:17-19 TLB

After the flood waters receded, the zebra didn't interact (sexually) with the giraffe!!!! Each animal reproduced with <u>his own kind!!!!!</u>

Animals were not to be crossbred (the mating of animals from two different breeds).
Man has a <u>mind</u> of his own! What did he do? How did he react after the flood?
Listen: Noah planted a vineyard, made <u>wine</u>, got drunk and laid naked in his tent.
Incidentally, alcohol clouds ones' judgement or makes it difficult to think clearly.

Ham saw his father's nakedness and went and told his two brothers. Shem and Japheth took a robe and held it over their shoulders; walked backwards into the tent and covered their father's nakedness. Noah awoke from his drunken stupor, learned what happened and what Ham had done. He cursed Ham's descendants. *"A curse upon the Canaanites,"* he swore. <u>*"May be the lowest of slaves to the descendants of Shem and Japheth."*</u> A curse is an utterance intended to inflict punishment on someone. Fact: It was not about what Ham had done because he did nothing wrong. It was what Noah did. He brought shame upon himself by indulging in wine and exposing himself. <u>Today, some blame others for their mistakes</u>. Noah chose to punish Ham unjustly by declaring a curse upon his descendants, the Canaanites. They spoke Semitic languages, constituting a subfamily of the Afro-Asiatic family...

And the sons of Noah, that went forth of the ark, were Shem, and Ham, and Japheth: and <u>Ham is the father of Canaan</u>. Canaan is the land which the tribes of Israel conquered after an Exodus from Egypt. Israel is the Promised Land where God's covenant with Abraham and his off springs was affirmed. God promised to be the God of Abraham's offspring and gift them the land of Canaan. *These are the three sons of Noah: Shem, Ham, and Japheth and of them was the whole earth overspread* (Genesis 9:18-19*). And all the days of Noah were nine hundred and fifty years: and he died.* O' what a life!

The Tower of Babel (meaning <u>confusion</u>)
There was one language; one speech in the whole earth. Noah's post-flood descendants remained in one location in defiance of God's command. They said let us build us a <u>city and a tower</u>, whose top may reach unto heaven. They had brick for stone and slime for mortar.

They said, "Let us make us a name for fear that we be scattered abroad upon the face of the whole earth." God is all-knowing and his eye is in every place. His timing is perfect! Listen to what God did.

Genesis 11:5-7: *But when God came down to see the city and the tower mankind was making, he said, "Look! If they are able to accomplish all this when they have just begun to exploit their linguistic and political unity, just think of what they will do later! Nothing will be unattainable for them! Come, let us go down and give them different languages, so that they won't understand each other's words!"* God scattered them all over the earth; and that ended the building of the city. God has the power to disrupt anything that is not His will.

PAUSE:
Sometimes there is confusion/division within the body of Christ (the church). One may not understand another. The church is under attack; not everyone is approachable. We know if a brother or sister has a problem with another, he should go to the member privately and confront him. However, some members are not willing to reason with others. Some are right in their own eyes. Jesus said, *"If a brother sins against you, go to him privately and confront him with his fault. If he listens and confesses it, you have won back a brother."* (Matthew 18:15)

CONTINUE:
Remarkable/God's Timing
There was a shortage of food in Canaan and the Israelites were forced to leave. Egypt's leader, Pharaoh enslaved them. While the children of Israel were held in bondage they cried. Their cry came up unto God and he heard their groaning. Scripture states: *God remembered his covenant with Abraham, with Isaac, and with Jacob. God looked upon the children of Israel, and God had respect unto them. And the Lord said, I have surely seen the affliction of my people which are in Egypt, and have heard their cries by reason of their taskmaster; for I know their sorrows...* (Exodus 2, 3 KJV). God delivered them out of the hand of the Egyptians.

The Deliverer: Moses, his Test

He was born in the land of Goshen during the Jewish enslavement in Egypt. His parents were Jochebed and Amram. During that time, Pharaoh decreed that all Hebrew male babies be drowned. Moses was placed in a basket in the Nile River. He was recovered and became the son of Pharaoh's daughter. He grew and in the course of time, God's people (Israelites) were in bondage over four hundred years in Egypt. God chose Moses to deliver them to the Promised Land. Moses encountered what many viewed as a problem: The Red Sea was before him and the Israelites; Pharaoh's army was behind them. Moses realized the situation was too big for him to handle in his own strength, but he had the assurance that God would do battle for him and the Israelites. They appeared to be trapped in a mercy situation. <u>Some of the followers blamed Moses for their predicament</u> yet, he put his trust in God. He believed if God brought them to the Red Sea, He would bring them through the Red Sea. Even with Pharaoh's army in close pursuit, Moses still trusted God.

<u>PAUSE...</u>
When the pastor gives orders in the church, the congregation trust that he is following orders from God. Although the members do not always understand the pastor's orders. We know that he is the under Sheppard (appointed head) and Christ is the head of the church. <u>We pray</u> that he is being led by God; <u>we pray</u> that God will give him understanding of His will. Should the appointed head fall, the body will fall as well. It cannot stand without a head.

<u>CONTINUE...</u>
When Moses stood on the rock which was solid, he was standing on <u>rock-solid faith</u>. He stretched out his rod and demanded the people to stand still and see the ocular demonstration: God made a highway through the Red Sea. I can imagine the mighty hand of God divided the waters with a swift wind, thereby providing dry land. After the Israelites crossed over, Pharaoh's army continued to pursue them. They met their fate and were drowned in the sea which overflowed or swallowed them up. Pharaoh watched God work. He gave orders, but he did not pursue the Israelites any further. He was DONE! When God says, "It's over," it is over. No one can fight a battle like the Lord. Amen! God will take care of our <u>enemies</u>.

You will look for your enemies, but you will not find them. Those who fought against you will vanish completely.

Isaiah 41:12 KJV

Did the complainers apologize to Moses after they crossed the Red Sea? What seemed impossible to them was an opportunity for God to show his power. Moses was the chosen one to lead the people out of captivity. He encountered God as he observed a burning bush that was not destroyed on Mount Horeb. There he accepted God's charge and followed His instructions. Perhaps the Israelites could not see what Moses saw. He believed God and his spiritual eyes were on the Way Maker. Sometimes our thoughts are wrong and we do not always understand, but we must trust God's process. We make mistakes in life; we must admit them and ask God for forgiveness. Yet, they are still behind us and time and time again someone will speak of them. Something happens and we are reminded. If one does not mention them, someone else will. That does not mean that we will dwell on them. The important thing to remember is: God will be merciful unto us; He will remember our wrongdoings no more. When they are brought to light, perhaps someone will learn a lesson; discover another pathway. Praise God, your past helped shape your future. Sometimes we need to re-tell the story; shed light on a specific topic. Face facts: The truth will stand; our sins will find us out. We must learn to deal with the facts!

I agree with Paul, God's peace will keep your thoughts and your hearts quiet and at rest as you trust in Christ Jesus. Fix your thoughts on what is true and good and right. Think about things that are pure and lovely, and dwell on the fine, good things in others. Think about all you can praise God for and be glad about it. Praise God today for all he has done for you. He has done "great" things for all of us. Truth of the matter is: All of us have a story!

We must have faith, hope and love; the greatest of these is "love." Apostle Paul explained the true meaning of love in I Corinthians 13: 4-7. He emphasized Love is patient and kind. When we mistreat our fellowman there is a lack of love. Nothing is done secretly because God has an all-seeing eye. His word say: Vengeance is mine, I will repay, so there is no need to try to even the score. There is always hope when we keep our minds stayed on Jesus! Our actions must be motivated by love and not hatred, jealousy or the like. Jesus is Our Rock, even when the whole world seems to be set against us. He is Our Way Out! Nothing is hidden from his view and he holds all our tomorrows in his hand. Perhaps one of the songs of the day for those who were enslaved was: Standing on the Promises of God. I might add: We are still standing on the Word of God because we know He will do just what He said. He is God and he cannot lie.

We remember Abraham...

<u>Abraham trusted God</u> and left home to go to a land far away. He was confident that God had his best interest at heart. He founded a new nation and is known as the father of the faithful. When we find ourselves in the valley of despair and face disappointments it is hard to say, "I trust God." But let us trust him anyway. At this time our courage is being tested, but God is still there! Recall he will never leave you nor forsake you. When it seems like God is silent trust him anyway. Keep calling him and I assure you He will answer. Sometimes things happen, situations become burdensome and we feel helpless. We cannot solve some problems. Take them to the "Counselor," step back and watch Him work. The battle is no longer ours; it is the Lord's.

The Light that Preceded the Illuminated Present

Jesus is the **light** of the world; he was in the beginning with God. When God said, "Let there be light" light appeared. And God was pleased with it, and divided the light from the darkness. This same Light which was in the beginning with God made it possible for us to become children of God. In the beginning of Jesus' ministry, Matthew recorded: *The people which sat in darkness saw great light; and to them which sat in the region and shadow of death light is sprung up. From that time Jesus began to preach, and to say, Repent: for the kingdom of heaven is at hand* (4:16-17 KJV).

God has called us out of darkness into his marvelous light. We must walk in the light and let our little lights shine. Let them shine so brightly the lost will find their way home. There is a home for prepared people. The lights will never go out nor be dim! Those lights are in that land where we will never grow old (The New Jerusalem)

Amen!

CHAPTER 2
The Love of God:
The Word was Made Flesh

Virgin Birth of Christ

Behold, a virgin shall be with child, and shall bring forth a son, and they shall call his name Immanuel, which being interpreted is God with us.
Matthew 1: 23 KJV

And Joseph went up from Galilee, out of the city of Nazareth, unto Judea, unto the city of David, which is called Bethlehem... To be taxed with Mary his espoused wife, being great with child. This message (good news) will continue to be told throughout the nation. It is the "Old, Old Story," yet it is a valuable one; it must be told in Jerusaleum and Samaria, and to the end of the world.

There is much controversy about "Christmas Day." We know that Christ was born of a virgin, Mary. That is the important fact and it does not matter that we know the exact date of his birth. God sent his Son to do what no other man could do because all are imperfect. Let us praise God today for Jesus!

O' what love! "Agape"

But when the <u>fullness of the time was come</u>, God sent forth his Son, made of a woman, made under the law, to redeem them that <u>were under the law</u>, that we might receive the <u>adoption of sons</u>
Galatians 4: 4-5 KJV

There was no room for them in the inn. Joseph and Mary were in need of shelter. Therefore, they accepted cover in a stable; there Christ, the Savior was born. Wise men brought gifts of gold, frankincense, and myrrh.

After eight days, the baby was circumcised (Jewish custom) and his name was called JESUS. Simeon, a man of Jerusalem was just and devout. And it was revealed unto him by the Holy Ghost that he should not die before he had seen the Lord's Christ. He was led by the Spirit into the temple and when the parents brought in the child Jesus (according to custom) Simeon took him up in his arms and blessed God, and said, *Lord, now let thy servant depart in peace, according to thy word* (Luke 2:29 KJV).

Old Testament Prophecy Predicted

The Messiah would be born in Bethleham. King Herod inquired of his wheareabouts stating he wanted to worship him, but not so. He initiated a murder to kill all the male infants two years old and younger. This was an attempt to kill the baby Jesus. Herod thought Jesus would overthrow his kingship. Jealousy led him to seek the death of Jesus.

Pause for a second: Today, centuries later man still seeks to kill others because of jealousy. For that reason many lives have been cut short. The evil act began when Cain slaughtered his brother Abel. It continues today...

CONTINUE...

From Egypt to Nazareth

Matthew recorded: Joseph came and dwelt in a city called Nazereth fulfilling the prophecy that Jesus would be called a Nazarene. Luke penned: *And the child grew, and waxed strong in spirit, filled with wisdom: and the grace of God was upon him.*

Luke 2:40 KJV

When the time was right, God sent his Son to pay the price that we could not pay. He came to die for sinful man. When God speaks, plans will be fullfilled. No one can obstruct or derail what God designs.

We know Jesus came into the world to save sin-sick souls. He came to die for us! It was <u>prophesied by Isaiah</u>: *But he was wounded for our transgressions, He was bruised for our iniquities: The chastisement of our peace was upon him; And with his stripes we are healed* (Isaiah 53:5). This was proclaimed by Isaiah long before the "Word" was made flesh, and he spoke as if Christ had already come. The fulfillment (birth of Christ) is recorded in the New Testament (Luke 2:8-16).

The Wisdom of Jesus

Jesus was teaching in the temple at the age of 12 years. He said, "I must be about my Fathers' business." After he ended his sayings, the people were astonished at his doctrine. Jesus taught as one with authority, and not as the scribes. He taught in parables which are earthly stories with a heavenly meaning. He came to seek and to save the lost and He lived a sinless life. He was identified as the carpenter's son and he was baptized by John the baptist in Jordan River. And a voice from heaven said, *"This is my beloved son, in whom I am well pleased."* Jesus went about doing good: He healed the sick, gave sight to the blind and multitudes followed him. He performed many miracles. Jesus called disciples to become fishers of men...

Miraculous Demonstration

We know that Mary and Martha's brother, Lazarus died and was buried. He was in the grave four days. Scripture tells us it was a cave and a stone lay upon it. The stone was removed at Jesus' command. Jesus called Lazarus to come forth. No one else has such power unless it is given him from God. Jesus raised Lazarus <u>from the dead</u> so that those who looked on would know that God had sent him (Jesus). Lazarus was raised from the dead a mortal soul and we know that he died again. Jesus has no respect of persons. He reaches out to the poor and needy. During a burial ceremony, Jesus arrived at the village of Nain and raised the son of a widow from the dead. Think of His goodness!

Jairus' daughter was raised from the dead; she was raised a mortal soul; she died again also. The point is: Jesus has supernatural power. He is God in the flesh. No one spoke like Jesus. <u>He is King of Kings and Lord of Lords!</u> There is no other god.

An Outspoken Character, Peter...

Peter, the Apostle, the Rock was one of the twelve Apostles of Jesus Christ. As a child, I heard the saying: "I hope St. Peter will let me into heaven." At that time, I did not know who St. Peter was. After studying God's word, I learned Jesus said to Peter:

"And I will give you the keys of the Kingdom of Heaven; whatever doors you lock on earth shall be locked in heaven; and whatever doors you open on earth shall be open in heaven!"
Matthew 16:19 TLB

Jesus was speaking directly to Apostle Peter. He meant that Peter would have the right to enter the kingdom himself. He would have general authority symbolized by the <u>possession of the keys</u>. Preaching the gospel would be the means of opening the kingdom of heaven (the spiritual realm over which God reigns as king or the fulfillment on Earth of God's will) to all believers and shutting it against unbelievers. By his sermon on the day of Pentecost, Peter opened the door of the kingdom for the first time. Bind or loose means to declare something forbidden or to declare it allowed. He used those keys on the day of Pentecost (Acts 2) when he announced that the door of the kingdom was unlocked to Jews and later to Gentiles (KJV).

Jesus told the disciples how he must go unto Jerusalem, and suffer many things of the elders and chief priest and scribes, and be killed, and be raised again the third day. Peter, the outspoken Apostle expressed disapproval. Jesus said to him, *"Satan, get behind me! You are looking at this only from a human point of view and not from God's"* (Mark 8:35 TLB). And Peter was with James and John on the Mount with Jesus during the transfiguration.

Triumphal Entry
Luke penned:
When Jesus had spoken, he ascended up to Jerusalem. After he mounted a colt, he came near to the mount of Olives. The whole multitude of the disciples began to rejoice and praise God with a loud voice <u>for all the mighty works that they had seen.</u> Don't be surprised when men falsely accuse you and say all manner of evil against you. They did the same to Jesus. Some of the same people who praised him turned against him.

After the Passover
Peter, the Out-spoken Character Denied Christ
Jesus said unto him (Peter), *Verily I say unto thee, that this night, before the cock crow, thou shalt deny me thrice* (Matt. 26:34). Scripture states, *Peter sat without in the palace and a damsel came unto him, saying, thou also was with Jesus of Galilee. But he denied before them all, saying, I know not what thou sayest. And when he was gone out into the porch, another maid saw him, and said unto them that were there, this fellow was also with Jesus of Nazareth. And again, he denied with an oath, I do not know the man. And after a while came unto him, they that stood by, and said to Peter, Surely, thou art one of them; for thy speech betrayed thee. Then began he to curse and to swear, saying, I know not the man. And immediately the cock crew* (Matt. 26: 69-74 KJV). Peter remembered what Jesus had said. But what will a man say or do in order to save himself? Choose Christ, he is the only one to depend on to be with you until the end.

Sometimes we are let down by those whom we trust, but Jesus is all-knowing and he said Peter would deny him! Today, we must walk closely with Jesus and the Holy Spirit will lead us around trouble. We must listen to the voice of the Holy Spirit.

Jesus was Betrayed
Judas Iscariot was one of the Twelve Apostles. Satan entered his heart, leading him to conspire with the priest and scribes to betray Jesus by disclosing his whereabouts for thirty pieces of silver. Money is the root of all evil and not all money is good money. Judas led men to arrest Jesus and identified him with a kiss. Listen: Not everyone who greets you with a kiss is your friend. Although Judas had walked with Jesus, yet he was motivated by Satan. Judas joined the disciples, who were in Bethany preparing for the Passover to celebrate in the upper room with his disciples. Passover celebrated God passing over the Israelites' home and not killing the firstborn males of each family.

WHAT THE TEAM DID TO OUR LORD:

They whipped Him and put a crown of thorns around his head. They teamed against Him and marched Him from one court room to another. There were two classes of Jewish courts which were called Sanhedrin Council. One was greater than the other. These were elders who were appointed to sit as a tribunal (bench of judges) in every city in Israel. Jesus was accused of <u>making himself the Son of God.</u> Were there some among the group who did not know the facts? Many had praised him for the mighty acts which they had seen. <u>Luke</u> declared: *When Jesus casts out demons, they fall down before him, and declare:* <u>*"you are the Son of God."*</u>

John the Baptist bears <u>witness</u> that Jesus is the Son of God (John 1:34*). Martha calls him the Messiah and <u>the Son of God</u>* (John 11:37). I call Jesus "My Everything." Who do you sat Jesus is?

The chief priest and officers raised their voices saying, "crucify him." Pilate said, "Take him and crucify him: for I find no fault in him."

Listen

When we do not find fault in our fellowman, we should not agree with the adversary or the enemy who claims to find fault in our neighbor. When we agree to get along with the one who is on the opposide side, we become as guilty as he! If the accused person is killed, his blood is on our hands. Pilate washed his hands, but Jesus' blood was still on them.

Thou shalt not bear false witness against thy neighbor.
Exodus 20:16 KJV

Solom penned, Lying lips are an abomination to the Lord.
Proverbs 12:22 KJV

On a hill called Calvary, they nailed Jesus' hands and riveted his feet to a cross; they lifted him up. I recall Jesus said, *"And I, if I be lifted up from the earth, I will draw all men unto me."* Our Lord and Savior was crucified; while on the cross, he was pierced in his side. Out came blood and water. We are saved because He shed his blood for us. Jesus could have come down from the cross, but He <u>decided to die to save you and me (sinful man). Jesus came into the world for that purpose</u>. If He had not died our souls would still be lost. This message is declared from pulpits, street conors, store-fronts across the country and all around the world weekly and possible daily by someone. Today, I declare it from the pages of this book. It must be told continuously and it will never be declared old. The blood of Jesus will never lose its power! The blood still works! All weary souls, come unto Jesus today!

The Call

Today is the day of salvation. O' sinner man, why not come to Christ today? We know not what tomorrow holds, but we know God holds all our tomorrows in his hands. He has the final say. We are aware that not all live to grow old, but some live as if they have no thought of dying. The sad thing is: Some don't make preparation to die either. Our forefathers said, "Come to Jesus while the blood is still running warm in your veins." One day the blood will come to a complete stop; the body will grow cold. Be ye also ready! <u>Please don't ignore the call. It's crucial!</u> Be reminded: The person who rejects Jesus Christ will receive a punishment greater than physical death.

CHAPTER 3
Prophecy Fulfilled

Carrying the Cross to Calvary or Golgotha

Jesus was made to carry his cross up the hill to be crucified between two thieves. He carried that weight for you and me. **A black man, Simon of Cyrene was among the crowd and he was compelled to give assistance.** Note: A black man has always been available and commanded to carry a load. Yet, today he is looked upon as a second-class citizen. He is often over-looked; disrespected time and time again, but he is conveniently used time and time again also.

CHRIST ON THE CROSS

In this picture which represents Christ on the cross, skin-tone has no specific meaning. We cannot verify that Christ is black or white. Let us be reminded: Differences in skin color ranges from darkest brown to the lightest hues. It is caused by variations in pigmentation, genetics and sexual selection. However, we know that Christ was conceived and born of a virgin and this was the work of the Holy Spirit. Christ was born unlike mankind. Nevertheless, Christ has no respect of persons; He died, paid a price that we could not pay. Amen! For that, I am grateful!

The European colonists (white men) have speculated that Christ is white. Artists have painted photos and displayed them depicting that Christ is white. Some blacks have said he is black. **They refer to the following description in Revelation**. Let us see what the Word of God says:

His head and his hairs were white like wool, as white as snow; and his eyes were as a flame of fire; and his feet like unto fine brass, as if they burned in a furnace; and his voice as the sound of many waters.
Revelation 1: 14-15 KJV

We must also consider the time-frame in which the book of Revelation was written and the circumstances. John, the Revelator was on the isle of Patmos and he had a **vision**. We cannot accurately describe Christ's appearance when he was with his desciples before his death. I am certain there was a difference (from the Revelation scripture). Had there not been, Judas would not have identified him with a kiss. This tells us that Christ's appearance was much like that of his disciples. Who can say precisely what race all the desciples were?

Death
The Crucifixion of Christ

But God commended his love toward us, in that, while we were yet sinners, Christ died for us.

Romans 5:8 KJV

For God so loved the world, that he gave his only begotten Son, that whosoever believeth in him should not perish, but have everlasting life.

John 3:16 KJV

Our sin was judged at the cross, it was at the cross that God pronounced judgement on the unbelieving world and on the enemy of our souls, Satan.

John penned: *Standing near the cross were Jesus' mother, Mary, his aunt, the wife on Cleopas, and Mary Magdalene. When Jesus saw his mother standing there beside me, his close friend, he said to her, "He is your son." And to me he said, "She is your mother!" And from then on I took her into my home.*

John 19:25-27 TLB

Jesus spoke from the cross 7 sayings:
- Father, forgive them for they know not what they do.
- Today shalt thou (the thief) be with me in paradise.
- Woman, behold, thy son! Behold, thy mother!
- My God, my God, why hast thou forsaken me?
- I thirst.
- It is finished (His work on earth).
- Father, into thy hands I commend my spirit.

O' what love! Jesus cried with a loud voice and after that saying, he gave up the ghost. Christ died on an old rugged cross. He died so that you and I might live and have life more abundantly. For that cause He came into the world. There's no love like my Father's love. O' PRAISE GOD TODAY!

Where were Peter and James, the other two of Jesus' inner circle? Why weren't they at the foot of the cross? They were beloved disciples of Jesus.

It was on a hill called Calvary...
Pilate allowed Joseph of Arimathea to take away the body of Jesus. **The bare cross**, is a symbol of suffering; reminds us that Christ paid our sin debt. He paid the price that we could not pay. All to Him we owe!

BURIAL OF JESUS

Joseph took the body of Jesus and wrapped it in a linen cloth. He laid his body in his own new tomb. He rolled a great stone to the door of the sepulcher. (Matt.27:59-60). Perhaps, the stone was to secure the door, but we thank God it could not prevent the resurrection of Christ. If he had not gotten up, our souls would still be lost. Today, we live because <u>He got up from the grave; we must tell the story.</u>

<u>PAUSE...</u>

<u>Today</u>, after a man dies his body is <u>embalmed or preserved</u> by arterial injection of a preservative. This takes place before the body is placed into a casket for burial. Scripture tell us: Our bodies will return to the dust of the earth. Christians will not get up from the grave until Jesus returns in mid-air. We (Christians) will receive a new body. The dead in Christ will rise first (resurrection of the just.)

<u>CONTINUE...</u>

Resurrection of Jesus

The stone was rolled away by an angel. *Jesus rose the third day* according to the scriptures (I Cor.15:4). He got up just as he said he would. Again, Jesus has supernatural power. He is God in the flesh; the grave could not hold him. Jesus conquered death. Amen! As I recall, a stone was laid upon Lazarus' grave but it was not final either. It was Jesus who said remove the stone and He called Lazarus to come forth. Jesus demonstrated his power. The difference or contrast is Lazarus died again, but <u>Jesus is alive forevermore! He died one time and He will not die again!</u> Now Christ is risen from the dead, (an immortal soul) and become the first fruits of them that slept. As forestated, others who were raised from the dead (mortal souls), and they died again.

By Christ (the second Adam), came the **resurrection** of the dead. In Christ shall all be made alive. Thanks be to God; we have victory through Jesus Christ. We are heirs of God and <u>joint-heirs with Jesus Christ</u>. We are children of God by adoption. Praise him for his love. Adoption as God's children is made possible by faith in Jesus Christ.

Ascension of Jesus

According to Luke, Jesus ascended. *While he blessed them, he was parted from them, and carried up into heaven* (Luke 24:50-51). He is seated at the right hand of the Father and He intercedes for us. Before Jesus ascended, He said,

But the Comforter, which is the Holy Ghost, whom the Father will send in my name, he shall teach you all things, and bring all things to your remembrance, whatsoever I have said to you.
John 14:26 KJV

No Greater Love

God loved us first. Let us love and honor him with our whole heart. Let us praise him because he is worthy to be praised. God sent His Son, (Jesus) who demonstrated his love toward us while we were yet sinners. He knew no sin. There is none like unto him. Praise Him! Let everything that has breath praise the Lord!

We Can't Find No One to Compare

- David was a man after God's own heart, yet he was not spotless or without sin. David had an affair and was a murderer.
- Gideon was a mighty soldier but he was afraid.
- Samson was a strong man but a womanizer.
- Noah was a righteous man who followed God's instructions and built a boat, but he got drunk.
- Abraham is the Father of the Faithful, he lied and said Sarai (his wife) was his sister.
- Therefore, neither of them was worthy to die for us; all of them had faults.
- Neither was any of the prophets worthy to die for us.
- Neither was any of the priests, all of them had faults. They were not allowed to continue by reason of death. All died and are still dead.

JESUS, OUR HIGH PRIEST IS ALIVE FOR EVERMORE!!!

God loves us so much. He was willing to sacrifice his only Son to pay our sin debt in full which no one else was worthy to pay. And unlike Man, God has no respect of persons. He loves the sinner, but He hates sin. Man could not keep the law to perfection. Christ kept it for us, He fulfilled the law. The just shall live by **faith**. Accept Christ as your Lord and Savior. In Christ shall all be made alive and thanks be to God; we have victory through Jesus Christ. Praise Him for His loving kindness. O' what love! O' what love!

We are heirs of God and joint-heirs with Jesus Christ. We are children of God by adoption. Praise him for his love. Adoption as God's children is made possible by faith in Jesus Christ. When one adopts a child it is by choice. The chosen one is truly blessed. This tells us that God truly loves us. Praise Him! If we follow the Light (Jesus), we will not walk in darkness!

But we are a chosen generation, a royal priesthood, an holy nation, a peculiar people; that we should shew forth the praises of him who hath called.
I Peter 2:9 KJV.

Our fore-fathers who accepted Jesus Christ as their Lord and Savior while enslaved recognized Him as the light.

Dark Past Chained: Inhumane Treatment

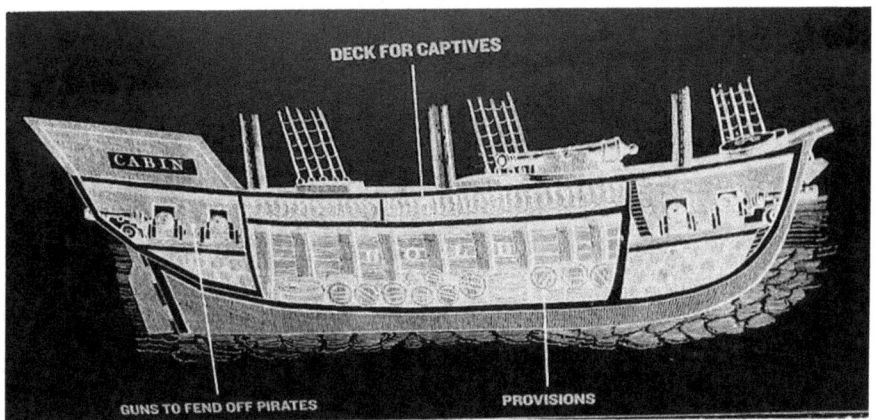

Photo was taken by permission
NCRM

While in grade school, I learned about the Mayflower Ship which transported the Pilgrims from England to the New World in 1620. However, I discovered later that the starting point to slavery in America dated back to 1619. **The privateer (armed ship) <u>The White Lion</u>** brought twenty enslaved Africans ashore to the British colony of Jamestown, Virginia. They established the Plymouth Colony in Plymouth, Massachusetts.

Slavery in America 1619---1863
"Declaration of Independence" Signed in 1776

America professed on paper: "All Men are Created Equal"
but, refused equal justice for the "black man"
This tell us: The black man was NOT considered.

Throughout the 17th and 18th centuries, people were kidnapped from the continent of Africa. They were **forced into slavery** in the American colonies and **exploited to work in the production of crops: tobacco and cotton.**

The Transatlantic Slave Trade Lasted more than 300 Years and Moved Millions of Africans Across the Atlantic Ocean. It was the Largest Forced Migration in Human History.

The black man, our forefathers were made to suffer physically and mentally. Pain was inflicted upon many as they attempted to escape slavery; many were hanged from a tree or lynched. The slave owners had no compassion for misery or suffering. In spite of the slave owner's brutal attacks and inhumane treatment, some chose to risk their lives to obtain freedom. I recall a familiar saying, "Before I be a slave, I will be buried in my grave and go home with my Lord and be free." I am reminded of another quote also.

"Give me liberty, or give me death!"

By: Patrick Henry

CHAPTER 4
Life of the Black Man

INHUMANE TREATMENT...

Photo was taken by permission
NCRM

PEOPLE AS PROPERTY

History lessons...
Slaves were freely bought and sold; they worked for slave owners. **The majority of slaves were born in the United States of America, not Africa.** Unfortunately, slaves were without power when their loved ones were sold as punishment, or as victims of changing laws. Children were separated from their parents. The cotton boom was the reason for the biggest exchange of people. Farmers were hungry for labor and willing to pay a high price for slaves. Slaves were moved through cities like New Orleans and Savanah. It was made known that by the outbreak of the **Civil War,** more than one million slaves had been sold. My grandfather made it known that there was no respect nor compassion for humankind! O' God of Our Fathers.
He said, "I hid under a bridge to keep from being taken as a slave."

The Civil War (1861—1865) was between the Union and the Confederacy. This was the discussion of the day by our forefathers. Mrs. and Mr. West were an elderly couple when I was a young child. They knew more than I could comprehend concerning slavery. It was beyond my wildest imagination. Mrs. West passed away at the age of 105years.

THE LONG BATTLE FOR FREEDOM

Sojourner Truth was an American women's rights activist. Her name at birth was: Isabella Baumfree, she was born into slavery.

According to the documentary
Harriet Tubman (Armenta Ross) was born into slavery; she was an American abolitionist. Her codename was "Moses." She had eight siblings and she escaped and made numerous missions to rescue enslaved people. They sang code songs such as "Wade in the Water," "Go Down Moses," "Soon I will be Done with the Trouble of the World," and "Up above my Head I Hear Music in the Air.

"The Custom / Rule"

Anyone who attempt to teach any free person of color, or slave, to spell, read, or write, shall be fined ...

<u>Bill Clarkson</u>, the father of my grandfather, Willie Clarkson was born in 1840.
He was reared in Ward 4, Red River Parish in Louisiana. He was married to Cloa Clarkson (my great grandmother). His mother was from the state of Georgia. <u>Enslaved people flowed through Savannah, Georgia.</u> My grandfather informed us of many things which happened during slavery.

In 1849, Harriet used the Underground Railroad and became the most famous "conductor" even though **she was illiterate and her life was full of hardships**. Let's remember Harriet for her courage and much needed leadership.

CREATING WEALTH THROUGH SLAVERY

Photo was taken by permission
NCRM

SLAVERY WAS BIG BUSINESS:
It is relevant that our children know in order to help them appreciate their options today. Investment in "human property" was said to exceeded investment in all of America's banks, factories, and railroads combined (a very sad situation).

From the teachings of professors:
Black men were freed from bondage of slavery (Emancipation Proclamation in 1863) by President Abraham Lincoln. My great grandfather was twenty-three (23) years old at that time. The proclamation declared that all persons held as slaves in the rebellious states were free. As a child, I was told: June 19, 1865 is the day that Union Army Major rode into Galveston, Texas and issued the message: African Americans there were free. They continued to work for meager wages as sharecroppers. They rented small plots of land to work for themselves. In return, they gave a portion of their crop to

the landowner. Thereby, they could not get out of debt; they were still bound by a form of **slavery**. It was declared to have ended; it was abolished in 1865. Sadly, Inhumane treatment continued <u>forty-six more years.</u>

REMINDER...
Dr. Martin Luther King, Jr. was a Civil Rights leader. He worked for justice for all man-kind. Yet he was assassinated in 1968 by one with a depraved mind. <u>Today, fifty-six years later</u>, the black man is still working for Civil Rights. Some with depraved minds are working to take the black man backwards instead of forward.

CONTINUE...
Field Order # 15
Our forefathers said...
Forty acres of land and a mule were promised to the slaves. That was part of a Special Field Order in 1865. The American Civil War was ending; land was to be allotted to 40,000 freed slaves. They were promised the land to start independent lives. So, what happened? The government didn't keep its promise after the assassination of President Abraham Lincoln. President Andrew Johnson was Lincoln's successor and he rescinded Field Order #15, a wartime order. Apparently, he was racist and preferred that black men remain slaves. He returned the land to White Confederate landowners. That was not fair by any means. The United States owe Black Americans for more than 200 years of labor. There is a battle cry for reparation (the making of amends for wrong) for slavery!!!! Yet, millions of acres of land were given to white peasants from Europe. America will answer to God! He is the true landowner!

Stature of Liberty
A souvenir (sewing thimble) was given to me by a co-worker, Irma D. Grant @ Louisiana State University Health Sciences Center

From my history class...

The monument, Stature of Liberty was given to the United States from France in <u>1884</u> as a symbol of friendship and liberty that citizens enjoy under a <u>free form of government.</u> We were told that it symbolizes **freedom and hope**. The black man was under cruel and oppressive government rule. History revealed: The stature was formerly designed to depict a black woman. However, the news was that some did not approve of the representation of a black figure which would stand atop a platform in the harbor. For that reason, changes were made to depict a white woman, the mother of the sculpturer. This was more acceptable or pleasing in the eyes of the white man. Although the black woman was the slave. The stature stands on Liberty Island in New York Harbor. It represents a woman donned in a robe which falls to the pedestal. Her right arm is held high; a large torch is in her hand held in the air. It has been said by visitors that it gleams at night with a powerful light as a <u>symbol of liberty</u> and sheds light upon the world. **A tablet is in her left arm. The Declaration of Independence date is written thereon.** A distinguished or unusual crown is on her head; at her feet is a <u>broken</u>

<u>shackle</u> which symbolizes the overthrow of tyranny.

We thank God for those who fought for liberty and the baton has been passed on to other believers. There must be liberty and justice for all; we must fight on and keep hope alive. White superiority is a myth. The white man has ruled for centuries, but his rule will come to an end. Christ is on his way back and he will set things in order.

Behold, he cometh with clouds; and every eye shall see him, and they also which pierced him: and all kindreds of the earth shall wail because of him (Revelation 1:7 KJV).

Be sure; very sure that your name is written in the <u>lamb's book of life</u>. Then and only then will you be declared **<u>independent; free</u>**, no shackle will have you bound. If anyone's name is not found written in the book of life, he will be thrown into the lake of fire. He shall be tormented day and night for ever and ever. Don't delay, but call Jesus today and gain salvation. The only way to escape torment is by accepting Jesus Christ as Lord and Savior. He is the door to heaven and it is written. Jesus answered, "I am the way and the truth and the life. No one comes to the Father except through me." John 14:6 NIV.

Lynching took place in 1911
Photo was supplied by a friend

History Lesson:

The National Association for Advancement of Colored People (NAACP) made an urgent request to government authorities. They shared concerns and a resolution of protest demanding action against lynching and cruel inhumane treatments. **<u>Lynching</u>** is such an extremely wicked act. How can anyone turn a blind eye to such atrocities? How could any human ignore the cries of the people?

Bible History in 979 BC
Unexpected lynching which was not ordered...

Absalom was the third and favorite son of King David. He is best known for his <u>betrayal of his father</u>. It was sparked by the fact that Amnon <u>raped his sister, Tamar</u>. He met his death surprisingly. Absalon (29 years old) was riding his mule, and as the mule went under the branches of a large oak tree, his head was caught in the tree. He was left hanging in midair, while the mule he was riding kept going. A very sad ending. We must be careful how we treat people.

The History Story Continues...
Notable Accomplishments despite atrocities

George Washington Carver will be remembered for his inventions of peanut products. The traffic signal and automatic elevator doors were invented by black men. Those men made daily life easier. A Muslim mathematician and astronomer is known as the father of algebra. Many tools were made in Africa and some thirty percent of the worlds mineral reserves are in Africa. The continent of Africa has forty percent of the world's gold (rich and fertile land). Whose home is Africa?

Black History...

Let's remember: <u>Many black men invented practical items which we use every day:</u> the ironing board, hair comb, hair brush and the list goes on and on. The history books do not contain all the records of black inventors. They are numerous and it is amazing to say the least. Every month is <u>"Black History Month."</u> America was built on what the black man has done. Yet, he is labeled a second-class citizen.

When black men had no resources to obtain a patent, who got the credit? <u>I didn't hear your answer.</u> In recent years, a renowned company took advantage of many, deceived them by assuring they would assist them in obtaining a patent/copyright. The company was paid a hefty price, but did not deliver as promised. They may have gotten by, but I assure you they did not get away. God does not miss anything! Man will reap just what he sows. There is no escape and God never fails!

Darkness Still Hovers Over the Land

Man has invented scores of items/products, but he used what was already available to him. After Man uses his brilliant mind to design a blueprint or a master-plan, he calls it an invention. He presents it for copy rights (Cheers)! We are so very proud! He has even made robots (mechanical men), but he cannot give them life. Robots cannot replace human being and in some instances they only complicate matters. Even though they can do certain things when man technically orchestrates the associated equipment. Even in communication, it is almost impossible to speak with a human being by telephone (automation). In today's world everything is high-tech and many are unable to comprehend. Is man smart?

BLACK LABOR
WHITE WEALTH

Like sharecroppers; tenant farmers did not own the land they worked. They rented it, paid landlords a portion of the crops. They had more independence than sharecroppers, but far less than landowners. On the farms: Every family was assigned a certain section of a field to work. As I recall, my grandfather and other family members worked in the cotton field. <u>A little cotton house</u> was on the property for family members to store the cotton. At the end of the season, the cotton was carried to the gin. My grandfather said he received a settlement. By the time that he paid for groceries which he had bought on credit, there was very little money left to receive. Our people were still enslaved.

Our Forefathers Endured Much Pain
My maternal great grandmother was a maid for a slave master. She was at his mercy. She gave birth to a son, Bell Hudson. He was a tall man, distinguished, of very light complexion and his eyes were hazel. He stood-out from the rest of his siblings (mix-breed). I am sure he felt privileged because he was different. His father was a white man. One of his sisters was Rachel Perry. Her husband owned a shoe-shine shop in later years.

Rachel Perry
Sister of Grandma Dollie Salters-Clarkson

Different Skin tones...

Maids birthed children for their slave masters thereby, our race is expanded. This accounts for <u>diverse skin tones</u> (yellowish, red, light brown, dark brown and black). The black man usually has a broad nose; many have a long narrow nose due to heredity. Our eyes are usually a shade of brown, whereas the Caucasian's eyes vary from brown, hazel or blue. They have thin lips whereas the average black man has thick or full lips. The black man's natural hair is usually black and kinky or curly; some have straight hair due to heredity or mixed breeds. The Caucasian's hair varies in color; it's straight and usually grows long in comparison to the average black man's hair. Only God knows the answer to some questions. All races vary in one way or in many ways. <u>Our cultures are also different. Yet, we learn from each other.</u>

Albinos

Let us not forget the Albino, a person who has a congenial absence of pigment (the natural coloring matter) in the skin, hair and eyes. They do not have an adequate amount of melanin which is responsible for tanning of skin in the sun. Albinism is an inherited condition. Even though Albinos are different, let us respect them. They are human beings (God's Creation) and no man is an island.

The Illuminated Present
Chains have been removed:
Freedom, Opportunities; Choices

Financial resources: Grants, government loans, scholarships and etcetera are available to those who qualify and take necessary steps to acquire them. By such provisions, choices and ideas are demonstrated and become focal points. Remember: God gave us all we need to be successful. We are complete in Christ!

Always remember that it is the Lord your God who gives you power to become rich, and he does it to fulfill his promise to your ancestors.
Deuteronomy 8:18 TLB

Keep in mind:
He who loves money shall never have enough. The foolishness of thinking that wealth brings happiness! The more you have, the more you spend, right up to the limits of your income, so what is the advantage of wealth----except to watch it as it runs through your fingers!
Ecclesiastes 5:10-11 TLB

Regroup
We must reflect on the former years: Man, broke God's heart. Let us tell ourselves we must strive to do the right thing; do justly, love mercy and walk humbly with our God. We were told to love our neighbor as ourselves; we are our brothers' keeper. God is our Keeper and Lover of our souls! Someone else is always in a worse situation than we are. Take a moment and reminiscence, look how far God has brought us. We are better by far than our forefathers were one hundred years ago. It is God's grace and mercy! Grace is an unmerited gift of

God. Walk on by faith each day! Remember: God has not dealt with us according to our sins; nor has he rewarded us according to our iniquities. Praise God!

The news bulletin (Bible) says Jesus is coming back again, but some continue to do things their way. They ignore or turn a deaf ear to the Word of God. When Jesus comes back it will be too late for many just as it was when the flood covered the earth. It will not be water, but fire next time. <u>Reach out to Jesus today!</u>

AFRICA: RICH COUNTRY MINING AND MANUFACTURING CENTERS

Our Roots, Listen

People of color were brought from **Africa** to America against their will. They were treated as property because they were called <u>slaves</u>. They were even placed into two groups: Field Laborers and House Laborers. They were actually called by a degrading name and some still use the offensive word, but all men are created equal! No one had, nor has a choice of skin color. Some people of color have brilliant minds! Martin Luther King, Jr. explained best how man should be looked-upon or defined. He referred to the content of one's character (ethical values) and not by the color of one's skin. As I recall, a local minister said, "Don't let nobody define you." The fact is, <u>we define ourselves</u> by our actions and that means weather we are just and fair among other values/standards. Sometimes man describes us by our careers, our life styles, <u>where we live,</u> appearance and etcetera.

Speaking of Territory:
This is God's Land

It does not matter who said they discovered America. God created the heaven and the earth before man was formed. Amen! Man claims to own property;

the earth is the Lord's, and the fullness thereof; The world and they that dwell therein.

Psalm 24:1 KJV

Apostle Paul penned:

For the earth is the Lord's, and the fullness thereof
I Cor. 10:26 KJV

Some say send the "black man" back to Africa where he came from. Have they forgotten the white man brought black men to America? Have they forgotten, or do they acknowledge life began in Africa? Therefore, the white man originated from Europe or Africa also. He separated families with no regard nor respect for mothers and children who were left behind. Now, truth of the matter is: Black men were born in America. This country is "our heritage." It is our home, but many white Americans do not want the black man in this country. They seem to think America is only the white man's present home. Yet, they sing "The Star-Bangled Banner," America's National Anthem which was penned by Francis Scott Key. <u>Thousands of black men have fought and died for this country!</u> What about the land of the free and the home of the brave? It was alright for black men to die for this country and many are still dying for America. It should be alright for black men to live in this country (God's land).

Man, Claims Ownership of Land

It is understood that we, the people want to claim land to be our own. We work to proclaim a <u>portion</u> of God's land as our own (a temporary dwelling place). Many years ago, the white man claimed the land of America according to history. The Indians were known to possess land here which was taken away from them. Since then, man has continued to be unfair with his fellowman. We should do unto others as we would them do unto us. That's the right way. However, many do not believe in doing what is right in God's eyesight. Some say, "It's my way or no way. God has the last say. The white man has always had the upper hand because his forefathers were in control of resources. They were and still are in charge of the majority of businesses, banks, manufacturing companies and etcetera.

The mind of man: The black man is smart and intelligent which is evidence because of the many inventions which were discovered by him. The sad truth is: When black men were finally able to work things out; discover how to manage, they were set backwards. Slave Owners never meant for the black man to live independently. Acts of violence were carried out due to jealousy.

ATTACK OF THE ENEMY WIDELY DISCUSSED UNTIL THIS DAY...

Black Wall Street, Tulsa, Oklahoma, Historical Landmark
1921, the year of the **Tulsa race massacre,** or the Black Wall Street massacre took place. White supremacist terrorists caused a riot. It is discussed even today; it's public news that guns and explosives were used and many people were injured. Hundreds were killed by a white mob. Greenwood District, home to about 11,000 people was known as Black Wall Street. It was a prosperous African-American community; more than one hundred businesses offered professional, retail and entertainment services. As a result of the evil/racist attack, blocks were looted, burned and many residents were left homeless. Although black wealth was drastically reduced, Greenwood was rebuilt.

What about reparation for the survivors? America pays reparation to others races (white peasants) but why not to the black race? They are also able to obtain loans at a lower interest rate. Black people were involuntary servants (slaves to white America). America is in debt to the black race! Every black person who is alive today is entitled to reparation if he or she were born before 1923.

It is Right to do Right

In spite of our differences, all races have **red blood.** God has made of one blood all peoples of the earth (Acts 17:26 KJV). All races of people are classified as "HUMAN BEINGS." We have some things in common and we need each other! God knows what we need; He knows the end of things before we know the beginning. Just trust God's plan.

SPEAKING OF BLOOD, THE LIFE OF THE BODY

Perhaps, William Harvey had a mind filled with curiosity when he discovered the circulation of blood. I was taught that an adult man has approximately 1.5 gallons of blood in his body. It is interesting to discuss the discovery of Dr. Charles Richard Drew, the African American surgeon who organized America's first large-scale blood bank. He was known for his work in blood plasma preservation. Man, still has ideas and continues to explore the human body especially by performing autopsies. Even before the postmortem examination surgeons performed scores of exploratory operations. Sometimes they were baffled (clueless). But somethings are a mystery and only God knows why. Nevertheless, man says there are four blood types: A, B, AB and O which is universal. There is also a protein, Rh factor which can be present or absent. Rh factor is an inherited protein. If your blood has the protein, you are Rh positive, but if your blood does not have the protein, you are Rh negative, per medical technologists.

After a vehicle accident in which serious injuries are caused the victim might lose a tremendous amount of blood. In some instances, he might bleed-out. History stated that Dr. Charles R. Drew's injuries from an automobile accident were so severe the attending physicians could not save him.

Some patients need a transfusion. In a hospital, the patient's blood is typed and cross matched. He is transfused if necessary with blood from an anonymous donor. No one is concerned about the <u>identity of the donor</u> who might be of a different race. In such case, race is not an issue. The concern is to transfuse the patient with the correct blood type. Otherwise, the patient might not survive; the objective is to save a life. The blood is the life of the body! We must keep in mind: God made of one blood all nations which tells us we are all related in a way which man will never comprehend. Let us keep that in mind.

Concerning Marriage (Medically)

Some physicians instructed couples in the past to learn their <u>blood types</u> before getting married. They were warned: There may be serious consequences when children are born. Two parents with sickle cell disease, or one with sickle cell disease and one with the trait are subject to have a child with the disease. This disease is common among black families. Most important: God is our healer and nothing is too hard for Him. O' the power of Almighty God!

It's good to know that the <u>blood of Jesus</u> can wash away all our sins. It has cleansing power. It will never lose its power. *"...Though your sins be as scarlet (red), they shall be as white as snow" (Isaiah* 1:18b KJV). Accept Christ today! He is a Miracle Worker. He can heal all manner of diseases. What He did in the Bible days, He can do today also.

In John 14:12, Jesus said, *"Verily, verily, I say unto you, He that believeth on me, the works that I do shall he do also; and greater works than these shall he do; because I go to my Father."*

No one has this power unless it is given him from God; there is no one else like Him.
God works through people as he will. He is in a class all by Himself! We remember Peter and John who were disciples of Jesus. They were at the Temple and there was a man lame since birth. Each day he

collected alms at the entrance. Upon encountering the man, Peter told him to look upon him and John. He took the man's hand and told him in the name of Jesus Christ to walk. The man proceeded to walk. It was the power of God in action. God is the giver of power; He rules and super rules. The poor does not always have money as needed.

The Elites...
Millionaires or the upper class are privileged to the best of the best with first choice of whatever is available to man. They are financially able to secure whatsoever their hearts desire. They are <u>accustomed</u> to having the best which is a carryover from slavery. Many Caucasians are where they are today because their parents or forefathers profited by owning slaves. The slave owners passed their wealth (inheritance) down to their children, and generations to come. Many physicians, lawyers and others who are financially blessed reside in well-kept areas. We expect nothing less. They can afford to live on a higher level than most. Today, many blacks are blessed to live on a much higher level than our forefathers ever dreamed of. In their subdivisions of choice, the speed limit sign is marked 25 miles per hour; the city lights are sure to glow. The city also ensures that a crew monitors the area weekly to remove any debris that might happen to be in sight and collect waste. In former years, the <u>workers</u> were expected to collect garbage from the back yards of homes. The crew consisted mainly of people of color (the unlearned or those who had little education), but they respected authority. The drivers of the trucks were white men. The black man's mind had been programmed. Although the chains had been broken or removed, old habits die hard. The black man learned to be loyal in order to survive. Even so, he expected to be paid what he rightly deserved.

Today...
<u>There are a few Caucasian people who will be fair with people of color.</u>
Those few are genuinely concerned about <u>human rights</u>. Some in this generation view things as they are. They are not afraid to <u>break their forefather's habits</u> and it is a fact that some will never change. They are cold-hearted haters of people of color; apparently, they are in darkness. Perhaps some would do more to ensure justice if they were not afraid of retaliation.

News Break Disclosure

I was informed of turbulent times in Mississippi. A New Yorker accepted a position in rural Mississippi on behalf of the civil rights group (Congress of Racial Equality). He and three other activists endured harassment by local thugs, policemen and Ku Klux Klan, in their attempt to assist African Americans secure their basic human rights. The three young men were murdered **(two whites and one black).**

A Concern for Justice

Doctor Martin Luther King, Jr. (01-15-1929 until 04-04-1968) was a humble servant for God and humankind. While his life was short-lived, packed with action, he was out-spoken; his voice traveled and echoed in the wind. Dr. King had many followers; there were many who despised him as well. He spoke with authority and sought justice for all. In March 1968, Doctor King traveled to Memphis, Tennessee on behalf of the Poor Peoples Campaign (striking sanitation workers).

Did the City Officials Turn a Deaf Ear?

I was a young mother when I heard the report: Two African-American sanitation workers were crushed to death in a garbage compactor when they took shelter from the rain. It was also reported that two men had died in the same way four years earlier, **but the city refused to replace the equipment which was not working properly**. "Black Lives" do matter! The black man labored during slavery and made the white man wealthy! That will be remembered until the end.

*Photo was taken by Permission
NCRM*

The Garbage Compacter, Death Trap

Dr. King knew someone should answer the call and stand with those who were helpless. He did not ask, "Who will go and be the voice of the poor?" He accepted the challenge and spoke bravely for those who needed attention, assistance and change for justice.

"The Ultimate measure of a man is not where he stands in moments of comfort and convenience, but where he stands at times of challenge and controversy."

Dr. Martin Luther King, Jr.

Photo by MPW

IN MEMPHIS, TENNESSEE

Photo by MPW

I had the opportunity to visit the location where Dr. King was assassinated. A large reef marks the place where he stood on the balcony of the Lorraine Motel before he was struck down by: James Earl Ray on 04/04/1968.

I am sure his presence was make known by curious spectators and enemies. Because of that, the assassin knew of his where-abouts. What a shame it was to kill him!

And they said one to the another, Behold this dreamer cometh. Come now therefore, and let us slay him...and we shall see what will become of his dreams.
Genesis 37:19-20 KJV

In Retrospect
Bible Days...
Joseph was a dreamer and his own brothers sort to kill him. More importantly, Jesus is King of Kings and Lord of Lords and many sort to kill him. Man can be evil and has no respect of life. But we know God is able to do all things well. He has the final say...There is a day of reckoning. Jesus died for mankind!

Dr. King had gone to Memphis to speak-up for the poor. That was his last plea for economic justice. Today, we acknowledge city workers need jobs and we need their service. Everyone must start somewhere. However, let us enlighten them; and hope they will be able to advance to better positions. They must have initiative and apply themselves. Adult classes are offered to those who are interested in furthering their education. One may consider how he might revamp or make changes to his work schedule. Thereby, he might improve his life style; prepare for the future if it be God's will. It has been <u>dark in the life of the black man for centuries</u>, but there is still a feeling of expectation and desire for change.

Chapter 5
Going Forward

Gifts From God: Children

We have been taught life begins at conception; we know a meticulous process takes place. After birth children began to grow, parents must teach them about the Lord. Write God's word upon the doorpost of thy house and on thy gates as a reminder. Some children will become preachers, teachers of God's word and evangelist. God has a plan for each one's life. After physical maturity, all travel the highways of life which are filled with challenges which test our strength, courage and determination. We must choose Christ for everlasting life. He is the way...Without Him, one will be as though he were blind even though he has his physical sight.

Children's First Example

Parents are children's first example. We must be cautious in our actions. Children learn what they live. Sometimes there is only one parent (mother) in the home. This is unfortunate because a boy needs a man (father) to teach him how to be a man. However, we usually teach our children to pray, "Now I lay me down to sleep..." As they grow, we teach them to pray the model prayer found in Matthew 6:9-

13 (KJV). That is good and it's necessary to know. But as they mature, life (the school of hard knocks) will teach them to call on the Lord in every situation. Cry-out to God and be specific every time. It alerts us to acknowledge God first; recognize our sins and ask for forgiveness. It teaches us to rely on God to supply our needs. It's the model prayer because it is our guide! Be vigilant because the devil is busy seeking whom he may destroy. He is the adversary for SURE!

Jesus Prayed
Recorded in John 17, Jesus lifted up His eyes unto heaven and **prayed to the Father**. He prayed for His disciples and He also prayed for (**us**) those who believed on Him through the disciples' word. We should pray to the Father in the name of Jesus. Biblically speaking: *We, the people of God ought always to pray* (Luke 18:1 KJV).

The writer of the book of Acts, Luke was a companion of Paul. He made it perfectly clear to us, *"Neither is there salvation in any other: for there is <u>none other name</u> under heaven given among men, whereby we must be saved."*

Many say call God by His name (Jehovah). The fact is, God has many names. He is the <u>great I Am</u>! *And God said unto Moses, "I Am That I Am: and he said, Thus shalt thou say unto the children of Israel, I Am hath sent me unto you"* (Exodus 3:14).

God is whatever we need Him to be: Way-maker when we don't know the way, Burden Bearer when the load seems unbearable to us. He is our Heavy-load Carrier when we try, but the load is too heavy and we fall. He is Light in darkness when we can't see, Healer when our bodies are sick, Mind Regulator when our thoughts are out of control. He is our Heart-fixer when it's not functioning right; its rhythm is off. And the list goes on and on! Jesus Christ is our Mediator; we must pray to God in his name. Your problem has a name and I assure you the great I AM can solve it.

Be Informed
Today, children learn quickly because of new technology. They have access to many resources and they search. We must teach them the

<u>Word of God</u>. A good place to start is the life of Jesus Christ, the greatest story ever told. Parents are held accountable for teaching/training children to know right from wrong. Do not kid yourself, they grasp things early in life.
For a solid foundation: Solomon penned.

Train up a child in the way he should go; And when he is old, he will not depart from it.
Proverb 22:6 KJV

Many times, our children get off-tract but sooner or later they make their way back to their parents' teachings. Some say: "They may stray, but they will not stay."

Some children are exceptionally smart, little geniuses. Others may be average or above, but no matter what one's level is, all are able to acquire knowledge. Everyone's intelligence quotient (IQ) is not and will not be the same. Many instructors are able to impart messages quite well. And many students learn well by listening while others need visual aids. They need to see examples. Some children have inborn or innate skills while others acquire skills by studying. The important thing is to LEARN!

Note:
In the past, some instructors had two groups of students. Some were on a higher level than others (more advanced). Therefore, they were allowed to complete assignments and move on to the next lesson. Today those students are allowed to take enriched classes. They begin studying college courses before they complete and graduate high school. That's a blessing which has not always been available. There are numerous opportunities if one has the initiative to take advantage of them.

CHAPTER 6
Respect For God's House

Enter into his gates with thanksgiving, And into his courts with praise: Be thankful unto him, and bless his name.
Psalms 100:4 KJV

When we enter God's house we must give unto the Lord the glory due unto his name. Worship him in the beauty of <u>holiness</u> as David declared. Peter, an apostle of Jesus Christ penned, *But like the Holy One who called you, be holy yourselves in all your conduct [be set apart from the world by your godly character and moral courage]; because it is written, "YOU SHALL BE HOLY (set apart), FOR I AM HOLY"* (Amplified Bible).

We are free to worship God; it is a privilege. The church should praise God when the Holy Spirit moves and not at the instructions of man. Praise God because we have reasons to praise Him. It is in God that we live and move and have our being. We must be grateful unto Him; we can do nothing without Him. It is God who gave us the breath of life. Praise Him!

The Church Should Have Standards...
When preparing to <u>dress for church service</u>, we should choose our attire carefully. Keep in mind where we are going and why. Dress respectfully and teach our children to do the same. Not only should we respect ourselves, but respect God's house, the house of prayer.

During my teenage years, my home-making teacher (Mrs. Lloyd) taught a class of <u>all girls</u>, "Put on your best attire when preparing to go to the house of the Lord." She continued, "Wear a hat and gloves." That was yester-years and today home-making is not taught in the public schools. We are well aware that clothes are NOT, nor should they be the main focal point, but we should respect ourselves and God's house. We must turn our attention to God for praise and worship. We must ask God to give us a clean heart; be grateful and praise His Holy name. We must also expect to be taught the **Word of God** in the house of prayer.

After Jesus was tempted by Satan, He told him, *"...bread won't feed men's souls: obedience to every **word of God** is what we need."* Matt 4:4 TLB

Newsbreak

Regardless of numerous <u>fashion trends</u>, some things should not change but take priority. Let's not remove the ancient guide which our forefathers have set. Now, many say, "Come as you are." Let's not misinterpret what it actually implies. If you only have a pair blue jean and a blouse or shirt, wear them. Now, girls/women if you have one skirt but it's too short or too tight, please don't expose yourself. Keep in mind where you are going (not to a night club).

If you are an alcoholic, don't say, "I will attend church after I put the wine bottle down." You don't know if you will live another day or get another opportunity. <u>Come as you are</u>, but leave the wine behind! In fact, put it out of sight; avoid temptation. Regardless of your addiction, the doors of the church must be open and inviting for you to enter. Everyone has or, had a habit/practice which needed to be broken. Come into the house of God; relax and listen for a word from the Lord! God is speaking to all generations, male and female, children and adults. He is speaking to those who might be confused as well. Please, please, listen to what the Lord is saying. Do not focus on the messenger, but please be attentive to the "word."

WHERE SHOULD YOU GO?

Choose a church where the Word of God is preached. Ask God for guidance and be led by the Holy Spirit. Focus on the Word of God; receive the word and hide it in your heart that you might not sin against God. Get on board "The Old Ship of Zion." It references The Church of Jesus Christ... Our forefathers taught us, "She has landed many a thousand and King Jesus is the Captain!" She is bound for Canaan land. Get on board if you want to see Jesus! We have the promise of eternal life, our inheritance.
Get this:

For whosoever shall call upon the name of the Lord shall be saved. How then shall they call on him in whom they have not believed? and how shall they believe in him of whom they have not heard? and how shall they hear without a preacher? And how shall they preach, except they be sent?

Romans 10:13-15a KJV

But how do you know whom God has sent?

Hear God's Word
And I will give you pastors according to mine heart, which shall feed you with <u>knowledge and understanding.</u>
Jeremiah 3:15 KJV

Ministers: If you choose to use terms which you learned in Theology School, it would be advantageous to hear the meaning of such words or phrases. Please be careful not to injure or insult the unlearned (do not drive them away). You don't help anyone by speaking over his head! Humbly come down to earth and you will possibly lead someone to Christ. Follow the example of Jesus! Humility...Low is the way! However, it is necessary to preach doctrinal sermons: The trinity (Father, Son and Holy Ghost), the virgin birth and the atonement of Jesus Christ or the sacrifice which Jesus made for us. Remember the old preacher may not be well-educated, but if he has been called by God, he has the <u>revealed word</u>. Revelations carry a heavier weight than any school of higher learning ever will. The Holy

Spirit is the Master Teacher and most elderly preachers have wisdom. There are many young men who have letters following their names, but they lack wisdom and one may say some lack <u>common sense</u> also.

Please keep in Mind

A well-rounded life consists of studying God's word in addition to making application. Thereby, we earn a living (we work) and incorporate other activities which allow for stability and a rewarding Christian life. "He who does not work shall not eat."

Some pastors are young and Apostle Paul penned to Timothy: Be thou an example of the believers in word, in conversation, in charity, in spirit, in faith, in purity. Our life style speaks volumes.

Moreover, whom he (God) did predestinate (fore-ordain) them he also called: and whom he called, them he also justified: and whom he justified, them he glorified.

Romans 8:30 KJV

Again, follow the lead of the Holy Spirit. Be not overly concerned about material things. God will equip you and your needs will be met!

A Wise Saying
A <u>tree</u> is known by the fruit it bears. A <u>pear</u> tree does not bear <u>apples</u>. Pay attention to what you are taught and especially by whom. When one sets a godly example, many will trust and believe in him. We must be an example in word and in deed. Some of the Jews believed Jesus' message yet, they had a need to be encouraged. Jesus knows the contents of every heart. So, He said to those Jews which believed on him, *if ye continue in my word, then are ye my disciples indeed;* <u>*And ye shall know the truth, and the truth shall make you free.*</u>

John 8:31-32 KJV

The Word of God leads men to true discipleship. We pray that our children will accept Jesus Christ as their Lord and Savior. Christ is not willing that any should perish. As time passes, children mature and life becomes complicated. All must be able to talk with God (Adonai or Lord and Master).

Note:
There are some who profess to be Atheists: They do not believe in God. Well, how do they think they arrived here? GOD is the Creator of life! At some point and time, I believe one admits: the seasons do not automatically change. One experiences pain; he is healed. It did not happen automatically. It was the grace of God. Sadly, I heard one say he does not fear burning in hell. <u>Remember we have choices!</u> When one is lost, it is no one's fault but his. Hell is real!

Apostle Paul penned: *For the invisible things of him (God) from the creation of the world are clearly seen, being understood by the <u>things that are made</u>, even his eternal power and Godhead; <u>so that they are without excuse.</u>*
Romans 1:20 KJV

Thunder roars, lightning flashes and zig-zags across the sky, rain falls, the wind blows and we cannot see it, but we can certainly feel it. Sometimes we witness a wind storm; we know it happens by the power of God. We know it is not the work of man, but the handy work of <u>Almighty God</u>. In Matthew 8:26 Jesus (Son of God) rebuked the wind and the sea; and there was a great calm. God is...God made everything that exist, the moon and the stars and etc.; we see the handy work of God. We know there is nothing here that he (God) did not make or speak into being. He created man!

I call to remembrance the Sadducees, a party which in contrast to the Pharisees-----rejected the oral traditions of the original teachings of Moses as authoritative. They did <u>not believe</u> in a bodily resurrection. They were said to often oppose Jesus and his teachings. If one does not believe in Jesus, he apparently does not believe in God. Jesus is the door to the Father. The Father, Son and Holy Ghost are the trinity Amen!

Changes/Decisions

A good foundation is vital and will make all the difference. It just might make the difference between life and death. Parents should teach children to choose friends based on Biblical teachings. If little Johnny-Bold-Boy has a habit of stealing, he is not a good friend. If Tommy-Do-Little practices lying, he is not a good friend either. We learned that association brings about dissimilation and some become like-minded. Although some skeptics disagree. Perhaps they will believe the <u>Word of God.</u>

> *Evil communications corrupt good manners.*
> I Cor. 15:33 KJV

Some say, "Men wrote the Bible." That is true and all scripture is given by inspiration of God and is good for reproof and correction in righteousness.

During adolescence, (the transitional period between puberty and adulthood in human development) our children become interested in the opposite sex (<u>usually</u>). That is natural and to be expected. They learn about the birds and the bees so-to-speak. Some even explore sex education classes, online dating and so forth. They have access to new technology and they search…Some may congregate with friends and associates and discuss sex rather than have a discussion with their parents.

Please Hear This

First, we must call to remembrance: God said everything which He made was good. He made Adam, the first man in His image after His likeness. God made woman after a rib was taken from Adam's side and she was perfect! She was fearfully and wonderfully made. They were in a perfect environment. It was Adam who messed-up by disobeying God. <u>There are consequences for our actions.</u> Because of Adam's sinful nature, Man was born in sin. Eve was at fault also and because of her participation women suffer during child birth.

Note:
When a young boy (maybe five years old or younger) wants to wear dresses; chooses to play with Barbie dolls, something is wrong. There is a so-called mix-up. It's not the child's fault but I assure you, there's a <u>hormone imbalance</u>. The same applies to the little girl. She wants to do things which a little boy normally does. She reacts as if she's a boy. There's a hormone imbalance. The child is not at fault and there are medical professionals who can administer medication in such cases. Hormones are chemicals that are produced by glands in the endocrine system. Who am I? I learned this from classes which I chose to study (Anatomy, Physiology and etc.) Will you question their maker? Have you ever thought were it not for the grace of God it could've, been you? Do you question those who have mental issues? Is there something which you can do to improve the lives of these? If you can do nothing, pray for them! Many children are withdrawn because they are different. They may not have friends and therefore they isolate themselves. We do not know what goes on in their minds. Only God knows their every thought. There are some things/conditions which man cannot correct. However, this is not a green light to request sex changes. We must be what God created us to be; that is either a male or a female.

Be it also known...

It's easy to speak out if you are <u>straight,</u> but remember there is at least one in your family who is not straight. Even though you may disown him/her, they are still your blood relatives and may I serve notice: There are no perfect families. Some people are different for whatever reason. God knows...Put mankind and all such matters in the hands of our Creator. He said cast all our cares upon Him. <u>Encourage/carry your children to the house of pray, they need to hear the Word of God.</u> Recall: God is a Miracle Worker.

We have been told down through the years that every family has a black sheep. Well, a black sheep has valuable wool just as the white sheep has! Although his wool is worth less, it is spun and woven into garments without dying, thereby eliminating an expense process. So don't be disturbed. There is still an advantage in having him. Keep hope alive, nothing is too hard for God.

Different Situations

Some children were <u>born with issues</u> which are beyond their control. Even the professionals are baffled by some children who did not develop normally. Some are born with more than ten fingers or toes, two babies conjoined, cleft lips, Down syndrome and more. Be reminded: some pregnant women <u>experiment with drugs, alcohol and smoke cigarettes even though they are carrying a child.</u> Amen! The child may be born deformed, but it is not his fault.

We remember Jesus healed a man who was <u>blind from his birth</u>. His disciples asked him, saying Master, who did sin, this man, or his parents, that he was born blind? **Listen to the question.** The man was born BLIND! Jesus answered, *Neither hath this man sinned, nor his parents: but that the works of God should be made manifest in him* (John 9:1-3 KJV). Jesus demonstrated his power! *He spat on the ground, and made clay of the spittle, and he anointed the eyes of the blind man with the clay. And said unto him, Go, wash in the pool of Siloam, ...He went his way therefore, and washed, and came seeing.* This was another miracle; Jesus demonstrated his power!

Think on this:

Some children grow-up and perhaps **choose to do things their way for whatever reason(s).** They will give account to God if they choose to be <u>differently</u> from what God made them to be (sex changes). Let's be clear: <u>Homosexual practice is sinful in the sight of God.</u> I am not a judge, but a messenger.

In today's world, there are many who accept the part of screenwriter or play writer for theatrical plays. Many are willing to participate during such acts of homosexuality. Money is the objective in many cases, the root of all evil.

For the wrath of God is revealed from heaven against all <u>ungodliness</u> and <u>unrighteousness of men</u>, who hold the truth in unrighteousness;...Wherefore God also gave them up to <u>uncleanness</u> through the lust of their own hearts, to dishonor their own bodies between themselves.

Romans 1:18, 24 KJV

...for even their women did change the natural use into that which is against nature.
Romans 1:26b KJV

And the men, instead of having a normal sex relationship with women, burned with lust for each other, men doing shameful things with other men and, as a result, <u>getting paid within their own souls</u> with the penalty they so richly deserve.
Romans 1:27 TLB

PARENTS...

Let's teach our children to pray specifically or more personally. Listen and retain the advice of Apostle Paul:

Don't worry about anything; instead, pray about everything; tell God your needs and don't forget to thank him for his answers.
Philippians 4:6 TLB

I ask that you do not make decisions on a spur-of-the-moment. Take time to think, pray, meditate and wait on God to inform you. You might have several thoughts, but ask God for confirmation before you finalize anything. Otherwise, you may regret your quick decision and bring sorrow into your life. My maternal grandfather once said, "When you're hurt, you did it yourself." That's true in <u>many</u> cases! I am a witness. Please do not lose focus on the one who has all the answers. God is our Counselor!

Please stay with the church, those who are born-again, baptized believers in Jesus Christ. We are not to judge who is or isn't Christ-like. Scripture says: let the wheat and tares grow together and Christ will separate them. Neither should we pattern our lives after anyone in the church. <u>Christ is our guide</u>. He set the perfect example. Fact is we must see Him for ourselves. Right living makes righteous! We must live right in order to have right standing with the Lord. We (mature women) want to be good examples, but we are subject to make mistakes. We will not reach perfection, but <u>we can try.</u>

Clarion Call

Time brings changes into all our lives. We (parents) must re-evaluate our life styles. Today, we are losing many of our children/young adults. Parents should know where their children are; who their friends/associates are. There must be guidelines/rules in the home. Your twelve-year-old son or daughter should not be free to roam as he or she chooses. We know Satan is seeking whom he may destroy. Parents, let us stay alert. For a moment let us allow our minds to go back to scripture: Luke 2:42.

In Jerusalem was the Annual Passover Festival. I recall Jesus was twelve years old. After he, his parents and others had been there a number of days, they returned home to Nazareth. Scripture says the child, Jesus tarried behind in Jerusalem; Mary and Joseph did not know it. They thought he was with the company. They went a whole day's journey and they looked for him among their kinfolk and acquaintances. After they did not find him, they turned back to Jerusalem to look for him. After three days they found him in the Temple, sitting in the midst of the doctors, both hearing them and asking them questions. All were astonished at his understanding and answers. His mother asked him, *"Why have you done this to us? Your father and I have been searching for you everywhere."* Jesus replied, *"I must be about my Father's business."*

Jesus was God in the flesh and not just another twelve-year-old boy. Parents, should young baby-boy Jim leave home without your knowledge, would you know where to look for him? Do you know what he might be doing when and if you find him? Would you be surprised to find him among drug addicts? Parents, we cannot allow our children to roam freely! They cannot be compared to Jesus. As I stated: Jesus was the Word made flesh and he was in the beginning with God. That makes him older than Mary and Joseph, his earthly parents. He was wise beyond the years of our twelve-year-old children. Yet, Mary and Joseph went to find him. Parents, go find <u>your children</u>!

Spring Season of Life

We as parents must practice living right in order that <u>we</u> may teach our children. During this <u>season</u>, children are generally very energetic, eager to learn and they remember what happens in their lives. Sometimes negative examples become stumbling blocks. As a child matures he or she is reminded of hardships of the past. They don't suddenly disappear. Even when they are in the past they are behind us and they will always be behind us. We do not have to look back. There seems to be no escape: The news media is full of life happenings. There is always one who can <u>relate</u>. One needs to ask God to give him strength to rise above the unfortunate situations. One must also focus on positive goals. Most times it's easier said than done. We can always tell others how to improve his/her lifestyle. There are many critics, but think about if you were wearing their shoes. You might not be able to walk a mile. Real truth of the matter: You might not be able to walk a mile in my shoes either. They were very, very uncomfortable and the road was rocky. The pain was excruciating. Today, I praise God for the storms He brought me through; I walk on by faith!

Focus on the Word of God
Let us not neglect our church meetings, as some people do, but encourage and warn each other, especially now that the day of his (Jesus') coming back again is <u>drawing near</u>.
Hebrews 10:25 TLB

Many choose to live in the moment, dangerously or on the edge. It is our job to inform them, "The <u>here and now</u> has consequences which are always costly if disobeying God." Some enjoy all they can and give no thought to what's right or wrong. Neither do they consider their home-training. Some have the audacity to tell parents what they think is outdated. "People don't do that anymore." Seriously, people are still dying and going to hell.

Solomon penned:
> *Hell, and destruction are never full;*
>
> Proverbs 27:20a (KJV)

My former Sunday School teacher, Mrs. Mary Jane Wilson brought this scripture to the attention of the class. I refuse to be silent about it, perhaps someone will take it seriously and make positive changes in his life (turn to Christ).

There are some who will not hear anyone!!! The people of Noah's day would not hear him either. When it began to rain continuously it was too late for them. The door to the Ark was shut and no one else was allowed to enter. They faced destruction because of their disobedience.

Listen to God
Why not come to Christ today? What are you waiting for?

Children…
Don't let the excitement of being young cause you to forget about your Creator. Honor him in your youth before the evil years come when you'll no longer enjoy living. It will be too late then to try to remember him, when the sun and the light and moon and stars are dim to your <u>old eyes</u>, and there is no silver lining left among your clouds.

> Ecclesiastes 12: 1-2 TLB

CHAPTER 7
Systemic Racism in America, the Beautiful

USA-LEADER OF THE FREE WORLD

America is beautiful: During the creation, God called the light "day" and he called the "darkness" night. He said, *"Let the water beneath the sky be gathered into oceans so that the dry land will emerge."* Then God named the dry land *"earth,"* and the water *"seas."* And he said, *"Let the earth burst forth with every sort of grass and seedbearing plant, and fruit trees with seeds inside the fruit, so that these seeds will produce the kinds of plants and fruits they came from"*
Genesis Chapter 1 TLB

<u>O' the wonders of God!</u> He supplied the needs of mankind then and he is still meeting our needs; making a way for us. O' how great Thou art!

> *And <u>God is able to</u> make all grace abound towards you; that ye, <u>always</u> having all sufficiency <u>in all things</u>, may abound to every good work:*
>
> II Cor. 9:8 KJV

<u>God made America beautiful</u>. The evergreen tree is an "evergreen." It can withstand the cold season of winter and still remain green. It stands tall and is strong; when storms beat it down it has resilience to rise-up again. During the storms: God allows the thunder to roar capturing one's undivided attention and the lightening zig-zags across the skies. As a child, I heard my mother say, "Be quiet while the Lord is working." She meant, respect God! Sometimes God allows the wind to do a job by wrapping around tree-toppings and uproot trees during storms! <u>O' the power of God</u>; Man cannot perform a job in such a powerful way. He must utilize equipment. Many times, storms tornados cut a clear path through the land. God speaks to man in many ways. He shows us who is in charge. So, how can anyone turn a blind eye or a deaf ear?

Deciduous trees are the direct opposite of evergreen trees. They shed their colorful leaves of yellow, orange and red in the fall, strip (becomes naked). They represent change of season. Even though they become naked, they survive the winter season. It's amazing how they began to bud and re-grow green leaves (cloth themselves) in the spring. Green leaves of spring and summer depict hope, renewal and revival. All this is the <u>timely</u> handy work of God. He covers the earth with a carpet of green grass in the spring and summer but, it changes: dormant in the winter. Let's say it is not dead, it is sleeping or taking a break. God's time clock is unlike the one made with human hands. Almighty God sends the rain to water the grain and cool the earth. <u>Thereafter</u>, a pastel, colorful <u>rainbow</u> may appear and capture ones' attention. At times there may appear a double <u>rainbow</u>.

The Rainbow

<u>...neither shall all flesh be cut off anymore by the waters of a flood; neither shall there be a flood to destroy the earth</u>. God set his bow in the clouds, a token of a **covenant between God and the earth.**

And it shall come to pass, when I bring a cloud over the earth, that the bow shall be seen in the cloud:
Genesis 9:14 KJV

How great Thou art!

Only God can roll back the clouds; hang a rainbow in the sky. It is held in place by his power divine. He demonstrates how awesome he is by painting it various colors with the stroke of his own hand. O' how marvelous; glorious and what a marvelous sight to behold!

Again, this is evidence that God is real. Yet many say they do not believe in God. He disseminates flowers of various kinds throughout the land. No one can arrange a bouquet to be more eloquent or expressive. Beautiful lilies are among them. Jesus said, *"And yet I say unto you, That even Solomon in all his glory was not arrayed like one of these."* It's God's work and not the work of man.

Color Meanings:
- Red means passion, enthusiasm, security or vitality.
- Orange represents endurance, perseverance and strength.
- Yellow represents awareness, cheerfulness and inspiration.
- Green represents growth, health, nature and wealth.
- Blue represents calm, peace, knowledge and communication.
- Violet represents creativity, luxury, royalty and imagination.
- Indigo represents awareness, wisdom and intuition.

God covers the earth with a white blanket of snow in places of His choice at times when He chooses. His wonders to perform because he is God. He set the Rocky Mountains on the West coast and the Appalachian Mountains on the East coast. They sit high above all else and seem to skip and hop while overlooking the land below.

They do not compete with each other. There is adequate space for all mountain-climbers; carved places are in sight and allows climbers to go higher with ease. Each mountain may have snow caps on its high peaks in the summer. Simultaneously, the valleys below may be dry. God is in control and He is awesome!

Many Americans and people from international lands choose to settle in the middle of these two beautiful mountains. Man may cultivate the soil on his chosen land; use it to work crops or gardens of his choice. He may grow organic vegetables and not concern himself about the store-bought veggies which may be over fertilized with unfavorable chemicals. His livestock may be allowed to grow naturally and graze which is more acceptable and healthier for the consumers. Choices are numerous, but we must have the initiative or the drive to prosper. God is our Helper! The Black Man (our forefathers) were accustomed to growing crops. Thereby, they survived. They preserved fruits and canned vegetables during the summer. They raised chickens and hogs. They followed the example of the tiny but industrious creature, the ant. They stored food away for the winter! Ants work together and each seems to know his obligations. Man should pause and learn a lesson from them! Never overlook the little one, he just might be the one whom you need.

Quilt: Beautiful Hand-Work   *Sister: Lessie P. Crowder*

Our mothers and grandmothers did not sit idle during the winter. They pieced quilts as they sat in front of the fire place. Grandfather supplied wood which he cut with the saw. He used his ax to split small logs for kindling which was used to start the fire. He placed the chips on the fire as well. Grandmother kept oil in the lamps. We did not have electricity at that time. Grandfather always kept a large flash light which was operated by batteries. He owned a lantern too. We also utilized a wood burning stove which contained two large round eyes which could be removed. Amazingly, the old stove had an oven too. The pipe extended from the stove throughout the ceiling of the house. That was the outlet to release the smoke. Our forefathers were very industrious to say the least; they were known for their work ethic.

As time passed, families moved to the cities. Many women worked as house maids and men worked as janitors. Some learned to work in factories and earned more money. They became more independent, bought cars and grew distant from each other. Time brought about change...

Now Watch God Work
We have the pleasure of watching the sun rise in the East; what a magnificent sight. We have the satisfaction of observing the gorgeous sunset in the West. God has made that possible too. Only He can display such wonders. On these two horizons, it seems that the sun touches the earth. <u>O' the wonders of Almighty God.</u> America is beautiful, a land of freedom of speech and many opportunities, but hard-hearted, stiff-necked, selfish, jealous man has incorporated racism and brought about hatred. Racism is prejudice or discrimination and God is not pleased with such. We must look closely at ourselves; ask God for mercy and amend our negative ways. God is Love and his word tells us to love our neighbor as ourselves. If we do, there will be less loss of lives. God has no respect of persons. It's mean, cruel man who is disrespectful, ungrateful, arrogant and very selfish. Let's be transparent: <u>This is not directed toward any particular race.</u>

It is noteworthy to say:
People of God, let's tidy-up, declutter our space. And let's not trash our city and expect someone else to do the dirty work. A wise saying: "Cleanliness is next to Godliness." Solomon penned the book of Ecclesiastes. *To everything there is a season, and a time to every purpose. There is a time to keep and <u>a time to **cast away**</u>*. Our forefathers said, "A good time to clean house is during the spring season." It is neither too cold nor too hot to get the job done. Let us properly **cast away** everything that no longer serves a purpose or is no longer usable. Don't delay for tomorrow may never come.

Psalm 51:10-12

This psalm was written by David. He repented for his sin and asked God: *Create in me a <u>clean heart</u>, O God; and renew a right spirit within me.* **<u>Cast me not away from thy presence</u>**; *and take not thy holy spirit from me. Restore unto me the joy of thy salvation; and uphold me with thy free spirit.* We should not only clean our house and its surroundings but, ask God to clean our hearts which are housed within us.

We should take pride in what God has blessed us with; respect our fellowman. If we have little or much, we should be thankful to God and praise Him! This is America, the beautiful! When (we) the occupants are untidy, we disrespect this land and show no appreciation. <u>This land</u> belongs to God!

CAN WE CO-EXIST PEACEFULLY?

We, the people of God should do better. It is time to build the "love" bridge to connect those who are disconnected; do justly according to God's command. In some nice, so-called upscale subdivisions there are a few black families who are blessed financially. They are able to afford a half million-dollar home located on two acres of land. However, some of the residents (obviously whites) do not accept nor respect blacks who relocate in their so-called area. They prefer to isolate themselves from black people especially those who cannot come-up to their standards financially. I also understand that many whites are as poor as some blacks are. However, the poor white man will be accepted before a poor black man any day. It's the people of color who are marginalized. Yet, this is America, the beautiful which is filled with a <u>rainbow of people from all walks of life</u>. Let's respect God's Creation! But if we cannot live together peacefully here on planet Earth, how do we expect to live forever with the Lord? There will be people of <u>every nation</u>. I assure you! It is imperative that we build a bridge to close the gap and thereby, eliminate the so-called differences. Let there be no respect of persons.

Segregationists

There are some who do not want people of other races to live anywhere near them. It was alleged that a Texas billionaire stated that he would build a "Dome City" and certain folks would not be allowed there. Apparently, he was in darkness. The news was brought to the attention of a renowned minister. The minister stated that a group of others (ministers) decided to address the billionaire. The group reminded the disrespectful, cold-hearted billionaire that diseases and death would enter his city. They also informed him of the city not made with hands eternal in the heaven. Obviously, the man had not accepted Jesus Christ as his Lord and Savior. The choice was his!

Let Us Face Reality: Organ Donations

Many patients experience kidney failure, depend on dialysis treatments and they sometimes await kidney transplants. Many patients have pacemakers and some need heart transplants and other organs. We are encouraged to sign-up to be organ donors. That means share our precious God-given organs with those who are in need. Amazingly, many patients are transplant recipients. No one questions the race of a donor. If one does not have a problem with receiving an organ from a donor of a different race, it should not be a problem to <u>live next door to one of another race</u>. Let us face reality!

Interracial Marriage

When two people of different races decide to marry you have a biracial couple. Today it is a common practice, but years ago the white man did not approve of a relationship which involved a black man and a white woman. Although the white man has fathered children by the black woman down through the years. They did not marry, but they used the black woman as if she were a tool (she had no voice). So, what has changed? Is love colorblind in this generation? The black woman's skin-color has not changed. The black man was expected to step aside when a white woman walked in his direction. He was expected to address her with respect regardless of her age. She was Mrs. or Miss to him even if she were half his age (she was the younger person). So, the white man has demanded respect from the black man down through the years. Most considered and some still consider the black man to be less important or insignificant. <u>I am right about it!</u>

Numbers 12:1
Moses, a Hebrew married an Ethiopian woman (referred to as a Black Cushite). Miriam, the sister of Moses and Aaron the brother of Moses spoke against him. Cushite refers to Africa. Many times, family members question one's reason for marrying a woman or a man. It is not always about race. The white man opposed the relationship of a black man and a white woman years ago and some still oppose biracial marriage. I reserve my opinion! I do know that <u>in the eyes of most white</u> men, a black man will always be looked upon as less important. The white man raped the black women but that was not considered a crime. They had no one to report to nor re-act against the rapist. A black man could not have a personal relationship with a white woman. They were not to look upon one as if they desired to have a relationship with her. Today, does the white man look upon the black woman through different eye-lens?

Speaking of Mixed-Breeds
According to the Bible, the Samaritans were mixed-breed people (of various nationalities). When Jesus met the woman at the well, He asked her for a drink of water. She responded, "How is it that you, a Jew ask a drink of me, a woman of Samaria?" The Jews had no dealings with the Samaritans. This was Jesus and not just another Jew; she was convinced because He told her all that she had done. I am aware that there is some good in the worst people and some bad in the best people. I am very well aware! It was a Samaritan who had compassion on a man who had fallen among thieves. The man was stripped of his clothes, wounded and left half-dead. Can you imagine a priest passed by on the other side of the road. His priorities were out of order; he did not value the man's life. A Levite came and looked on the man and passed by on the other side also. But a certain Samaritan came where he was and had compassion on him. He was a good Samaritan, a half-breed!

Today:
Many black professional athletes and actors have personal relationships with white models and actresses. Money talks! They get married, have children and should they divorce, the wife gets child support and she gets alimony (she takes him to the bank). Perhaps she

clears the account. Usually when a poor black man marries a white woman, she is usually poor also. He apparently thinks he has <u>scored</u>. A few white men marry black women and it depends upon her career among other things. I didn't ask if anyone agrees; it doesn't matter! We must love each other although we do not always like each other's ways.

If anyone says, I love God, and hate (detests) his brother in Christ, is a liar; for he who does not love his brother, whom he has seen, cannot love God, Whom he has not seen.

1 John 4:20 Amplified Bible

HATE CRIMES IN AMERICA...

A must-read story) Hatred...If this does not stir your emotions, you must not be human!

ACCORDING TO THE DOCUMENTARY

In 1955, a young 14-year-old black boy from Chicago was brutally murdered (shot; his body was mutilated; disfigured). His killers were so angry they tossed his body into the Tallahatchie River. To add insult to injury: His body was affixed to a weight (large metal fan with barbed wire). The weight allowed his legs to extend out of the water and his feet were seen by a fisherman according to the documentary. The young boy had been taken in the middle of the night by two white men who were carrying weapons. They angrily went to the home of the young boy's uncle; gave no explanation to the elderly black man, but continued through the house. The elderly man asked what was the problem, but he didn't receive an answer. He tried to tell the two men if the child did something wrong he didn't mean any harm, but the men ignored him. He even gave the men permission to whip the child; that was not sufficient. The boy was asleep in bed at the home of his relative. Why did they take him? He had allegedly flirted with a white girl (he wolf-whistled at her) four days earlier. He never laid his hands on her! Yet, she became infuriated or extremely angry.

The racist officials in Mississippi rushed to bury the remains of the young boy the same day his body was removed from the river. The boy's mother sought assistance from the Civil Rights Activists. She had her boy's disfigured, mangled body brought back to Chicago by train just as he had left for Mississippi. At the service, she had the casket open for viewing. She wanted the public to see what the racist men did to <u>her boy</u>. Many mourners and spectators filed past the casket. They observed what racist men did to the teen-aged boy. The heinous murder brought nationwide attention to racial violence; injustice to the senseless acts which took place in the deep south (Mississippi). It was reported that the accuser allegedly recanted her allegations after 60 years! She <u>lied</u> on a 14-year-old black boy. The young boy was Emmett Till!

A faithful witness will not lie, but a false witness breathes out falsehoods.
Proverbs 14: 5 Amplified Bible

What price will she pay? What price will his killers pay? They didn't spend one night in jail but should spend eternity in hell. They were acquitted by an all-white jury, but they will not bypass the judgement!

The White Rule
When I first heard of the rule from a school teacher, I was appalled. In 1954, Claudette Colvin (a black girl) was arrested at the age of fifteen in Montgomery, Alabama for refusing to give-up her seat to a white woman on a segregated bus prior to the Rosa Parks incident. **Everyone in America should be aware: News flashed via the airwaves.**

In 1955, Rosa Louise McCauley Parks (a black woman) was known as an American activist in the civil rights movement. She rode at the front of the bus and refused to give up her seat to a white man which was required by law. This was known as the Montgomery Bus Boycott. <u>This was echoed by Civil Rights Activists.</u> She was jailed and paid a fine. In 1956, the Supreme Court ruled that the bus segregation violated the <u>Fourteenth Amendment</u> which led to the successful end of the bus boycott. This subject has been discussed for decades. We must respect Rosa Parks even in death. She started the Civil Rights Movement.

Light has Come, Yet it is Dark in America

Obviously, it will continue until Jesus Christ returns. Our children must be taught to obey the laws of the land; respect the laws. Respect those who are in uniform who are expected to enforce the laws. Even though many officers are racist and seem to join law enforcement in order to act-out without consequences. They expect the law to be on their side even when they use excessive force to arrest individuals who violate the law. Some black officers use excessive force against other black citizens as well. They follow in the footsteps of their racist leaders. They must remember they are accountable to God also. There is a day of reckoning.

Our children must be taught: You do not need to fight in every battle. Sometimes motorists are compliant, yet officers use excessive force against them. Most officers travel in pairs and sometimes call for back-up before they stop motorists. Every stop is not justified. If one has an outstanding warrant, he is likely to be stopped. There are other reasons drivers may be stopped, but that is not the time for motorists to resist those who confront them.

The writer of II Chronicles 20:15(TLB) penned:
"Listen to me, all you people of Judah and Jerusalem, you O king Jehoshaphat! "*he exclaimed.* "*The Lord says, <u>Don't be afraid</u>! Don't be paralyzed by this mighty army! For the battle is not yours, but God's!*

Jehoshaphat feared the multitude which was coming against him. He acknowledged God's sovereignty over the current situation; took comfort in God's promises and he committed the situation to God.

Young people visualize yourself standing before an army. A war is going on! Call Jesus to come to your rescue because you need back-up. Recall a scripture to quiet your anxiety! We know fear creeps in when we face danger.

Notice to Parents:

<u>Two children of color</u> were adopted by a white couple. The mother of the adopted children stated to News Media: "It will cost more money to protect my children in court because of their skin color." That statement speaks volumes. By this, the mother admitted that <u>racism</u> is a problem in the United States of America.

Racism...The false and tragic notion that one particular race is responsible for all the progress; insights. It is the theory that another group or another race is totally depraved, innately impure; innately inferior. Racism is evil because its ultimate logic is genocide.
Dr. Martin Luther King, Jr.

Why Racist Slayings?
The world needs Christ...

These are perilous times which the Bible states would come. Satan is seeking whom he may devour. When he enters the mind of man he becomes hard-hearted, committees murder, steals, robs and performs every evil act. When man obeys Satan his heart has grown cold and he does not feel his brother's care. He has no love for his fellowman; hate consumes him. He does not even love himself; he demonstrates violence and unrest. Thereby peace cannot abide. He is walking in <u>darkness</u> and likes <u>darkness</u> more than light. That's when men stumble, lose their way and sometimes fall. Many are possessed by the devil, but there is hope in Jesus Christ.

Luke penned, *Mary called Magdalene, out of whom went <u>seven devils</u> (Luke 8:2).*

Mark penned; Jesus casted out <u>devils</u> from a man who had his dwellings among the tombs (Mark 5). We know God is able...What He does one time, He can do again!

Apostle Paul advised mankind to live peaceably with all men (do not discriminate). The love of God is not in haters and lovers of violence. Apparently those who display such actions have become filled with anger, greed and the like. Greed suggests a ruthless desire in pursuit of material things. Lovers of violence destroy that which belongs to his neighbor. God's word says: Love thy neighbor as thy self. He who obeys Satan is in a very dark place in his life. Man becomes a servant to whom he obeys. Let us not become servants of Satan and perform his evil works.

Apostle Paul penned: *Know ye not, that to whom ye yield yourselves servants to obey, his servants ye are to whom ye obey; whether of sin unto death, or of obedience unto righteousness?*

Romans 6:16 KJV

When one listens to Satan he becomes his servant; commits sin. Sin brings forth disappointment and the soul that sins will face death. Whereas, if one is obedient to God, he will live forever. Even though he were dead (asleep in Jesus) yet, shall he live. Thus, righteousness exalts a nation!

Jesus brought light into the world, but it has allowed darkness to take over; the land is sick because of sin. There is not sufficient "light" in the world because people love the creature more than the Creator. Therefore, change must be made in order for light to shine through and the land will be healed.

Reflect on this: Plant life

Photosynthesis is the process by which plants use **sunlight;** water and carbon dioxide to create oxygen and energy. Plants need sunlight! Plants need chlorophyll, a green pigment, present in all green plants responsible for the absorption of **light** to provide energy for photosynthesis. The world needs **"Light"** and that light is Jesus! Light and darkness cannot co-exist. In order to bring about change, Christians must pray without ceasing; make disciples of men. We have been informed: We must be transformed by the renewing of our minds! We must come out from the world and be separate. The world needs to see Christ-like examples and we must conform to righteousness. Amen somebody!

The writer of II Chronicles penned:

If my people, which are called by my name, shall humble themselves, and pray, and seek my face, and turn from their <u>wicked ways;</u> then will I hear from heaven, and will forgive their sin, and will heal their land (7:14 KJV).

Hear and Receive This:
Search me, O God, and know my heart (out of it comes the issues of life): *Try me, and know my thoughts: And see if there be any <u>wicked way</u> in me, And lead me in the way everlasting.* Amen!
Psalm 139:23-24 KJV

Darkness remains in <u>America and in the world</u> while hatred continues to destroy relationships.

Problem: The Absence of Love

God is not pleased! He speaks to us via His word: **Love** <u>the Lord thy God with all thine heart, with all thy soul and with all thy mind.</u> **Love** <u>thy neighbor as thy self.</u>
1. **The Storm (Hate) Rages…**
   When the Devil motivates man to do his dirty work
2. **The Storm Intensifies…**
   When man obeys the devil
3. **The Storm Destroys Lives…**
   When man is possessed by the devil
4. **The Storm Causes Division…**
   When man disregards human life
5. **The Storm Continues…**
   When man refuses to see the error of his ways

Parents, we must pray always and when we do not know what to pray for, we must rely upon the Holy Spirit.

...for we know not what we should pray for as we ought: but the Spirit itself maketh intercession for us with groanings which cannot be uttered.

Romans 8:26KJV

The Solution to the Problem in America and in the world:

1. We must confess our sins to God; agree with God: <u>All unrighteousness is sin</u>, turn away from sin to God. Acknowledge we have disobeyed His commandments.
    Thy shall not kill.
    Thy shall not steal.
    Avoid covetousness
2. Ask God for forgiveness
3. Accept Jesus Christ as Lord and Savior.
4. Be baptized in the name of the Father, Son and the Holy Ghost to identify with the death, burial and resurrection of Jesus. Amen!
5. Recognize: Faith without works is dead. We must become doers of His word.

CHAPTER 8

Skin Color, the Barrier
DISCRIMINATION

The brown or black man is last on the list for jobs and etcetera. Man has respect of skin color. However, in this twenty-first century some children choose not to follow their fore-fathers pattern. They have a mind of their own.

There has been discrimination within the black race. Many fair-skinned blacks have not always been receptive to people of very dark complexion. Some seemed to think they were a few steps ahead of the dark-skinned individual. This was brought about by the white man who would not keep his <u>hands off</u> the black woman. **He raped many and thereby, the black woman birthed mixed-breed babies.** Some light-skinned blacks chose to pass for white. They believed their chances for employment were better. In the late fifties and early sixties, that was true. Some employers would not hire a person of color if his / her complexion was dark. Qualifications did not matter. It was skin color which grabbed their attention and it was skin color which qualified the applicant for the job (in the employer's opinion). That was all that counted, but God is not asleep! Today, there is much hatred (black-on-black crime). It is not about whose complexion is darker, but jealousy and every evil act. Many have no concern for the lives of people in general.

The Rule of the People

Democracy means rule by the people, simply put! It is said to provide equal rights for the citizens. The Preamble to the constitution states that it exists to establish justice as well as insure peace. That brings us to the need for laws. We have here three branches: Legislative which makes laws, executive which enforces laws and the judicial which interprets laws. That's great! But there is something here in America which I do not see the relevance of: Republicans and Democrats! This seems to be an open-gate to division. Why do we have two major parties? Republicans seem to only see individual rights whereas the Democrats seem to observe equal rights. I believe the majority of black and brown people are Democrats while the majority of whites are Republicans. Many of our people are poor, at the poverty level and don't be fooled, many whites are at the poverty level as well yet, they vote Republican. It should not be about a certain party, but rather what is the right thing to do. We only need one party, a **Unified party!**

Printed on our money (United States of America): In God We Trust. Obviously, all people do not trust in God. There is division here. I believe the same imprint is on the money which belongs to the atheists, but they say they do not trust in God.

NOTICE:
God's word says: Do justly, love mercy and walk humbly with thy God! END of STORY! Does anyone expect to have individual rights in heaven? Those who don't believe in the "Trinity" (Father, Son and Holy Ghost) will not enter into heaven.

The War of Change/Integration in the South

This took place when I was an elementary school student. For many years, Man chose segregation (apart from certain people) over integration which is bringing people together. That is why we walked miles to public school. We used books which were handed-down to us after the white students had used them. In some instances, the black and brown man functioned fine before the big change was made. Especially in our public schools, the teachers took time to assist the little black students in their classes. They showed concern when they noticed one who was unkempt, or they sensed that something might not be right at the child's home. We acknowledge the black and brown children were transported to better schools for an opportunity to excel. But most whites were not receptive to other races. Many said they did not want blacks to attend their so-called schools and some white parents were out-raged. Most have always reacted as if the black man does not belong. Apparently, this is what they were taught by their parents or forefathers. Children learn what they live!

National News Echoed...In 1957, the Little Rock nine was a group of African American students who enrolled in Little Rock High School. I was twelve years old; as I recall, this school was for whites only. The black students were initially prohibited from attending the school by the Governor of Arkansas. Obviously, he was white and prejudiced! He ordered the Arkansas National Guard to prevent violence by blocking the access of nine black students to Little Rock High School. It's a shame and disgraceful that the Supreme Court had to be called upon to intervene. We still need the higher court to speak-up for justice to be served in many cases. We must keep in mind that God has an all-seeing eye. He rules and super-rules. Those who are a part of law enforcement are accountable to God also. No one is exempt; neither is anyone above the law. America seems to <u>still</u> have two sets of laws: One set for people of color and another set for the white race.

It's noteworthy to report that the brave group of students (Little Rock Nine) took a stand for justice. Over the years (centuries), our people have been mistreated and still are. Many have been used and abused, worked but were underpaid and still are. Our people are murdered and there is much <u>black-on-black crime</u>. Many times, no one is held accountable; after a period of time: Law officers say, "It's a cold case." Many of our church buildings, our places for praise and worship have been burned to the ground. Our leaders (those who fought for equal rights) have been killed because they spoke-out for what is just. America is accountable to God. O' prejudice man, how will you answer when you stand before God? You will not escape.

Chapter 9
Partners in Love

Brian and Denise LuBom
Brian is the Great, Great Grandson of <u>Willie Clarkson</u>

Consult God: Choose Your Mate

Brian is a Shreveport native and a graduate of Poteet High School in Dallas, Texas. He furthered his education at the University of Pine

Bluff, Arkansas. He is currently the owner of On-Sight Printing & Apparel and a full-time mechanic. His wife, Denise is a Licensed Esthetician/Cosmetologist and Hair Stylist. She is Hispanic and has a unique and fascinating Mexican culture heritage. Brian and Denise are residents in the state of Idaho.

The Second Season of Life: Summer

Young Men:
Now you feel that you are all grown-up…In your mind you are ready to discover what life is all about. You are mature young scouts and you believe you can handle a man's job. You are bursting with energy and your hormones have shifted from neutral into the drive mode.

Not-so-Fast
We are familiar with the saying: "I will not buy a pig in a sack." First of all, you should not compare your so-called lover (girl) with a pig. Fact: A pig is a swine! So, if you refer to her as such that means you are also a swine! We know that it's a swine's nature to wallow!!!! Take a moment to think! In addition: You should not consider her to be a THANG (an inanimate object). Hello! She is fearfully and wonderfully made in the image of God after His likeness. It will be by her that your children <u>might be born</u>. Amen! Now if a young lady is right for you, you will know before you expect to hit the sack. <u>Wait patiently</u>! The standards were set by God.

Apostle Paul pinned: ***Love is patient****, love is kind. It does not envy, it does not boast, it is not proud. It does not **dishonor** others, it is not **self-seeking**, it is not easily angered, it keeps no record of wrongs.*
I Cor. 13: 4-5 KJV

May God help us!
Some men say you must spend time together in order to know each other. That's true and while you are interrogating your friend, be careful to treat her like you would expect another man to treat your beloved sister. RESPECT is the word!

The So-called Significant Other

In this case, significant is used to refers to a person's partner in an intimate relationship. If the couple truly loves each other they should be willing to do the right thing. It is not respectful to continue in a long-term personal relationship without making a commitment. Yes, it takes two. If a man is not willing to commit, he has a problem. He does not love you; he is interested in someone else or he is going along to meet his needs only (lust of the flesh). Neither is it respectful to be in a leadership position and make announcements about your, or other's significant partners. In some cases, it might be degrading depending on the duration of the relationship and past occurrences.

Mate Selecting

Young Men before you choose your mate, pray that God will direct you and do not search for outward beauty only. Consider the whole package (contents). Sometimes a package has a gorgeous wrapping but you might be surprised when you remove all the decorative covers. There may be more than what meets the eye. Today, women have choices; they may purchase padded bras, other underwear with pads, waist clinchers, false eyelashes, eye contacts of color and wigs (unlimited) of several colors (shades or hues) and we represent ourselves!!!

Remember, out of the heart comes the issues of life: evil thoughts, murders, adulteries, fornications, thefts, false witnesses and blasphemies. These are the things which pollute or make one impure or **morally unclean**.

You should also know each other's spiritual beliefs. This is important; my suggestion is: Do not become unequally yoked. Think about the Prophet Amos. *Can two walk together unless they are agreed*? There is a problem when a married couple is not spiritually aligned.

Apostle Paul wrote: *Be ye not unequally yoked together with unbelievers: for what fellowship hath unrighteousness with righteousness? And what communion hath **<u>light with darkness</u>***?
2 Cor. 6:14 KJV

God's word is our road map; if we follow Jesus, we will not walk in darkness nor be ignorant.

<u>Notification</u> for Young People

Be aware that as time passes and physical changes take place, the figure eight may soon become figure zero. Remember beauty is vain; without real significance, value or importance. The long beautiful hair may soon turn gray and become thin and stringy. Also be aware that she who is <u>disrespectful</u> while you are dating will likely remain or continue to be disrespectful when marriage takes place. In spite of that, marriage is honorable and he who finds a wife, finds a good thing.

Note: It is not respectful nor a godly example to shack, take-up, or decide we're just going to try it out first (live together). You may not get married, so why tarnish your reputation? Every decision does not require an immediate course of action! Think about it. <u>Why live-in sin</u> and sleep with the <u>devil's advocate</u>? Should a couple do so it does not mean they will learn everything about each other. It may very well be the so-called Norm today, but it does not make it right. **Sin saturates the mind, affects one's joy and takes away one's testimony!** It also causes separation from God. Seriously speaking, the "Norm" has caused many disgraceful failures. Remember <u>we represent ourselves</u>. We do not have to keep up with the status quo. Yes, family members and others may have practiced such down through the years. We know better so **break the cycle**. The paper document is important, but it is also about respect and obedience. Many disagree because they have low moral standards or no standards at all. In today's world any and everything goes...There is no shame in their game and they say they are grown and could not care less what anyone has to say. God's word said, "<u>marriage is honorable.</u>" God would not have said what He did if it is alright to shack.

Don't follow every pattern. <u>Let's ask ourselves:</u> Is God pleased with the way we live, if not, we must change the way we walk (our life style), and change our language as well. Using profanity does not make us look good either (bad habit). It takes away from us; damages our character. When people are young most don't have wisdom. Some speak much fiery and colorful language; become very dramatic and plain disrespectful. When they gain wisdom, they have lost their youth. It is a fact that old habits die hard; we must strive to change from our former ways.

Young women the macho six-pack or Mr. Good-bar may become a keg so-to-speak. He just might lose his hair (become bald). So, look for precious, lasting, godly qualities. The same advice to the male applies concerning <u>respect</u>. Should Mr. Good-bar's behavior be unacceptable while dating, he will likely continue to display the same behavior after marriage. If he does not respect his mother, he surely will not respect you. His mother was his first example of a woman and I do hope she was or is one of integrity. Know this: We are not responsible for whatever our parents' actions are or were. Let's not make excuses! Right living makes righteous! Follow after it! We should want "right-standing" with God. By all means, don't demoralize the one whom <u>you say you love</u> because you were informed of his/her past. Remember you also have a PAST! You should either accept each other or move on. You cannot change your past. Although it may haunt you the rest of your life. Hindsight is 20/20 and no one is <u>lily white</u>; all have sinned. Some of us made foolish mistakes during our growing years; many people are not aware of the whole story. They only know in part and sometimes it's too painful to share all the details and it's <u>not</u> to your advantage!

Mind Preparation
Marriage should be taken seriously. I must remind or inform you, there is a time for <u>everything.</u> You must prepare to deal with mental, physical and emotional changes when Mother Nature takes her course. Women go through or experience menopause and with it comes its companions: Hot flashes, mood swings, crying-spells, irritability and more. Each woman's experiences may differ. However, Ms. Lydia E. Pinkham may be able to help. She has been around many years. Let's hope she is still available although she has been hard to locate. The sleep pattern also changes. One may have

more restless nights, choose not to disturb the other; many things should be taken into consideration. A trip to the doctor may or may not prove to be helpful.

You Need to Know
Men go through changes when Father Time interrupts their lives. Do not be surprised should your <u>marriage partner</u> choose to sleep in a separate bedroom. It does not mean he does not love you, rather it does mean the thrill is not as it was at age twenty-five. The hormones are not kicking as high or maybe <u>not kicking at all</u>. It does not matter how fancy the negligee, or how bouncy the long sexy hair. Many men experience what is known as ED (erectile dysfunction). They become frustrated, irritated and sometimes embarrassed. That's life! We must adjust and accept changes. Nothing remains the same all of our lives. Be reminded: We either live to get old or we die young.

Medical issues such as diabetes causes some men to experience problems when it comes to performing sexually. The diet might seem to minimize the problem but it still exists. In such a case, some men become delusional. Don't be so quick to call <u>Mr. Viagra</u>. He just might put you out of existence. Mr. Arthritis volunteers to come by and sometimes decides to stay. If he chooses to stay you will find a way to deal with him and yet live. Would you choose Mr. Viagra over Dominate Arthritis? Let's be real!

Men, there is no need to chase after a younger woman. After all, what do you THINK you can do with her? Your problem goes wherever you go. If you cannot perform with your wife, you cannot meet expectations with a younger woman. First, her question will be, "What is in your wallet or your bank account?" She will empty it and leave you with zero. Her next question will be "What do you own?" Men, don't embarrass or make a fool of yourselves.

Keep in mind
There is quite a contrast between men of today and men of the Bible days. Men of yester-years were able to father children in their old age. They also lived longer lives. Think about Methuselah who lived 969 years. Adam lived 930 years, Seth lived 912 years and Lamech lived 777 years. WOW!

Women, some of us look good for our age, our size and we still have the ability to go about our daily routine, but let's keep it real! We are seasoned saints! Let us strive to be worthy of emulation for the younger women! Amen somebody...

Children, Gifts From God
Innocent and in the dawn of their lives...

Aria Woods

Zayden R. Williams

Asia LuBom

Rilynn Rose Horton

Most couples desire children. They are a gift from God. At this time, clubbing, happy hour at the juke-joint, partying at Sally and Bill's place, hanging-out with the gang should be over. Mothers' obligations should change and so should Dad's. You are now adults! Put away the magazines, don't try to copy Mary and Mark's Guide. It may not be designed for your marriage. Pick up the Bible, study, teach your children, carry them to church and talk with God daily. He has an answer to every question and he can solve every problem. He is our Source. God is a very present help in times of <u>trouble</u>. It will surely come. Please believe me.

Today, many women are not able to conceive for whatever reason(s). Although they search for answers and seek help from medical professionals and sometimes to no avail. I am sure many women have asked themselves why? <u>In some cases</u>, reality sets in: **Abortions**

- They feel or felt guilty after choosing abortion while pursuing an education.
- They were caught-up in a situation with multiple sex partners or one sex partner.
- They became pregnant, but felt they could not afford to support a baby.
- Some may have concluded while pregnant: "I was taught better than this; it is disgraceful to be pregnant without a husband."
- And the list goes on.
- One might be reminded: Some single women have several children for several men. They have no husband and seem to feel no shame!

ABORTION/PRO-LIFE

Let's Differentiate

In some cases, a <u>spontaneous abortion</u> (miscarriage) occurs. That is premature expulsion from the uterus of the products of conception (embryo or nonviable fetus). In such case, the fetus could not survive by any means. It may be that the fetus was not developing properly or other reasons. Some spontaneous abortions occur after two months. The expectant mother-to-be might be pro-life, but was unable to carry the fetus full term.

When a woman is with child or pregnant, after two months of development that time is considered the fetal period. <u>The placenta is functioning</u>. It is the special structure through which the exchange of materials between the fetal and maternal circulation occurs. **If an abortion takes place before the placenta begins to function,** <u>there is no circulation at that time.</u> When there is no circulation, the fetus is not in a state of survival.

I obtained this information while working in the health-care field. In many cases, abortions have been sort due to many, many personal reasons: Rape, incest and etc. After sexual assault (abuse), a <u>victim</u> may be seem by a health care provider. He will utilize a rape kit to collect forensic evidence. If one is impregnated by a rapist, she does not normally want to carry a baby for him. In such a case, the physician will give her advice or inform her of other options.

One who uses birth control medication (estrogen and progesterone) uses it to prevent pregnancy. It works to prevent ovulation. In such cases, the female cannot get pregnant if there is no egg to be fertilized. In other words, **her intention is to abort the possibility of becoming pregnant.** She is engaging in sexual relations. If she is not married, she is committing fornication. That is willfully sinning. Amen. Who has not been there?

God formed the **first man (Adam),** from the dust of the earth. He was not <u>alive</u> until **God breathed** into his nostrils the breath of life and he became a **<u>living soul.</u>**

Today, some babies are still-born and physicians are helpless and have no explanation. Only God can give life!

The 6th commandment: You shall not kill. This commandment forbids intentional killing (sinful). Commandment #7: You shall not commit adultery; fornication is also a sinful act. All are sinful in the sight of God. Who can justify one over the other?

Women Who Choose to be Mothers

When some married women cannot conceive, they choose in vitro fertilization, artificial insemination or a surrogate mother. It's not strange that some women are barren. It was in Biblical days and it is today also. May I remind you: Rachel gave Jacob her maidservant, Bilhah, to be a surrogate mother for her. Sarah was initially unable to bear children and she gave Abraham her maidservant, Hagar. As I recall Hannah was barren, and she prayed specifically unto the Lord. She was blessed with a male child and she called his name Samuel. Some women are mothers to children of other women. That's a good thing. Finally, some choose adoption and provide a loving home for children who need a home and a caring family. Make no mistake, some children are reared by foster parents and the out-come is better than if they were nurtured by biological parents.

Today, we know adoption as the legal act of giving status of a family member. Let's reflect on adoption during Biblical Days:

Listen:

When Esther's father and mother were dead, Mordecai took her for his own daughter. That was love in action! Let us say he adopted her. She became Queen Esther, went to see the king, and found favor with him. Queen Esther put her life in danger to save the Jewish people from destruction. She was a brave woman who showed compassion for others!

When adopting a child, parents should pray, and cry out to God Almighty. In many cases the couple does not know the biological parents, their background or inheritance. There are so many unknowns in this life, but God...Only He knows what the child has inherited. Call on our Maker!

Pray For Our Children

Man ought to pray always and we as parents should pray mightily for our children. Women who are pregnant should not wait until they have given birth to pray for their child, but pray while the child is developing. Women should ask God for a healthy baby. Afterwards, they must continue to pray daily that God will cover, provide and sustain their family. All our help comes from the Lord. We must pray for directions and instructions in righteousness. We know God will take care of us, yet it is <u>up to us to ask.</u> Tell God what you want and ask if it be His will. Sometimes we ask God for things which are not in our best interest. He knows what is best. Also, our time of choice may not be the right time for certain things to take place in our lives.

Remember God sent His Son, Jesus who was born in the fullness of time. God had a specific <u>time for Jesus to be born to the virgin Mary</u>. She did not choose to be the mother of "The Savior." It was God who willed it to be at the appointed time.

Headline News
Be very careful when choosing a mate who has children from a previous marriage. It has been proven that some stepfathers have sexual interest in their partners' teen-aged daughter. Women, if you notice your hubby watching young Candy-Girl more than usual, you need to find out what's going on with that attention. How does she react when she's around him? How does she dress; what's her language about? Have you noticed her checking him out?

Some uncles, brothers and cousins cannot be trusted to be respectful. Incest has taken place since Biblical days. Molestation takes place now as it did in the past. Some men have no respect for family members, especially young children. Many girls appear to be older than they actually are. They mature much earlier than in yester-years and they are aware of the role which women play in relationships. Sometimes women become careless while children are in their midst. Women let us conduct ourselves in a respectful way.

Listen:
Amnon, the son of David took hold of <u>his sister Tamar</u>, a virgin and forced her to lay with him. He would not listen to her, but being stronger than she, forced her, and lay with her (2 Samuel 13 KJV). He <u>raped</u> her. Amnon raped his own sister.

Reality Check
Such is not always the case. There are some decent men who are

respectful and caring. <u>Where are they?</u> You must pray and ask God for guidance. Do not be in a hurry to engage with Mr. Good-bar because he speaks <u>what you think is your language</u>. He has checked your pulse and perceived what you like. Don't be fooled as many have been. Sometimes the "front" seems to be real, but there is an ulterior motive. Allow plenty of time if necessary because the real man will show up. No one can constantly practice a lie; he will be exposed for who he actually is.

> *...and be sure your sins will find you out.*
> Numbers 32: 23 KJV

CHAPTER 10
Church of Yester-Years

Mount Olive Missionary Baptist Church Grand Bayou, Louisiana

IN THE COUNTRY

The pastor was Reverend George Washington Holmes from Natchitoches, LA. He rode the trailway bus to Grand Bayou on second Saturdays and spent the night at one of the deacon's house.

That was commitment. Apparently, he did not have transportation of his own or, maybe he chose to travel by bus for another reason.
Service was held every second Sunday of the month; Sunday School was taught <u>every Sunday morning at nine o'clock A.M.</u> The pastor was <u>not</u> present for Sunday School other than on second Sunday.

Speaking of Transportation:

Today most pastors have multiple vehicles. There are several modes of transportation available to choose from today: Rail transport, Bus, Air transport and cars of course. That is if one has financial resources available. It's a known fact that one might have breakfast on the East Coast and have dinner on the West Coast on the same day. Even during the days of horse and buggy, not every family had transportation. I don't believe cars were available until the 1800's. During my early education days, I was told about the car which was invented by Henry Ford. I am sure the rich were more than elated when automobiles were made/manufactured.

The Pastor

Reverend Holmes was knowledgeable. I am sure he could read God's Holy Word. <u>I am aware also of God's revealed word.</u> Of course, I was just a child and I had respect for him. Mother taught us to respect our elders. I do know that he introduced us to Jesus Christ. That is what church was all about, saving souls and we fellowshipped with other born-again, baptized believers in Jesus Christ.

When it was time to collect money, we paid dues to our assigned tribe leaders. Sometimes I had fifteen cents and many times I had nothing to give. <u>We heard nothing about tithes and no one ever told us to be a blessing to the man of God</u>.

When communion was served, we read the church covenant. **Note:** …contribute **cheerfully and regularly** to the support of the ministry, the expenses of the church, the relief of the poor and the spread of the gospel through all nations and so on…

But do we provide financial support for the poor? I believe the pastors of yester-years had a clear understanding of the <u>covenant.</u> And the ones who wrote the covenant considered much. <u>Support of the</u>

ministry: The pastor was given whatever monetary donation the congregation could afford. We had the right attitude toward giving: We gave from our hearts. We were residents on Marston Plantation; the overseer was Mister Jim Dick whose residence was the "white house" and the owner was Mister Randolph. He lived in Shreveport (Louisiana), and he flew his airplane to Grand Bayou to check on his business, his plantation.

Pastors knew that God is our Sustainer and He will repay! <u>Doing those days most pastors worked a job</u> and they could not depend upon the church for a comfortable salary. They pastored churches which had service once per month; sometimes a pastor had two churches. They held their monthly services on different Sundays and the members supported each other. I believe the pastors supported each other also. No special offering was raised to give to the visiting minister. If they were paid to preach for each other we were not aware of such transaction. We do know that preparation is required when one is to deliver a message to the people of God. However, most have access to computers today. Thereby, messages may be prepared in a matter of minutes.

Note: <u>Apostle Paul worked</u>. He was a tentmaker and he reasoned in the synagogue every sabbath, and persuaded the Jews and the Greeks (Acts 18:3-4).

Apostle Paul penned: *Wherefore comfort yourselves together, and edify one another, even as also ye do. And we beseech you, brethren, to know them which labor among you, and are over you in the Lord, and admonish you; And to esteem them very highly in love for their <u>work's sake</u>...*

I Thess. 5: 11-13 KJV

Members seemed to genuinely care for each other. Today, most members have his or her own transportation and they are more independent and selfish too. Time has brought about changes and many who were farm laborers now reside in cities. Jobs are available and most have benefits and more money to support their families, the church and ministry. God has brought us all the way! Praise Him!

Our Forefathers Had Rules:
A Rule of Conduct

Some years ago, when a woman gave birth to a child out of wedlock, she had to go before the church. No member of the church is a judge or juror; Jesus is the JUST JUDGE. He will judge all after the resurrection. No member nor anyone else is qualified to pass judgment on another.

Someone decided it was time to change the rule. They didn't want to bring the married Christian man or pastor before the church for committing adultery. The woman and the man committed sin and they should have gone to God and asked for forgiveness. To put her on display before the church was not right. As a result, the church should have restored her back to the membership in meekness considering themselves. After all, who is without sin?

Apostle Paul wrote to the people of the church at Rome:

You, therefore, have no excuse, you who pass judgement on someone else, for at whatever point you judge the other, you are condemning yourself, because you who pass judgment do the same things (Romans 2 NIV) **AMEN!** Paul shows that all have sinned and need the righteousness that only God can provide. He summarized the sin of all, Gentiles and Jews alike. He later pinned, "There is none righteous, no not one."

The Pharisees did a similar thing to the woman who was caught in the act of adultery. Jesus, who is perfect did not condemn her. Her accusers could not either because they were all guilty of something also, sin. We need to look at ourselves. Don't be so quick to point an accusing finger at our neighbors. We are all guilty! We cannot judge others because we are guilty of the same thing, sin! However, the Church should have rules regarding right and wrong (according to God's word).

Reverend Curtis F. Roberson, Sr.

A MAN OF GOD

Apostle Paul was grateful and praised God for gifts from the Philippians.

He pinned:

> *Not that I was ever in need, for I have learned how to get along happily whether I have <u>much or little.</u>*
>
> Philippians 4:11 TLB

Where are the leaders today who have the attitude of Paul?

Apostle Paul stated further*: But though I appreciate your gifts, what makes me happiest is the well-earned reward you will have because of your kindness.*

Philippians 4:17 TLB

This explains: Paul did not ask for gifts from the Philippians.

However, he was grateful for their <u>thoughtfulness</u>. He also wanted them to know that God would bless them for giving to him from their hearts. The Philippians apparently gave because they desired to do so. They were compassionate and they also knew that Paul traveled. He was on his third missionary journey when he wrote the book of Romans. He was likely ready to return to Jerusalem with the <u>offering from the mission church</u> for poverty-stricken believers in Jerusalem. And I didn't read anywhere that Paul owned any type of transportation, but he did a great deal of missionary work. He and a group of companions <u>sailed</u> from Troas to Neapolis, located on Macedonia's eastern shore. Today, most pastors have more than one mode of transportation.

We know that <u>gifts should be given **voluntarily** from the heart and not just because you are told to do so.</u> We also know we will be blessed when we be a blessing to the poor. We must be kind to them, too. Although they do not always ask for assistance. Christians should have a discerning spirit. When we recognize a true NEED, we should plant a seed (in good ground). God will give the increase (harvest) in due time.

Anniversary Day

On Pastor's Anniversary Sunday, two chairs were placed up-front for the <u>pastor and his wife</u>. They were a couple and whatever was given to the pastor was for the wife also. <u>Frankly, that's how it should be</u>. There was no need for division. I am not sure of the amount of money which was collected for <u>them</u> because it didn't seem to be just about "<u>the money</u>." It was appreciation/recognition and praises to God for all He had done for us. God takes care of His own. He promised to supply all our NEEDS! He didn't say GREED! The members were not assessed to pay any amount of money. I am sure the pastor graciously accepted whatever the members gave him. No one can pay or reward us like the LORD!

On first Sundays, we attended service at New Star Baptist Church, Abbington, LA. On second Sunday, we attended Mount Olive Baptist Church. We were members there. On third Sundays, we attended service at Bright Morning Star Baptist Church. Those pastors did not teach the members to pay tithes. As a matter of fact, they preached the life of Jesus Christ. Even when they preached from the Old Testament, they did not preach tithes, but why didn't they? They had the King James version of the Bible. Let us say they prayed to God for understanding and they were aware: The Priests and Levites had a commandment to take tithes of the people according to the law. **The law was** our tutor to bring us to Christ. The Word (Christ) was made flesh. He was crucified, died for our sins, buried and rose from the grave the third day according to scripture. By one man's (Adam's) disobedience many were made sinners. So, by the obedience of one (Christ) shall many be made righteous (Romans 5:19 KJV). The New Testament Church is under **grace** (Romans 6:14 KJV). Could it be that those ministers understood this? <u>They knew via the "Revealed Word of God."</u> What say you ministers of today? How many will admit: "When we learn better, we should do better?" As I recall, a well know minister did admit, "Some of the books which I penned were in error and "<u>we are under grace</u>." Who can say differently? Since then, some pastors have said, "We should be grace givers." I realize tithing is not for God's benefit because He does not need our money. Everything belongs to him. Sacrificing a portion of our income reminds us to rely on God to meet our needs! <u>We give to support the church and the ministry</u>.

Study to show thy self-approved unto God, a workman that needeth not be ashamed, rightly dividing the word of truth.
II Timothy 2:15 KJV

We study God's word because it is a lamp unto our feet and a light unto our path. God's word tells us His will and how we should live. Amen, and to God be the glory! When light shines, darkness disappears! Let us walk in the light. If we follow Jesus we will not walk in darkness.

Big Meeting Day in 1955

August 7th was a special Sunday because it was after two weeks of revival. After candidates were baptized, the girls wore white dressed (white represents purity). A large white handkerchief was tied around each one's head (the practice is no longer followed). The handkerchiefs were removed after the pastor shared the covenant with the converts. If one chose to join a different church that candidate was not given the right hand of fellowship. He or she was sent to the church of his or her choice. That <u>Sunday night,</u> (during the service) each candidate sat on the first pew and each one prayed (one after the other). Why did the modern-day church choose to discontinue the practice? I became a junior usher and my mother fashioned my uniform. All were expected to get busy!

CHRISTIAN DUTIES

The members were faithful about visiting the sick. Many did not own transportation, but by the grace of God they managed to go from one house to another. Many lived within walking distance. They prayed, cooked, baked (tea-cakes filled the crock bowl) and they cleaned house. Every woman disciplined the children who were unruly. It did not matter who was the child's parent(s), and that was our way of life. Sister Millie Ann did not curse nor threaten Sister Hazel Jo because she told her teenaged daughter to respect her elders. Today the difference is: No one can tell another woman's child when he / she is wrong. The parent is the one who will have a problem!

The members' focus was on what is pleasing to God and keeping Jesus in the forefront of their minds. Living on a plantation was hard to say the least. Teenagers were in a hurry to be grown-ups just as many are today. They didn't have the many ways and means of communicating as children have today (computers, iPads, cell phones were unheard of). If a family had a **radio and/or a television** that was considered to be high-end. Some owned an old-fashioned record player. Today, we are grateful for new or advanced technology.

Philco Floor Model Radio
An oil lamp was used for lighting before we had electricity
Owner: Mattie Oliver, my great auntie

In Retrospect

During the former years (late forties and early fifties), children were required to work in cotton fields. We chopped cotton during the spring; we picked cotton on the farms during late summer and early fall. I utilized a <u>pillow case as a cotton sack</u> at the age of four years. At the age of five, I was a baby sitter at my dad's command. Today, some children are not required to work, nor do chores. Most homes are fully equipped with electrical appliances. Some children will not load the dishwasher. They do not clean their own bedrooms until they are demanded to do so. In such cases, there is a lack of training and discipline. Every household should have rules and they should be followed; enforced. However, it is not a child's responsibility to work at age four. Today, I ask why wasn't there a "Child Labor Law?"

Sign of the Times

Regardless of all the different gadgets which are available today, some children are more disobedient now-days. They have more than children of yester-years and yet, they have the audacity to be disrespectful. Many mothers sacrifice to put food on the table and provide other necessities. Teenagers have access to Mother's vehicle and Father's credit card, but they still want more; they are never satisfied. Many seem to think they are entitled to whatever they desire. They are ungrateful to say the least! Nothing is new under the sun!

The Prodigal Son (From the book of Luke)

A man had two sons. The younger son told his father, I want my share of your estate **now**, instead of waiting until you die. He had some nerves! The boy's father agreed to divide his wealth between his sons. The younger son packed his belongings and took a trip to a distant land; there he wasted all his money on parties and prostitutes. After his money was gone a great famine swept over the land, and he began to starve. He accepted a job feeding swine and what he fed them looked good to him. It took all of this to bring the son to his senses. He remembered, at home the hired servants had food to spare. He said to himself, "I am dying of hunger." He returned home to his father who gladly welcomed him back. Despite how disrespectful the son had been, the father showed him love. The same is happening today.

CHAPTER 11
Quiet Time/Before Work

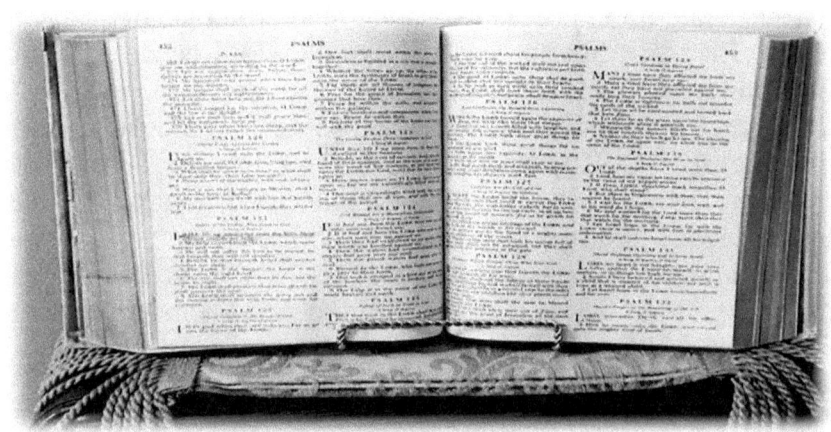

The Holy Bible
Psalm 121

MORNING DEVOTION

Read a scripture and say a prayer before leaving home. Psalm 121 is ideal. <u>Choose your scripture</u>. There are multiple daily devotionals available to the public and most are free of charge. More importantly, we have access to many different translations of the Bible. If one prefers the Amplified Bible, The Living Bible, the King James Study Bible or the New International Version they are all accessible. Many have concordances and Bible dictionaries also to aide them in studying God's word. We have access to the Word of God by way of cellular phones. We can even hear the pronunciation of words and names too. There are scriptures for every situation: Sickness, health, death, encouragement, and etc.

The law of the Lord is perfect, converting the soul: The testimony of the Lord is sure, making wise the simple (those whose understanding and judgment have not yet matured). The statues of the Lord are right, rejoicing the heart: The commandment of the Lord is pure, enlightening the eyes.
Psalm 19:7-8 KJV

IN TIMES OF DISTRESS

A phone call to inform us about one's sudden death can be devastating. When we receive news about a tragedy, we may be shocked and overcome by grief. It is understandable. That is a time when we need spiritual support; <u>strength</u> to go forward and the hand of God to guide us.

Strength when weak

God says to *"fear not, for I am with you; be not dismayed, for I am your God; I will <u>strengthen</u> you, I will help you, I will uphold you with my righteous right hand"*.
Isaiah 41: 10

The Lord is my rock, my fortress and my deliverer; my God is my rock, in whom I take refuge (Psalm 18).

We must trust God to do what we cannot do for ourselves. He assures us he is with us and yet, we feel alone and deserted even after he has said, "I will help you." He knows our weaknesses and he will <u>strengthen</u> us.

Sickness:
"But I will restore you to health and heal your wounds, declares the Lord."
Jeremiah 30:17 NIV

Sometimes God heals in a way that we may not be prepared for. He calls one home. Physicians may do all they are able to do, but God has the last word. Other times, God heals in a miraculous way. Physicians are astonished, amazed and left in awe!

Sinned:
Have mercy on me, O God, according to your steadfast love; according to your abundant mercy blot out my transgressions.
Psalm 51 KJV

Peace:
Peace I leave you; my peace I give you. I do not give you as the world gives.
Do not let your hearts be troubled and do not be afraid.
John 14:27 NIV

The world may give one material things, money and even food, yet he feels no peace. God wipes away tears, wraps us with mercy and gives us strength to continue the journey.

Burdened:
Come to me, all who labor and are heavy laden, and I will give you rest.
Matt 11:28

Anxious:
But my God <u>shall</u> supply all your need according to his riches in glory by Christ Jesus.
Philippians 4:19 KJV

In Danger:
I will say of the Lord, He is my refuge and my fortress: My God; in him will I trust.
Psalm 91:2 KJV

Depressed:
The Lord is my light and my salvation; whom shall I fear? The Lord is the strength of my life; of whom shall I be afraid?
Psalm 27:1 KJV

Go to God in prayer when you feel as though the weight of the world is on your shoulders. When you feel as if you cannot go on, call Jesus. He will come to your rescue, lift the trouble which weighs you down and give you safe passage to your destination. I know God will! He did it for me.

<u>Trouble</u> comes even though it's never invited. Life happens and we must deal with all situations under all circumstances. Sometimes it floods our lives like a river but, I read in God's word: *When thou passes through the waters, I will be with thee, and <u>through</u> the rivers, they shall not overflow thee: when thou walkest through the fire, thou shall not be burned; neither shall the flames kindle upon thee.*
Isaiah 43:2-8 KJV

The prophet gave words of encouragement: When we go through <u>great trouble</u> God will be with us. When we go through <u>rivers of difficulties</u>, we will not drown (we will keep our heads above the waters). When we walk through the fire of oppression, we will not be burned up, the flames will not consume us (TLB).

Government
Its role is to protect citizens from sinful conduct of others. Neighbors inflict harm upon other people, cause the death of our love ones. They take that which does not belong to them, then we have oppression; riots. Government must step-in and bring about order. Government is to help preserve order and people must respect God's creation. However, we live in a world of sin.

Isaiah penned: *For unto us a <u>child is born</u>, unto us a Son <u>is given</u>: And the **government** shall be upon his shoulders: And his name shall be called Wonderful, <u>Counsellor</u>, The mighty God, The everlasting Father, <u>The Prince of Peace</u>.*

Isaiah 9:6 KJV

Isaiah, an Old Testament Prophet spoke as if Christ had already come in the flesh.
He pinned: <u>A child is born.</u> Christ was in the beginning with God; when He came into the world He was God in the flesh. Today, He **is** and always will be! Choose Jesus for life everlasting!

ON THE JOB

Most employees work eight hours per day and some work in the health-care field on twelve-hour shifts. If your job is a cook, seamstress, environmental worker or whatever, do your job well. Whatsoever thy hands find to do, do it with all thy might!

During me-time we pamper ourselves, rest, relax and meditate. **Meditation** is a good thing, time to hear instructions from God. It is alright to separate ourselves from others; clear our minds for a while and talk with God. Everyone needs <u>quiet time</u>. Solitude is good! Some call this me-time. After we care for others, take care of all or most of the household chores, yes, we need <u>me-time.</u> Sometimes we need to separate ourselves from our closest friends. Remember Jesus took His inner-circle: Peter, James and John to a garden grove, Gethsemane. He told them to sit down and wait while He went ahead to <u>pray</u> (Matthew 26: 36-37 KJV). Jesus prayed and He is perfect; without sin. So, what about us, sinful man?

Right Mind-Set

"Lord God please clear our minds that we may focus on You and condition our hearts. <u>Please</u> give us listening ears and receptive hearts to do what's right! Help us make application of your word in our lives." We declare it done in the powerful name of Jesus, Our Provider. Amen!

God works in mysterious ways in which we do not always understand, but we must trust Him. He makes no mistakes. When we have a conversation with God we must listen closely for an answer to our questions and directions how to proceed and etcetera. Sometimes we need an answer right now, but that is not how it works. We call the Lord and <u>when it seems like we are on</u> <u>hold, I tell you hold on!</u> God has not forgotten us. He will give us just what we need and it will not be too late. Know that we cannot change somethings, but be assured, we will survive. I know so, be encouraged! God has brought me through **many storms.** Now I can tell...My story is to strengthen someone else. Sometimes it is necessary to re-tell the story!

I penned the book after years of hardships; darkness in our lives. I chose to use the pen name: Hannah T. Merritt. The book was published by iUniverse Publishing Company. God has been and still is good to me! He brought me out of darkness into His marvelous light! Praise God...

Patience on the Job

On any job the duties or requirements can and will be overwhelming at times. Some co-workers/managers become belligerent or disgruntled. We must remember who we are in Christ and ask Him to come to our rescue. Not every employee has accepted Christ as his Lord and Savior. The devil is on his job seeking whom he may devour. Some workers are jealous-hearted. They are not interested in climbing up the ladder, but they do not want you to move-up either. They are known to have carb-mentality. It is also possible that they are enslaved to the manager.

Please be attentive. There is always the So-called Know-it-all person. There is also the: Complainer, the Yes-person and the Do-Nothing person.

Listen:

Most employees are scheduled to work an 8-hour shift, but some refuse to do all their assigned duties. They re-act like children and grumble about what another worker should do. <u>It is a serious problem when one pretends to be hurt on the job and expects to be compensated.</u> Be careful, if you are the pretender, you might actually become disabled. That is what you spoke into your Spirit.

Death and life are in the power of the tongue: And they that love it shall eat the fruit thereof.
Proverbs 18:20 KJV

Remember God's eye is in every place. One might get by but I assure you he will not get away. We reap just what we sow. We find in life what we put into it! Many try to be on the receiving end regardless of how much they have. They are selfish.

When we desire to do good evil is present on every hand, but we cannot let the devil win the battle. So, we speak peace in the workplace and ask God to fight our battles. We must be alert, sometimes bold, yet respectful. By all means try to stay within the so-called "blue or cool zone" of professionalism and know that God is in control. He has the power to elevate or remove whomever he chooses. Remember promotions come from God; while you are displaying patience, believe God is working in your behalf (the next job). This just might be a great opportunity to take a break (vacation) from the work-place. We need a bit of space to rethink things, explore other options and consult God. A change of scenery for a spell will make a difference. We know that God works in mysterious ways. The saying goes: "His wonders to perform." Sometimes we think what's happening should not happen to us. That's because we report to work in a timely manner and we do the job correctly. Our team goes above and beyond to accomplish the goals of the establishment and our attitudes display gratitude. Guess what? The boss still makes unrealistic demands. Many times, things work out for our good. Something else: Employees have been treated as if they were possessions. Maybe, just maybe the boss's mind went back to the days of Pharaoh!

Sometimes the pay does not equal the responsibilities. However, we find pleasure in our work and we believe that right will win in the end. We do hope the manager is aware and believes that we should do unto others as we would them do unto us.

> Look at it this way: *Pay everyone whatever he* ought to have...
> Romans 13:7 TLB

Yet, there are those who grumble (mangers and co-workers), find faults and are never satisfied. So, we ask ourselves, "Why don't they show us how the duties can be performed more efficiently?"

Perhaps they cannot do the job as well as the ones who completed the many tasks. There may be some jealousy for whatever reason.

The Zoo in San Antonio, TX

Take a break and see how well things go. A walk in the park; a trip to the <u>zoo</u> may be exciting. Watch the animals and observe how they get along with each other. Even the American Bisons take a break from each other (give each other some space). One may want to relax alone sometime. Rest and relaxation are good for the mind. Quite often, we need to refresh our thoughts in order to gain a new perspective on life. Most adults deal with many difficult situations and some require more than one plan of action. Man is the crown of God's creation and we are expected to be intelligent. We should know how to agree to disagree. When there is a problem and there will be many, remember no question is ever settled until it is settled right. One man said, "Even a clock which has stopped is right twice a day."

Come now, and let us reason together saith the Lord.
                                                                Isaiah 1:18 KJV

If the disgruntled employee refuses to reason, take him to the next-in- charge. If the issue is not resolved, leave it in the hands of the Lord. He can and will work it out. Sometimes we cannot comprehend the actions of co-workers. Neither can we understand the procrastination of the one who is in charge. The situation may be liken to a **<u>wind storm</u>** that blows with great intensity. That is when we say, "Lord this is too much for me to handle, it's bigger than me." Step back, get out of the way. God will do what we cannot do. There is no limit of His understanding and neither of His power. Always recall a scripture(s) to help you regain your composure.

Think about this...

Jesus said to his disciples, *"Let's cross to the other side of the lake." ...A terrible **storm arose**. High waves began to break into the boat until it was nearly full of water and about to sink. Jesus was asleep at the back of the boat with his head on a cushion. Frantically they wakened him, shouting, "Teacher, don't you care that we are all about to drown?" Then he rebuked the wind and said to the sea, "Quiet down!" And the <u>wind fell down</u>, and there was a great calm!*

Mark 4:35-39 TLB

When Jesus said, Let's cross to the other side of the lake, that should have been comforting to the disciples. Jesus was with them; He knows the end before we know the beginning of everything. With God all things are possible and Jesus was God in the flesh. Perhaps that was an afterthought. It is a fact that we do not always recognize what we need is at hand or in our midst. Why was Jesus asleep on the boat during the storm?...He identified with mankind; he was 100% human. After his disciples woke him out of his sleep, He demonstrated his power as the Son of God. Jesus is 100% God. He can calm any storm! My point is: When situations escalate to a level that is higher than you can handle, make a call to Jesus. He was with his disciples during the storm, He is omnipresent today.

Behold, he that keepeth Israel shall neither slumber nor sleep.

Psalm 121:4KJV

Jesus is the great "Counselor." He is Lord of Lords, King of Kings, the Commander-in-Chief. It is never too early, nor too late to call him. When he speaks, there will be order in the camp. "O' Lord, Our God, Our Help in ages past, Our Hope for today and tomorrow, Our Strong Tower, please have mercy on your people, strengthen us in weaknesses, condition our hearts and regulate our minds (our thoughts) in the mighty name of Jesus, Our Lord and Savior." Amen!! We must rely upon God, The Father!

Reflect on Paul's Experience

God can change cold hearts

Saul of Tarsus was one who persecuted Christians. *"I used to believe that I ought to do many horrible things to the followers of Jesus of Nazareth. I imprisoned many of the saints in Jerusalem, as authorized by the High Priest; and when they were condemned to death, I cast my vote against them. I used torture to try to make Christians everywhere curse Christ."*

A Change Took Place

Paul said to the King, *"I was on such a mission to Damascus, armed with the authority and commission of the chief priest, when one day about noon, sir, a light from heaven brighter than the sun shone down on me and my companions."*

According to scripture, they all fell down and Saul heard a voice speaking to him. He heard the Lord call him by name, *"Saul, Saul, why are you persecuting me?"*

The Lord replied, *"I am Jesus, the one you are persecuting.*

*But rise, and stand upon thy feet: for I have appeared unto thee for this purpose, to make thee a minister and a witness both of these things which thou hast seen, and of those things in the which I will appear unto thee. Delivering thee from the people, and from the Gentiles, unto whom now I send thee, To open their eyes, and to turn them from **darkness to light,** and from the power of Satan unto God, that they may receive forgiveness of sins, and inheritance among them which are sanctified by faith that is in me.*

Acts 26: 16-18 KJV

Saul's name was changed to Paul after his Damascus Road experience (he was blinded). He turned his life around and began **working for the Lord**. <u>Allow God to use you on your job</u>. Not all will be receptive to the Word of God. As I recall, King Agrippa was asked, *believest* *thou the prophets?* Then Agrippa said unto Paul, *"Almost thou persuadest me to be a Christian."* When the world refuses to receive the "Word of God, "they are not rejecting the messenger, but God himself.

Reminder:
Paul said there was given him a thorn in the flesh. We do not know what the actual thorn was, but we do know it was not a thorn as the 72 which were placed in the <u>crown of thorns</u> for Christ. Paul sought the Lord three times that it might depart from him. Get this:

And he said unto me, "My grace is sufficient for thee: for my strength is made perfect in weakness."

If you are disturbed by a thorn in your flesh, call on Jesus, the Problem Solver. He knows when and I assure you He knows how to remove the thorn. Ask, "Lord, Please do it for me." Our time is not His time neither is our way his way. Trust God's process and things will work out and you will be the better person in the end. Jesus never fails! We become <u>perplexed, disturbed, anxious and more</u>. God's time is not our time. He knows what's best and even though he may delay his answer, it does not mean that He has denied our request. He still comes through in time. Trust God! Remember we will have seasons of struggles in our lives. I learned that struggles help mold our character. Apostle Paul calls such times <u>light afflictions</u> which are for a moment. Know that God has a time of deliverance. Sometimes the burden seems unbearable. Guess what? I made it through…and you will too! There is joy on the other side of through! God has an answer to every question and I assure you, He knows how to solve every problem. Trust him! He will not let you down nor disappoint you. O' how good He is! The good thing is He has no respect of persons. You can depend on God! He will see you through whatever occurs or happens in your life.

The Eunuch was Enlightened
Some are in **<u>darkness</u>** and are willing to discover a better way **<u>(walk in the light)</u>**. *And the angel of the Lord spoke unto Philip, saying Arise, and go toward the south unto the way that goeth down from Jerusalem unto Gaza, which is desert. And he arose and went: and*

behold, a man of Ethiopia, an eunuch of great authority under Candace queen of the Ethiopians, who had the charge of all her treasure, and had come to Jerusalem for to worship, was returning, and sitting in his chariot read Esaias the prophet. Then the Spirit said unto Philip, Go near, and join thyself to this chariot. And Philip ran thither to him, and heard him read the prophet Esaias, and said, understandest thou what thou readest? And he said, How can I, except some man should guide me? And he desired Philip that he would come up and sit with him.

Acts 8:26-31 KJV

Philip preached unto him Jesus and they went their way. The eunuch was convinced because when they came to a certain water, the eunuch said, *"See, here is water; what doth hinder me to be baptized?"* And Philip said, *"If thou believest with all thine heart, thou mayest."* He answered and said, *"I believe that Jesus Christ is the Son of God."* Philip baptized the eunuch.

CHAPTER 12
In Times of Loneliness

"Mattie" Granddaughter of <u>Willie Clarkson</u>

Look-Up and Live

Reminder: The Psalmist penned: Lift up your heads...
I decided to walk on by faith each day, breathe slowly and never let go of hope!

Psalm 121:1-8 (KJV)

I will lift up mine eyes unto the <u>hills</u>, from whence cometh my help. My help cometh from the <u>Lord</u>, which made heaven and earth. He will not suffer thy foot to be moved: He that keepeth thee will not slumber. Behold, he that keepeth Israel shall neither slumber nor sleep. The Lord is thy <u>keeper</u>: The Lord is thy shade upon thy right hand. The sun shall not smite thee by day, Nor the moon by night. The Lord shall <u>preserve</u> thee from all evil: He shall preserve thy soul. The Lord shall preserve thy going out and thy coming in from this time forth, and even for <u>evermore</u>. Amen!

When we are all <u>alone</u> the days seem long <u>and dreary</u>. The nights seem dark as a thousand midnights. There seem to be no stars in the sky and even the moon seems to be invisible. In reality, things are not always the way they seem to be. Our thinking is not clear and our vision is obscured. Our imagination becomes magnified; we sometimes become frightened, angry, disappointed but still try to rationalize the situation.

Reflecting on the writing of Paul:
We are troubled on every side, yet not in distressed; we are perplexed, but not in despair.

II Cor. 4:8 KJV

We find ourselves pondering over what we think went wrong. We roll back the calendar in our little minds and try to pin-point the root of the actual problem. We ask ourselves who, what, where and why? In all of our reasoning, something still seems to be off. We beat ourselves up and still cannot fathom what is actually happening. Sometimes we tell the whole truth <u>only to hear it used against us</u>. After all, we were taught honesty is the best policy. Immediately, we feel isolated in a very dark place or fenced-in, or even backed into a corner. We sometimes feel as though we are in a **horrible pit** and no one will come to our rescue. Think on the Word of God, call our Redeemer, Jesus Christ.

David penned: *I waited Patiently for the Lord; And he inclined unto me, and heard my cry. He brought me up also out of a **horrible pit**, out of the miry clay. And set my feet upon a rock, and established my goings.*

Psalm 40:1-2 KJV

We suddenly find ourselves at crossroads in life. I have been there too; that is disturbing! There is always a need to consult The Counselor, Jesus. He is our way out of whatever the situation is. Sometimes we cannot solve the problem, but I know God can and He will in his own time. Step back and watch God work. The battle is not yours, it's the Lord's.

Remember, Robert Frost pinned a poem: *"The Road not Taken."*

In Matthew 7 we are reminded of the broad road...

When we come to crossroads in life we must pause and gather our thoughts. Two roads diverge and we want to carefully choose which one to take. One will possibly be well traveled and the other might seem to be seldom traveled. Recall, the road that leads to destruction is wide and has a lot of travelers. While the road which lead to eternal life is narrow and has few travelers. Thus, the road which we want to take is the straight and narrow which lead on home! (for eternal life). Be sure, be very sure you are traveling the right road!

Continue the Journey (in the meantime)

How do we go forward after interruptions on this **earthly journey**? We ask ourselves the question and quickly recall: *In all thy ways acknowledge him, (God) and he shall direct thy path.* If you were reared in a Christian home your mother's teachings will quickly ring in your ears. *Trust in the Lord completely; do not ever trust yourself.*

In some situations, we cannot even trust our so-called friends or acquaintances. They might be part of the problem. Sister-Girl might advise you to have a one-night-stand. Your childhood best-friend-forever may tell you to lose yourself in strong drinks and forget everything. Pretty-Playboy might tell you to crash at his place for the night (big mistake). Neither of those is the answer. Should you be fooled or deceived by either one you will quickly discover that you made a humungous mistake. Reality will shake you to your true-self then you will be dumbfounded. At that time, you will realize that you are in a mercy situation! Good news: No one can fall so low that God cannot reach down and pick him up. One must humble himself in the sight of All Mighty God; acknowledge his sins and ask for mercy. He will hear our humble cry and <u>He will answer</u>! We really need guidance and God's word is the best. Call on him and do not delay. He waits patiently to hear from us.

Listen to The Voice of God
I will instruct you (says the Lord) and guide you along the best pathway for your life; I will advise you and watch your progress.
                                                          Psalm of David, 32:8

We know sheep will sometimes stray; they need help to find their way. In the Bible days a shepherd had a staff which was used for more than one reason. When he realized one sheep had wondered off, he went to find him. The sheep possibly had fallen into a place that prohibited him from being able to pull himself up. After the lost sheep was located, the shepherd lifted him out of the trapped place. There was much rejoicing. Today, how many shepherds even notice the absence of one sheep? There are some who lead mega congregations. Some may never notice the absence of one member who might have lost his way. The pastor's job is multi-faceted! The good shepherd seeks for the lost sheep and I believe Matthew and Luke agree. However, this part is the responsibility of the <u>entire church</u>.

Be Honest
Let us be honest with ourselves and with God. When we deliberately do wrong, or we realize we did something wrong by mistake, we need to repent which mean turn away from sin to God. There are consequences for our actions. Every action causes a reaction. Sometimes we make mistakes; that's life. When we fall, we don't have to crawl, linger in the lowest place or wallow in the polluted

space. We can get up, brush ourselves off and begin again. Sometimes one needs a little assistance. He might need instructions in righteousness as well. In order to help our neighbor, we must be able to impart the Word of God to the fallen one. Let the Holy Spirit be our guide. Remember we have a friend in Jesus. We must tell Him all our problems because He has all the answers. Jesus has an all-seeing eye and He can see way down the road (into the future). He will lead us around all the curves; pitfalls in life. Jesus knows where all the roadblocks (nay-sayers) are. He will steer us clear of them if we trust his guidance. We need Grace and Mercy as our traveling companions. They are magnificent, a bridge over troubled water, and a **light in darkness**. The Lord knows it gets dark in our lives sometimes, trouble gets in our way and we cry many tears! We know God will wipe all our tears away and give us new directions too.

Jesus said, Let not your heart be troubled: ye believe in God, believe also in me.

John 14:1 KJV

Jesus reminds us that God is Our Father; we believe in Him. We have confessed that we believe in his Son, Jesus. Now we must put our trust in Him. Believe that Jesus will see us through all hurtful situations. He understands our sorrow because he was acquainted with grief. Jesus suffered through pain, He walked with his disciples and he ate with sinners. Jesus was humble and he demonstrated how we must live.

Lift up your head, tomorrow will be the beginning of a brand-new day. You will see the sun rise in the East and cast a bright light on your pathway. Your roadmap will be without error. Tell yourself, "Jesus is speaking to me." Get up, start moving into your destiny. This will be the beginning of a new chapter in your life. As you pray and seek God's guidance, follow his instructions and you will not walk alone. You will discover while you were disheartened, tucked away and all alone, God was working in your favor. While you were sitting idle, shedding wild tears and had no song in your heart, God had a blessing with your name on it. And what is for you, it is for you! Sometimes we need to be patient, stand still until God's will is clear.

The Psalmist pinned: *"Be still and know that I'm God."*

You will be fine; be encouraged. In fact, encourage yourself.

For I know the thoughts that I think towards you, saith the Lord, thoughts of peace, and not of evil to give you an expected end.
Jeremiah 29:11

Now that you know this, rejoice!

CHAPTER 13
The Power of Prayer

Grandma's Hands

THIRD SEASON OF LIFE: FALL OR AUTUMN

Many women are grandmothers; we should be seasoned saints. Our prayer life should be constant or steady. Sometimes it is necessary to "fast and pray." Fasting is preparation to hear from God. It is motivated by desire; to declutter our lives. Fasting also prepares us when trying to discern right from wrong or greed from needs. Seasoned women should be prepared to counsel younger women. When we do so, we must remember we were not always mature Christians. We had to grow by studying the Word of God and asking God for guidance. We also had to amend our ways. Let us be careful not to injure others with our words. When one is overtaken in a fault we who are spiritual are to restore such a one in the spirit of meekness. Remember if we did not do one thing, we did another doing our growing years. Thank God for grace and mercy! They are new every morning, His compassion never fails; great is thy faithfulness! Because of God's love, we are not consumed. He <u>held back</u> that which we deserved and showed us favor. Praise God today! Let us not be lifted up in pride and proclaim that we DESERVE anything!

Young men need advice; they need a father figure. Many men are grandfathers in the Fall or Autumn of life. Men you must be careful how you correct or advise younger men. When they ask questions, you must be trueful and let them know you learned from your mistakes. All have sinned and come short of the glory of God. **We (men and women) did that which He told us not to do...**

Apostle Paul pinned: *When I want to do good, I don't; and when I try not to do wrong, I do it anyway* (Roman 7:19 TLB). A war is going on!

We must be ready to pray at a moment's notice for any need, concern or situation no matter how devastating it may be.

The effectual, fervent prayer of a righteous man availeth much.
James 5:16b KJV

THE CHRISTIAN'S DAILY WALK

Once we confess Jesus Christ we are called by his name. We are God's representatives and we must pray often to keep our relationship intact. If we draw nigh to the Lord, He will draw nigh to us!! Prayer should be a part of our daily routine. Many times, we don't consult God because we want to do things our way. We depend on our little knowledge and do not consider the consequences. We also know things happen by God's permissive will or his divine will. He has the final word. Prayer may be <u>uttered or unexpressed</u> and we pray to God in the name of Jesus. He is our mediator, the door to the Father. No one can prohibit us from praying. There is no divider/curtain between us and Jesus Christ. We remember the veil was the curtain in the temple at Jerusalem which was rent (torn) from top to bottom when Jesus died on the cross.

Luke penned:...*it was noon, and* **darkness** *fell across the whole land for three hours, until three o' clock. The* **light** *from the sun was gone---and suddenly the thick veil hanging in the Temple split apart.*
Luke 23:44-45 TLB

Today, no one and nothing stands in our way to the Father. We must pray to the Father in the name of Jesus. He is the door. We heard that prayer was taken out of schools. That may be the decision which was made by man but actually, we can pray every time the Spirit moves upon us to pray. Glory to God! First, we acknowledge God as our father and Jesus Christ as our Lord and Savior. We confess our sins for all have sinned and fall short. We thank God for every blessing and we petition Him on behalf of our family, others and this <u>whole nation.</u> We are our brother's keeper. We must pray for those who are chained and bound. Many are behind prison walls. Ask God to take out the stony hearts of the jailers and give them hearts of flesh. Thereby, they may be mindful of their behavior as well. Always pray for the unsaved and do not forget to pray for the back-sliders too. If we pray, God will hear our prayer! We must seek Him with all our heart!

James tells us that the prayers of a <u>righteous man</u> have an advantage. There is power in prayer; always ask if it be His will. We ask God for blessings, believe, and thank Him because of our faith in Him. In other words, we call those things that are not as though they were, but we must also prepare ourselves to accept His will. Sometimes God does not answer the way we want Him to. He knows what is best just as a mother knows what is best for her child.

Remember Jesus prayed in Gethsemane before He went to the cross.

Saying, Father, if thou be willing, remove this cup (of suffering) from me: nevertheless, not my will, but thine, be done.
Luke 22:42 (KJV)

*For he hath made him (Jesus) to be sin for us, who knew no sin; that we might be made **righteousness** of God in him.*
2 Cor. 5:21 (KJV)

Think about the ten commandments. Sinful man could not keep them to perfection but, Christ is perfect and He kept them for us. We should strive to live right and expect our prayers to be productive. Living right produces righteousness! Abraham, the father of the faithful believed God and it was counted unto him for righteousness. It is a fact that we can do nothing without God. We may talk with Him repeatedly because there is so much to thank Him for. We need guidance in everything that we do and without God, we will fail.

Trusting God/Faith on Trial

We must gird up the loins of our minds. Put on the whole armor of God knowing that this journey called life takes us through valleys and we have mountaintop experiences too. We are fighting a war against Satan. This is intense spiritual warfare. Wickedness is in high places, but we must bind every evil act. We must call things that are not as though they were: Sickness and diseases are healed in Jesus' name. We must believe in the power of prayer and claim victory in Christ. We shall win with Christ as our Commander.

Children of God have power to pray for the sick that they may be healed and we know that all sickness is not unto death. When talking to God, you shall have power when the Holy Ghost is come upon you!!We have faith in God and we call on the name of Jesus, our healer. There is healing in his name. There is deliverance in His name and we pray that it be God's will to heal our people, but not all will be healed on this side. Some will be healed when soul and body separates. In the meantime, read God's Holy Word, pray, believe, and trust God. How strong is your faith? If you have little faith, ask God as the apostles did. "Lord increase our faith." How does one activate his faith? The answer is: Do what God said, believe Him, trust Him and react accordingly. Recall the many miracles which Jesus performed. If one is sick with a fever, recall Jesus healed Simon Peter's mother-in-law. She was suffering with a high fever. The apostles sought Jesus on her behalf because they believed he could heal her.

And he (Jesus) stood over her, and rebuked the fever; and it left her: and immediately she arose and ministered unto them.
Luke 4:38 KJV

Jesus demonstrated his power and Peter's mother-in-law was made whole. Who has witnessed such a healing miracle in this day? Jesus is not walking among us in the flesh today, but He is still in the miracle working business. I tell you, "Lay your hands on your loved one; call Doctor Jesus. He is waiting to hear from you." Ask if it be His will; have faith in God. If one cannot see recall blind Bartimaeus, the beggar. He could not see, but he could hear. He heard the crowd and that Jesus was passing by; he had faith. Bartimaeus cried-out to Jesus. He ignored the crowd's plea for him to be quiet. In fact, he cried louder because he had a need. He received his sight because he asked, "Thy Son of David, have mercy on me." He was in **darkness, but Light** came where he was. Jesus is the Light! He is still giving sight to the blind. Those who have not accepted Jesus as Lord and Savior are spiritually blind. The woman with the issue of blood had faith in Jesus. After ten years of what we may call pure agony, she pressed her way through the crowd to get to Jesus. She touched the hem of His garment and she was made whole. The fountain of her blood stopped. We must press our way: Remove all that may hinder us which may be jealousy, envy, arrogance or the like. Those are weights which we need not carry. Run to Jesus!

Beloved, I wish above all things that thou mayest prosper and be in health, even as thy soul prosper.
III John 2 KJV

As children of God, we pray for this nation! Many have turned away from God but there is a remnant that will continue to trust, praise and believe Him and we are sure of our salvation! We have power to pray for our wayward children and especially those who have gone to a very dark place, far-away land, LoDebar. We can leave the light on for them, but they need the prayers of the righteous.

The young play-mom was familiar with the dark place of LoDebar; unfortunately, no one left the light on for her. There was no turning back and she could not hear nobody pray until she went into the house of the Lord. She could not say who prayed for her either. It was heartbreaking to be "way-down yonder all by herself." All of her home-training kicked-in. She prayed and God answered her prayers! Finally, she got what she needed, but not what she wanted. God is a Way-Maker; He knows what is best. Pray because unlike our so-called friends, King Jesus is listening; He will answer. People of God, we must pray for our enemies, if they be hungry, give them bread to eat; if they be thirsty give them water to drink.

For thou shall heap coals of fire upon their head, And the Lord shall reward Thee.
Proverbs 25: 22 KJV

We know that it's right to do right. Our conscience tells us what we should do. The Holy Spirit is our guide. Let us not override the Spirit. All of us have the ability to make a difference in a positive way. Jesus said to His disciples, *the harvest truly is plenteous, but the laborers are few.* And so, it is this very day. In the meantime, be encouraged:

…and it doth not yet appear what we shall be: we know that, when he shall appear, we shall be like him; for we shall see him as he is.
I John 3:2 KJV

Christ is on His way back! Are you prepared to meet the King?

CHAPTER 14
Remembering the Clarkson Legacy

THE LEGACY WHICH WE LEAVE IS A TESTIMONY OF OUR LIVES

PROFOUND ADVICE:
Always keep God in the fore-front of your mind; let Jesus lead the way. He is a mighty good leader; He can lead you all the way from earth to glory!

Descendants of Bill & Cloa Clarkson (7 Children) (DOB. 1840 & 1849)

1. **Likely Clarkson and Mary A. Pinesett-Clarkson (9 Children)**
   Applas (Cuff), Billy, Cato (Dude), Georgia, Annie Lou, Judge (Honey), Hezekiah (Dobelly), Revelation (Papp), and William (Jack)
2. **Louiza Clarkson (3 Children)**
   Malissa Clarkson, Lizzie Clarkson, and Menerva Clarkson
3. **Willie Clarkson and Dollie Salters-Clarkson (3 Children)**
   Ellis Clarkson, Sr., Annie B. Clarkson-Turner, Susie B. Clarkson-Taylor
4. **Matt Clarkson and Parthine Dale-Clarkson (4 Children)**
   Matt Jr., Jessie, Twins: Mary Clarkson-Williams &Martha Clarkson-Young
5. **Bulow Clarkson and Sarah A. Hampton-Clarkson (4 Children)**
   Isaac Clarkson, LePatry Clarkson, Mary Anna Clarkson, Elva Mae Clarkson
6. **Noble Clarkson and Pearlean Smith-Clarkson (1Child)**
   Clarafene (Beanie) Clarkson-Washington
7. **Walter Clarkson**

God Has Plans for Our Lives
The Clarkson Legacy Lives On!

For I know the plans I have for you, says the Lord. They are plans for good and not for evil, to give you a future and a hope.
                                    Jeremiah 29:11 TLB

Idonia Clarkson-Farrell
Granddaughter of <u>Bulow Clarkson</u>

IDONIA CLARKSON-FARRELL'S STORY

Idonia resides in Arcadia, LA. She is the daughter of Isaac and Idries Hartwell-Clarkson. Prior to her husband's death, she was a housewife and served as the first black female <u>volunteer firefighter</u> in Bienville Parish. <u>We salute her</u>! She was married to John Earl Farrell, who is now deceased. He served this country with the United States Marine Corps. He fought in the Vietnam War; we appreciate his service and bravery. Three sons were born to the couple. The eldest son, Randell L. Farrell served with the United States Navy and their youngest son, Demetris A. Farrell, Master Sergeant served with the United States Army. He worked in the White House and was working in the Pentagon on Tuesday, September 11, 2001 when a plane hit the building (Pentagon). We thank God, Demetris was unharmed. The same day, the World Trade Center known as the Twin Towers (North and South Tower skyscrapers) were hit and destroyed by terrorists.

The iconic World Trade Center (WTC) was located in New York City. The destruction and the loss of lives changed the course of history.

Richard, Anika, and Aria Woods
Anika is the Great, Great Granddaughter of <u>Willie Clarkson</u>

ANIKA'S SUCCESS LADDER

Anika graduated from Caddo Magnet High School in Shreveport, LA in 1996. She continued her education at Louisiana State University and graduated with a <u>Bachelor's Degree in Criminal Justice</u> in 2001. Anika relocated to Atlanta, GA and began her career as a Probation Officer at Atlanta Municipal Court. During her 12 years in Atlanta, she also worked for Fulton County Superior Court as a Judicial Assistant. In addition, she was employed by Dekalb County Juvenile Court as a Public Relations Manager.

She met Richard Woods in 2014 at a National Court Management Conference. They got married a few months later. Anika moved to Phoenix, Arizona and worked as a Compliance Specialist at the Arizona Supreme Court. She was the first black Court Supervisor at the Mesa Municipal Court. Her husband, Richard was promoted to District Court Administrator of the Harris County Supreme Court in Houston, TX where they currently reside.

Willie Clarkson: Military Draftee for World War II Place of Residence: Grand Bayou, Red River Parish, LA

In Memory
Minister Ronnie Young, BS
Grandson of <u>Matt Clarkson</u>

Ronnie was a Shreveport, LA native; the son of late George and Martha Clarkson-Young. He graduated from Fair Park High School and furthered his education at Northwestern University in Natchitoches, LA. He majored in <u>Business Administration.</u>

Ronnie served his country in the United States Marines Corp and was honorably discharged. During his career he was the manager of several local restaurants and the District Manager over Jazz's. He performed duties in the department of Nutrition Services for Caddo school system. He sang with the Avenue Baptist Church Male Chorus and was a soloist at the chapel in the Veteran's Administration Hospital. Ronnie often ministered in songs at the 80th Street Church of God in Christ where he also assisted with the Feeding Program.

Lastly, he enjoyed meeting and witnessing to all the veterans at Veterans Administration Medical Center.

Armanda Clarkson, MA, BS
Granddaughter of Likely Clarkson

Career Story

Armanda is the fifth child of Judge and Lucille Anderson-Clarkson. She attended Booker T. Washington High School in Shreveport, LA. She continued her education at Grambling State University and graduated with a Bachelor's of Science Degree. Amanda earned her Master's from Texas Southern University in Houston, TX. She worked at numerous public schools in Caddo Parish. Armanda retired from Eden Garden Magnet (K-5 grade school) after thirty-three years of dedicated service.

Well done Armanda! We thank God for your <u>ability and patience to impart lessons</u> to children of all walks of life.

LaDuska James, MA, BSN, RN, LP, FP-C, CEN
Great, great,great granddaughter of <u>Louiza Clarkson</u>

Climb to Higher Heights
(**Credentials:** Master's of Art, Bachelor's of Science Nursing, Registered Nurse, Licensed Paramedic, Flight Paramedic-Certified, Certified Emergency Nurse)

LaDuska is a Shreveport native who graduated from Parkway High School. She furthered her education at Bossier Parish Community College and obtained an <u>Associate Degree in Science-Paramedics; a Bachelor's of Science Degree in nursing from Northwestern State University.</u> She worked in the ER, ICU and Neonatal ICU. LaDuska was the first black female Flight Nurse at three air-medical companies which she worked for. She received a Master's of Art in Human Services Counseling:Crisis Response and Trauma Cognate from Liberty University, Lynchburg, VA. She holds two national certifications.

During LaDuska's nursing career she has had the oppurtunity to be a Nurse Manager of an Observation Unit and interim Nurse Manager for an ER Department. During the first surge of Covid in the U.S., she had the opportunity to successfully facilitate the opening of the first Monoclonal Antibody (MAB) Infusion Clinic; the first Covid High Acuity High Flow Oxygen Unit for the facility where she was employed at that time. These two additions opened a door to provide advance care to the patients in the surrounding communities. Thereby ensuring to succeed their goal in providing quality care. She is currently a Clinic Program Manager.

Accolades include:
- Three-time recipient of a system award in Quality and Patient Safety in three different categories
- Texas Nurses Association District 9 Nurses Hero
- Houston Chronicles Top 150 Nurses in Houston
- Recognition by State Represenative Babin for Covid Response Services
- Two-time recipient for excellence in Nursing Good Samaritan as a Bronze Medalist
- Outstanding Nursing Leadership of the year

The Clarkson Family is grateful to God. We thank Him for blessing LaDuska to provide excellent professional and compassionate care to patients during such perlious times. We look forward to future endeavors along with her and believe God will be her guide.

In Memory of
Clarafene Clarkson-Washington (Beanie)
Daughter of Pearlean Smith-Clarkson and <u>Noble Clarkson</u>

Clarafene confessed Christ at an early age at Oakdale Baptist Church, Gayle, LA. She later united with Galilee Baptist Church on Highway 1. Clarafene served faithfully as an usher until her health failed. She was known as "Beanie" and she was married to M.C. Washington; she was the mother of four children.

Noble Clarkson: Military Draftee for World War II in 1942
Place of Residence: Red River Parish, LA

Walter Clarkson:Military Draftee for World War II in 1942
Place of Residence: Sample C. Ward 4, Red River Parish, LA
He was married to Arenna Clarkson. To this union, no children were born

CHAPTER 15
Those Who Serve / Served Our Country
BRAVE HEROES OF THE CLARKSON FAMILY

Randell L. Farrell
U.S. Navy

Cheryl Cuningham
U.S. Navy

Demetrius A. Farrell
U.S. Army Master Sergeant

Randell is the son of Idonia C. Farrell and John Earl Farrell. He served in the United States Navy.

Cheryl is the daughter of Mattie P. Wilson and Manuel Wilson. She served in the United States Navy during Desert Storm. She is also a Licensed Vocational Nurse at Dallas Regional Hospital.

Demetrius is also the son of Idonia C. Farrell and John Earl Farrell. He served in the United States Army.

Nikeya D. Clarkson *Naomie Clarkson-Kinsey* *Cedric Brown*
Army II Lieutenant *U.S. Navy* *U.S. Army*

Nikeya is the son of Jimmie and Dorothy Clarkson, both of Arcadia, LA. He is the grandson of Isaac and Idries Hartwell-Clarkson. Nikeya graduated from Arcadia High School in 1995 and received a Bachelor's Degree in the year 2000 from Southern University in Baton Rouge, LA. He is an executive officer assigned to Charlie Company 168th Medical Battalion.

Naomie is the daughter of Isaac and Idries Hartwell-Clarkson. She joined the U.S. Navy in 1971 after graduating from Arcadia High School. She and many others came from a military family. We thank them for their service to this country.

Cedric is the son of Willie and Shirley Brown. He joined the United States Army in February 1999 and served his country (6.5 years) until

November 2005. Basic Training was completed in Ft. Jackson, South Carolina, Advance Individual Training (AIT) at Ft. Lee, Virginia. While at Ft. Lee he signed-up for Jump School to become a Paratrooper. From there, he went to Ft. Bragg, North Carolina. He spent three (3) years in 82nd Airborne Division, re-enlisted and went to 7th Group 3rd Battalion where he deployed for 6.5 months in Afghanistan Operation Enduring Freedom (OEF). Thank you for your service!

OTHER BRAVE MEN AND WOMEN

United States Navy Graduates in Great Lakes, Illinois
Cheryl C. Wilson, fourth from left on 2nd row

Many soldiers have served and continue to serve our country in spite of the danger which they encounter. They put themselves in harm's way to protect and preserve our freedom. Words alone cannot express the gratitude which we owe to those who serve this country! Thank

God for many who were blessed to return home, but many with amputated limbs, troubled minds and more.

Multiple veterans are homeless after serving this country. It's a disgrace to know that many return home and for whatever reason they sleep on the streets. Some live in shelters, under tents, in the woods or wherever. This should not be because they have no place to reside decently. Shelter should await them upon their return home to America. Resources should be readily available to any and all who are in need.

Some veterans say it is hard to get medical attention. In such cases, they spend hours waiting in medical facilities. Yet, we say we are grateful for their service. Sadly, I recognize: Many brave warriors have given their lives and their bodies were returned to the USA in coffins. Many bodies have not been returned and their families do not have closure.

Body of an American Soldier

An On-going War

Many men served our country in other ways: Martin Luther King, Jr., Congressman John Robert Lewis; Medgar Evers. Evers was a World War II veteran who served in the Unites States Army; fought hard for equal rights for all. We must not forget James Meredith who was also an American civil rights warrior and Air Force veteran. He was shot down like a dog while marching for civil rights by a <u>white sniper</u>. We thank God for sparing his life. Let's not forget Malcolm X. He fought for justice and in his words, "By any means necessary."

War in America continues because of injustices. Ruth Bader Ginsburg was a spokeswoman for Women's Rights and many others have paved the way...This generation must carry the baton (responsibility) forward...We have not reached our goal and we are in no way satisfied. Many of our every-day citizens are at war with each other over petty things and in gangs. At times our subdivisions or neighborhoods seem to be battle-grounds. Shots ring out and innocent people are killed. Many lives of children are taken during senseless drive-by shootings. Sometimes whole families are eliminated by gang members. Where is your conscience? Violence is not the answer. It only begets more violence. Our children are fighting with the wrong weapons. That is the work of the devil. It is time for change: Put down the AR57 or Smith & Wesson firearms and other weapons of war. We must teach our children to pray, be transformed by the renewing of their minds and fight with the Word of God. To do so, they must study God's word, receive it and transformation will take place. God will fight our battles. Nobody can fight a battle like the Lord!

Dearly beloved, avenge not yourselves, but rather give place to wrath: for it is written, vengeance is mine; I will repay, saith the Lord.
Romans 12:19 KJV

Rivalry

I am reminded: Cain and Abel were brothers and Cain slaughtered his brother, Abel. Cain was apparently jealous and became angry because his brother's offering was acceptable to God. Therefore, Cain developed a negative attitude toward his brother. Abel's blood cried out from the ground to God and today, the blood of many is crying out from the ground! Many families have been torn apart. God said, "Vengeance is mine I will repay." He will!

Chapter 16
Opportunities of Today

MAKING A DIFFERENCE

Despite hardships, "Black" men are blessed to succeed in many professions. Beyond doubt, they have played a very important part in American History, but they have not always been recognized! God is good... Blacks can be found working/participating in just about every profession there is. Many have made history, broken records in sports, theater, the medical field and poetry. There is no end to music/entertainment and voice. Some of the world's greatest singers and performers are black. Educators have done and continue to do a great job. There are other occupations as well (the list goes on and on). There is much talent within the black race!!! Thank you God!!!

Blacks can do more than be gardeners and maids for others. However, there is profit in all labor and man must consider how he may better himself. Some may consider landscape design & installation as a career. There must be a desire to accomplish something; leave a worthwhile legacy. Do more than live in-the-moment; don't be satisfied with just anything. Don't have the attitude of: "This will do." All we need is a chance.

Mary L. Clarkson, Clinical Assistant
Granddaughter of Willie Clarkson

Mary L. Clarkson, a Shreveport, Louisiana resident began her tenure at Louisiana State University Health Sciences Center in 1997. The facility is currently Ochsner Health System. She has proven to be a dependable worker for twenty-five years and performs her duties with care and concern. For the reasons stated, she is recognized by the staff as an "Outstanding Worker." Mary has a passon for those who are in need of medical assistance.

And whatsoever you do, do it heartily, as to the Lord and not to men.
                                                           Colossians 3:23 KJV

Malique Cannon, Medical Assistant
Great, Great, Great, Grandson of <u>Willie Clarkson</u>

Malique Cannon resides in Shreveport, Louisiana. He graduated from Remington College in Shreveport, LA in 2023 at the age of 21 years. He successfully completed the curriculum for Medical Assistant and plans to continue his education at Southern University in the fall (2023). Malique's goal is to become a Registered Nurse. His philosophy is, "<u>Believe</u> and set your mind on what you aspire to accomplish and it can be done." He holds to the words of Jesus,...but with God all things are possible.

Matthew 19: 26 KJV

Gionreicho Dale Lynch, BS Criminal Justice
Great, Great Grandson of <u>Willie Clarkson</u>

Gionreicho D. Lynch is the Great, Great grandson of **Willie Clarkson.** He is gifted in music and sports. He writes and produces songs, plays drums and keyboards. Gionreicho graduated from Evangel Christian Academy where he participated in football and track events earning several awards and recognitions including state championship for javelin and discus. He earned a track scholarship to Grambling State University where he graduated with a <u>Bachelor's of Science Degree</u> in Criminal Justice. He was employed at Lew Sterrett Prison in Dallas, TX.

When Behind Prison Walls…

P………. Prison: punishment for unlawful conduct, crimes, or sinful acts etc.
R………. Reminder: A time to recall past mistakes [Reformation]
I………...Isolation from family and friends; associates
S………. Sign of disobedience, disrespect for the laws of the land; moral laws
O………. Observation to be informed; improve conduct
N………. Now, be transformed by renewing your mind (right living)

Wrong Actions are Followed by Consequences

Prisons Have Rules
They have a scheduled time for everything; inmates must follow the rules. Unlike in the comfort of one's home with Mom and Dad, inmates do not rebel against authorities (not without consequences). They line-up for head-count and are given work assignments.

Employees:

Some chose a career in law enforcement and changed their minds because of harsh treatments, ugly attitudes among other things. This job is not meant for mild-mannered individuals. They are subjected to become cold, bitter and un-Christlike.

Reicho decided to make a change. He is now the owner of a trucking company; doing well by the grace of God.

Clarke Lemar Jackson, BS, Paramedic EMS Officer
Great Grandson of <u>Likely Clarkson</u>

Clarke L. Jackson is the son of Rosetta Clarkson-Jackson and Leroy Jackson III. He graduated from Southwood High School where he was a state basketball stand-out. His team won multiple district titles and 2003 state runner-up.

Clarke received multiple individual awards including 1st team all-district, all-city, and all-state during his tenure at Southwood with the class of 2004. He attended Centenary College of Shreveport, LA, played basketball and later transferred to Louisiana State University in Shreveport. He graduated in 2009 after studying Education & Kinesiology and obtaining a Bachelor's Degeree in General Studies. Clarke is married to Jacquelle Dixon-Jackson; the couple has two children. Clarke has been a Paramedic/Firefighter with the City of Shreveport Fire Department since 2013; was recently promoted to an Emergency Medical Service Officer in the Division. He is also a basketball coach/trainer with HeartWork Athletics, an organization which he and former team-mates organized to mentor and aid local youth to achieve their goals utilizing the game of basketball.

Kelvin B. Taylor, Barber
Great Grandson of Willie Clarkson

Kelvin Taylor is a Shreveport, LA native. He attended Fair Park High School; graduated from Captain Shreve High School. He furthered his education at Southern University and relocated to Dallas, Texas in pursuit of better opportunities.

Kelvin stated, "I remember my childhood barber, Mr. Jerry Bowman and I was inspired by him and his reputation as the legendary "Jerry Bowman" in the world of barbering. Since then I developed a passion for cutting hair."

Kelvin enrolled in Larry's Barber College and in 1993 he became a Class A Licensed Barber. In 2005 he started Tight Edge and Styles in North Arlington, Texas. At Tight Edge one can get all the latest styles, cuts, and **designs.**

Kamela Horton, Great Granddaughter of Willie Clarkson

Kamela Horton resides in Shreveport, Louisiana. She has been employed with The Arc Caddo-Bossier Missions for over twenty years. She currently serves as a Mail Clerk Specialist on Barksdale Air Force Base in Shreveport, Louisiana. Kamela processes packages to over 35 mail locations on base with an overall 98 percent accuracy rate, and zero customer complaints. She is a faithful and dependable employee.

Kamela has been a member of the Union Springs Baptist Missionary Church, Shreveport, Louisiana for over forty years. During her membership, she has served in the Youth Department, Vacation Bible School, Music Ministry and other auxiliaries as needed. Her commitment and dedication are examples to her team members, peers and family members.

Stephanie LuBom-Dawson and Ronald Dawson
Stephanie is the Great, Great, granddaughter of <u>Willie Clarkson</u>

The couple, Stephanie and Ronald graduated from Lakeview Centennial High School in Dallas, Texas. Stephanie furthered her education at Southeastern Oklahoma State University. She currently works as a Life Insurance Annuity Claims Examiner of Benefits and Beneficiaries.

Ronald, her husband furthered his education at Eastfield Community College. He is a Dispatcher for UPS. They are residents of Dallas, Texas.

Mrs. Iva Youngblood

Iva has worked in city government for over a decade with the city of Shreveport Department of Community Development. She is passionate about encouraging others and ministering God's love. She believes in the redemptive power of God and stands firmly on Hebrews 4:16—*Let us, therefore, come boldly unto the throne of grace, that we may obtain mercy, and find grace to help in time of need* (KJV).

Lennard Holden, Bachelor's Degree in Music (Maestro)
<u>Renown Community Leader</u>

Lennard Holden received his Bachelor's Degree in Music from Mississippi College, Clinton, MS. He is and has been the Director of Bands at Southwood High School since 2007. Previously, Mr. Holden held a position at Clinton High School in Clinton, Mississippi.

Currently, Mr. Holden directs the Freshman Band, Percussion Ensemble, Brass Choir, Woodwind Ensemble, Marching Auxiliaries, Southwood Symphonic Wind Ensemble, Jazz Band, Pep Band and Marching Band.

Under his precise directions at Southwood High School, the band program has grown from 23 members to over 120. Southwood's Band has been recognized for numerous awards and honors. The school's ensemble has performed in multiple states:

Washington D.C.   Houston, Texas
Orlando, Florida   Memphis, Tennessee
Atlanta, Georgia   Jackson, Mississippi

The Southwood Symphonic Wind Ensemble was featured in USA Today in 2015. The group was also chosen as Featured Artist in the Shreveport Magazine and the Shreveport Times.

The Southwood Symphonic Wind Ensemble competed in 2019 at the Southern Star Music Festival in Atlanta, GA. In a field of 35 other ensembles from across the country, the Symphonic Winds won the title of Grand Champion.

Mr. Holden is active as a judge and clinician in Louisiana and Mississippi. As a performer, Mr. Holden plays trumpet in the Shreveport Regional Jazz Ensemble and the Red River Wind Orchestra where he has served as guest conductor. His professional affiliation includes: NAfME, Louisiana Music Educators Association, the National Band Association, Phi Mu Alpha Music Fraternity and Minority Band Directors National Association.

Lennard is an active member of the <u>Praise team</u> at Calvary Missionary Baptist Church, Shreveport, LA 71108 where Reverend Joe R. Gant, Jr., is Pastor/Teacher. We have utmost respect for such an accomplished and talented member of the congregation!!! All praises to our God!!!

A NEED FOR CHANGE

Many students drop out of school for a variety of reasons. They find themselves caught-up in gangs, selling drugs, teen pregnancies and more. If something is not right it can be nothing but WRONG! <u>Some children are disobedient</u>. They will not hear instructions; neither can they see the error of their ways until it's too late.

Children, obey your parents; this is the right thing to do because God has placed them in authority over you.

                                                                          Ephesians 6:1 TLB

We as parents teach our children, pray for them, and tell them to pray for themselves. They must face the facts and want to make positive changes. At some point, parents conclude: "I'm going to leave you in the hands of the Lord." I am a witness that it hurts when our children are disobedient, but we can only do so much for them. Some do not learn until they are caught between a rock and a hard place...They must realize that they cannot rely upon their parents the duration of their lives. Some parents instruct their children or warn them about being unruly. Little Bad-Boy-Blue seems to think nothing will happen to him. He thinks he has things under control. As I recall the saying, "Some think they have the world in a jug and the stopper in their hand." Little Bad-Boy-Blue is a bully, large for his age and robust. Not only that but he is an athlete. In his mind, "I'm cool." Being cool is no comparison to being obedient, educated and successful.

Many times, it's the company which they keep which lures them to practice dangerous habits. They want to fit-in but become hooked so-to-speak. They seem to realize what is going on but tell themselves, "After I collect X amount of loot, I'm going to shake this habit." They find themselves in deeper trouble than they could have ever imagined. At that point they are likened to a broken vessel. They must repent of their sins or disobedient actions. Fact is, the Potter wants to put them back together again. He can make them whole again; make their lives brand new. Jesus is the Potter; the Great I Am! He is waiting to hear from them. They <u>must humble themselves,</u> reach out to God and follow his instructions.

In most cases children seem to think they are grown-ups before they are actually grown. They deceive themselves by claiming they can be successful without getting an education. They still have childish ways and thoughts. When one becomes a man, he should put away childish things; grow-up and be transformed by renewing his mind. Yes, some are blessed to find their way into business without additional learning/training. Perhaps one's family has a prosperous business which the child chooses to continue or might inherit. Young Johnny just might be thoughtful and learn to manage well. He might even have his priorities in order, become a good protective family man who takes his family to church, praises, and worships God!

I urge all students to be the best they can be. Take advantage of the opportunity to learn some useful trade or profession. A trade might be the better choice due to the fact that many businesses/companies have chosen to utilize robots. In most professions unnecessary and expensive classes are required. Thereby, students are left with a mountain of debt which they must work many years to repay. Grants are available for those who qualify; loans and scholarships are readily available also. It is alright to work at <u>fast food businesses,</u> but do not expect it to be your job until retirement. Yes, there are some who do well and eventually advance to a management position, but do not expect that to be the case. Statistics prove: Scores of employees work for minimal wages and they retire with barely enough income (poverty level) to support themselves. In such cases, many return to the workforce!

I strongly advise adolescents to read, "DEFINE YOU!" We define ourselves, but the public describes us by our careers and life styles among other things. No one has to be defined by his or her past.

Neither should one give-in to disabilities. You can still do great things; accomplish what you believe you can. You determine how far you want to go in life and trust God to achieve your goals. You can do it! You define yourself. Opportunities are boundless.

Don't count on flapping your wings like birds; going nowhere. Spread your wings and soar like eagles to higher heights. Tell yourself that God is the Wind beneath your wings. He can take you to heights unknown! You can discover new territories. Metaphorically, you may also tread swift waters! You can break old records! You can... Put your faith to the test. By all means, believe in yourself.

Parents must encourage children to do their best and pray for them. Pray with them to show love and support. Encourage them to read the Word of God that they may be strengthened thereby.

For the Needs of Others

Gwendolyn LuBom Foster, BD, C-PP
Great granddaughter of <u>Willie Clarkson</u>

<u>Early Childhood Educator</u>
Gwendolyn LuBom is a Certified Para Professional in Shreveport, LA. She holds a <u>Bachelor's Degree in General Studies</u> with a concentration in Social Science from Louisiana Tech University. She is employed by Caddo Parish Public School System and has rendered 38 years of dedicated service.

Different Categories
Unfortunately, some children have serious health concerns or disabilities. They may require more attention than the average child. Many learn at a slower rate than others. They are educated in a way that addresses their individual needs. The process involves individually planned and monitored arrangements of teaching

procedures. So, the children attend special classes which are taught by Special Education Professionals. Many students are able to make tremendous progress. Disabilities (physical or mental) do not discriminate. They are among all races.

More concerns...

In some instances, counselors meet with students occasionally at school during assigned times. This takes place with <u>high school students.</u> When other students are aware of the meetings, some make fun of the ones who are mentally challenged. The child becomes embarrassed and sometimes refuse to continue the counselling sessions. They are not strong enough to know how to overcome the adversaries; they may be afraid of being bullied. Thus, they become withdrawn, agitated and sometimes hurt themselves. We must show love to all children and encourage them to do well!

Dyslexia

These students are said to <u>take longer to retrieve words,</u> thus they may not speak or read well. We must understand they require more attention and should they transpose numbers, it is understandable.

Autism

This is a disorder which refers to challenges with social skills, speech and nonverbal communication among other conditions. My first experience with an autistic patient was at Louisiana State University Health Sciences Center.

Bipolar

This is a disorder associated with mood swings...

ADHD

Attention-Deficit/Hyperactivity (attention difficulty) Disorder is a treatable, neurodevelopmental disorder that occurs in children, teens, and adults. Yes, adults are said to suffer from the disorder as well.

<u>Adderall Drug</u> is said to improve focus and reduce impulsivity. <u>Ritalin Drug</u> is said to cause insomnia (lack of sleep). In such case one drug may be helpful while the other creates another problem.

Other Conditions
Some children are hypo (below normal) or hyper (unusually energetic) and may appear to be fearful or insecure. In both cases, we observe the difficulties and we are aware that the cases are unfortunate. While we cannot begin to comprehend their struggles, we can show empathy.

The Graduates/High Achievers
Those students who graduated with extremely high grade-point averages are abundantly blessed. This age of new technology has made it possible to access materials immediately and easily. Thereby, decreasing the length of time to research and compile information. Students no longer need to await assistance to communicate with registrars of colleges/universities. They have the capabilities to complete applications for grants and federal loans via internet. We are thankful to God for the achievements of all students. While some choose to attend junior colleges, others choose trade schools. It's important for all to choose which direction they believe will best suit them. Sometimes students complete their studies at a trade school and still decide to attend a university. Many students graduate with a double major. Praise God for His goodness and His mercy.

The Disadvantaged
A high percentage of our children (young adults) are incarcerated. People of color are arrested or killed at a higher rate than their white counterparts. The justice system is biased. A person of color is subject to do more time in prison than a Caucasian person who does the same crime. The facilities are filled with 85% blacks.

In the 1970s...
Many people were working in factories. Thereby, they earned a living. Manufacturing began to decline due to automation take-over. One may say that skills were lost. Those who had very little education or no education were at a loss. Some turned to using drugs and especially selling them to make a living.

Facts:
A black man was sent to prison for possession of three pounds of marijuana with intent to distribute. He spent twenty-five years there; he did not hurt nor kill anyone. He was a victim of Satan's because he allowed himself to be caught-up in the devil's trap. Sometimes what looks good is enticing, but it is not the right thing to grasp and try to profit from it. All money is not good money. The man was expected to serve seventeen more years, but thank God for the governor who commuted his sentence.

While men are physically bound behind locked doors, they are imprisoned but we pray that their <u>minds are still free</u>. Remember <u>Apostle Paul</u> was behind bars in Rome, but he wrote a letter to the Ephesians. He was working for God even though he was held in prison. No one can put chains on our thoughts. Even when incarcerated, men are still free to think, pray, repent and plan how to return to a free society.

<u>Peter</u> was put in prison. King Herod arrested him during the Passover celebration. He was placed under the guard of sixteen soldiers. Herod intended to deliver Peter to the Jews for execution. Earnest prayer was going up to God from the Church for his safety all the time he was in prison. The night before he was to be executed, he was asleep, <u>double-chained</u> between two soldiers with others standing guard before the prison gate. An angel of the Lord stood beside Peter; slapped him on the side to awaken him and said, "Quickly, Get up!" The <u>chains</u> fell off his wrists! The angel led Peter out the cell; through the iron gate to the street. Peter said, "The Lord has sent an angel and saved me from Herod and from what the Jews were hoping to do to me" (Acts 12:3-19).

Conclusion: Everyone in chains is not guilty. We hope they put their trust in God and pray daily. He is able to provide a way of escape if it be His will. Perhaps some are behind bar for their own protection and they are not aware. We pray to God for them and believe they will mature while incarnated. Some are model prisoners and have an opportunity to learn a trade. They can look back on their lives; recognize how and why they allowed themselves to become caught-up in Satan's trap. Thank God, some will have another chance.

Unfortunately, many are people of color who are locked away behind bars; some are innocent but spend decades there. Where is the justice? After DNA testing, a few men are released to return to public life. Where do they begin after twenty or thirty years behind bars for a crime which they did not commit? Some said in the beginning they were innocent, but they did not have adequate representation. Some appointed attorneys advise their clients to plead guilty (plea bargain). In such cases, it is unfair because it leads to innocent people being coerced to plead guilty.

Danger and Set-backs
Some men are killed while in prison and families may never know the real reason. There are many very sad situations: Minors are in juvenile detention. When they are released, some of them become repeat offenders. Even if they do not become repeat offenders, they have made or set a negative record for themselves which follows them <u>all the way to employers</u>. When they cannot find work sometimes it's their own fault. They crippled themselves.

Many are free to pursue a career but have no role models. They tend to follow the bad examples of parents and others<u>. Even when parents encourage them to do better, they still choose to be care-free</u>. They may be influenced by the flash of cash which they think was easily obtained. Truth of the matter is, some parents work two jobs to make ends meet. Some children think they are entitled to sleep all day while Mom and Dad work eight hours per day, pay all the bills and etcetera. Athletic Jim will not cut the lawn, he implies, "The yard is too big or it takes too much time to do such." The parents are at fault in this case.

Alarm
<u>Parents conduct yourselves as parents should! Your baby is now an adult</u>! He needs to learn to be independent; he will not always be able to rely on Mom and Dad (He needs to grow-up)!

CHAPTER 17
The Dutiful Housewife
And Mother

SHE EXEMPLIFIES THE WOMAN OF PROVERBS 31 HER JOB

Many housewives are mothers; their jobs are fulltime. Their work begins at the break of day; it is never done, but continues the next day. The Christian mother rises early, starts her day with morning devotion, awakes the children and prepares breakfast for the family. She assist the little ones to assure they are properly dressed for school and transports them for safety. Many times, she assures the teens are off to school as well. She might even pack lunch for her husband and prays that God will protect him from danger and keep his mind stayed on Jesus. She trust God to direct his thoughts and do not allow the devil to tempt him with worldly ideas or ungodly deeds. He must do his part to stay on the right tract as well; do not lose focus on what is right. He will do well to remember there are consequences for committing sinful acts.

After the school rush, Mother begins the many daily tasks which include house work, running errands and paying bills as needs dictate. She makes dental and medical appointments in a timely manner. She balances the budget and makes necessary changes to include the unexpected expenses. Mother is careful to include a portion of the income for savings when available. She is careful to be on time to greet the children at the end of the school day. She prepares dinner; Father or Mother says a prayer of thanksgiving (blessings) when all are seated at the table. In times past, it was a tradition for each one to say a Bible verse before dinner. Each child also shared his or her problems with parents and they made decisions for them. If necessary, Mother paid the teacher a visit. Today, routines are different. Mother instructs the children to do their chores and complete homework assignments. The mother of little children might read a bedtime story as I did when my children were small. She might sing a lullaby song to put the baby to sleep and say a pray also. The dutiful housewife will remember to encourage her older children to talk with our Lord and Savior before closing their eyes for a restful night's sleep.

Today, most children have cellular phones. They tend to talk until...When they are disciplined for being disobedient, they rebel against the parent who looks out for them, provides and tries to protect them from harm.

Christian mothers teach their children:
Children, obey your parents; this is the right thing to do because God has placed them in authority over you. Honor your father and mother. This is the first of God's Ten Commandments that ends with a promise. And this is the promise: that if you honor your father and mother, yours will be a long life full of blessings.
Ephesians 6:1-3 TLB

It is of utmost importance to pray with children before they hurry off to school. We are living in perilous times and many children have left home for school, but did not return because of some evil person possessed by the devil.

HER HUSBAND'S JOB

He must love his wife as Christ loved the church and treat her with respect. He must not belittle, humiliate, or devalue her. Neither should he verbally or physically wound her. It is Father's responsibility to make provisions for his family; his work ethic must be good. He should be the bread winner or head of the house. He must set a good example for his son(s); he cannot be idle. Father must be a model of the future husband of his daughter. An idle man will suffer hunger and so will his family as stated by Solomon. He must not be a heavy drinker of wine or glutton because he will come to poverty. Amen somebody!

The Lord will not let a good man starve to death, nor will he let the wicked man's riches continue forever. Lazy men are soon poor; hard workers get rich.

Proverbs 10:3-4 TLB

Parents

Christian parents must teach their children to respect the elderly, be kind and respect the rights of others. Apply the golden rule: Do unto others as you would them do unto you. The family must attend church service and worship God in spirit and in truth. Children's first teachings must be done at home by the parents. They must be taught to be tidy and to prioritize. It is a good thing for the family to attend Sunday School to study God's Word. Thereby, they gain knowledge and a better understanding when taught by one who is well versed. Thereafter, children will likely decide to accept Jesus Christ as their Lord and Savior. Parents must be careful to set an example in conversation as well as lifestyle. Children learn what they live. We do not want to be stumbling blocks for our children. God holds parents responsible for discipling their children. They are gifts from God. As children age, parents must give them instruction based on their ability to comprehend. It is a good thing to keep them busy, an idle mind is the devil's workshop.

Extracurricular activities are a plus when children are able to maintain good grades. Parents should be mindful of the student's choices. Girls may take a class to learn etiquette (polite behavior or good manners): They practice being polite and respect themselves, peers, siblings as well as the elderly. They learn to carry themselves in a way that is pleasing to their parents and to the Lord. Thereby, others will recognize they are well trained. They should also participate in church activities: Their faith will be strengthened.

Time passes quickly, children graduate high school and prepare to attend a school of higher learning (college, university or trade school). When packing to travel, they must be sure to pack their weapon, the Bible. It is a valuable book of information. They must consult God and ask for instructions concerning a career. He knows what they are best suited to become.

In all thy ways acknowledge him (God) and he shall direct thy path.
Proverbs 3:5

Mother's Helper
After the children become adults and have little ones of their own, most grandmothers share the responsibility of caring for their grandchildren. They give instructions and nurture them with love and concern. They ensures that the little ones are properly cared for. Not only are they Grandmothers, they are early childhood instructors.

CHAPTER 18
Marriage/Divorce

Wives, submit yourselves unto <u>your own husband</u>, (not to another woman's husband) *as unto the Lord* (Ephesians 5:22). *Husbands, love your wives*, (not another man's wife) *even as Christ also loved the church, and gave himself for it;* (Ephesians 5:25).

Paul was inspired to write by the Holy Spirit; God gave directions for the family.

PRESTIGIOUS WEDDING

This was prevalent yesterday and it continues today.
Some brides-to-be plan extravagant weddings and their parents are usually supportive. That is fine when one has planned well in advance. It usually happens when the bride-to-be's parents are in a certain financial category also. Most brides wear a designer's white wedding gowns of her choice and style. She chooses her Tierra or vail and her maid of honor usually wears a different style formal dress than her maids of honor. Some brides select two flower girls and a ring bearer. They choose candle lighters and a unity candle is likely in place. The groom usually wears a tuxedo and the groom's men usually wear suits with selected shirts/ties of a specific color. The wedding venue is usually one located in a five-star hotel and decorated to please the bride. Her wedding arch may be decorated

with gorgeous white roses with baby breath and greenery. Her wedding planner usually ensures that the bride's cake is fit for a queen. The groom's cake is usually fit for a king. They are short of nothing. The honey-moon may be planned in advance also. Most have a plan to build a nice home in an upscale subdivision which will be child-friendly.

Many marriages last a life-time, but some end in divorce also. When the later happens and the couple has children, they may be hurt during the break-up. Some couples chose to start a relationship with someone else and marry a second time. In such cases, little children become step-children. In some cases, they become abused or torn between Mom and Dad. They may be transferred from one to the other for periods of time. In such cases, the children do not have a stable place to call home. They do not always adapt to step-parents. Neither do they recover from the break-up.

Deuteronomy (5th Law Book)
Moses' Address to the People of Israel

If a man does not like something (uncleanness) about his wife, he may write a letter stating that he has divorced her, give her the letter, and send her away. If she then remarries, and the second husband also divorces her, or dies, <u>the former husband may not</u> marry her again, for she has been <u>defiled</u>; this would bring guilt upon the land the Lord your God is giving you.

Deuteronomy 24:1-4 TLB

The Pharisees asked a question: Is it lawful for a man to put away his wife for every cause?

Matthew 19:3b KJV

Jesus answered and said unto them, Have ye not read, that he which made them at the beginning made them male and female, And said, For this cause shall a man leave father and mother and shall cleave to his wife; and they twain shall be one flesh? Wherefore they are no more twain, but one flesh. What therefore God hath joined together, let not man put asunder (separate). V.4-6

The Pharisees asked a second question: Why did Moses then

*command to give a writing of divorcement, and to put her away? He said unto them, Moses because of the hardness of your hearts suffered you to put away your wives: but from the beginning it was not so. And I say unto you, Whosoever shall put away his wife, except it be for **fornication**, and shall marry another, committeth adultery: and whoso marrieth her which is put away doth commit adultery.*
Matthew 19:8-9 KJV

So, why polygamy= the practice of marrying multiple spouses? Why bigamy=the act of going through a marriage ceremony while married to another person? Apparently, man has his own rules and thereby, he disregards the Word of God. O' Self-willed man, how will you answer to God?

Apostle Paul wrote:
*For sin shall not have dominion over you: for ye are **not under the law**, but under **grace** (Romans 6:14 KJV). The meaning is NOT that the Christian has been freed from all moral authority. The moral law will not change. Know ye not, brethren, (for I speak to them that know the law,) how that the law hath dominion over a man, as long as he liveth? For the woman which hath a husband is bound by the law to her husband so long as he liveth; but if the husband be dead, she is loosed from the law of the husband. So then if, while her husband liveth, she be married to another man, she shall be called an adulteress: but if her husband be dead, she is free from that law; so that she is no adulteress, though she be married to another man.*
Romans 7:1-3 KJV

Uncomfortable Marriages
In some marriages one partner refuses to believe the other. The two cannot live together in peace. If that be the case, you surely can live separately. Tell the Lord even though he already knows what you are dealing with. You have to let go of any toxic relationship. In some marriages one becomes abusive, combative, and or a narcissist. He has a sense of entitlement, monopolizes conversations, belittles others and exaggerates his talents. A narcissist will take advantage of you!!! If a marriage to one is to survive, the narcissist must change his behavior, attitude and show love and respect. He must love his wife as Christ loves the church. Amen Somebody!

Need for Counseling

Sometimes parents divorce and the children are caught in the middle. They do not always recover from the separation. They are scarred for life. Even though the things which happened were in the past, yet they are reminders which will not die. The children may be teased by others and made to feel ashamed. They may become withdrawn. History has recorded that those children sometimes become depressed, need counseling and even more. Parents must face reality; admit their children's lives have been affected and pay the price for the part they played. Regardless of the situation, children are wounded. Their lives are affected for the duration of time on planet earth.

Some couples decide to go forward together for the sake of the children (they remain married-in-name only). Some try to save face because of their positions; goals which were set for the children among other things. The trust has been broken and the marriage will never be the same. In such cases, misery will not cease, the couple becomes roommates until the children are of age. It is no longer a home, but merely a house. Some couples live out their lives in the same house, but communication is minimal and financial responsibilities are shared.

DISAPPOINTMENTS

Many marriages end in divorce for various reasons: Jealousy, dishonesty which includes lying, cheating, being deliberately deceptive and more. Everyone has faults which he must confess for a better relationship and a clear conscience. To conceal our faults is to continue in darkness which represents ignorance. Thereby, many stumble and fall.

> *<u>Confess</u> your faults one to another, and pray one for another...*
> James 5: 16a JKV

Some (men and women) are disrespectful, will not listen, they are right in their own eyes. Many become belligerent and have double standards; some are good as gold, but too controlling. Many men refuse to keep a steady job; therefore, they are not dependable. Some men have two wives (they separate from their wife and decide to shack with another) and have a mistress. They say: "What you don't know, won't hurt you." Some say, "What you didn't see, you can't prove." They seem to forget God has an all-seeing eye. His eyes are in every place. He beholds the evil and the good and His record is correct! Remember what is done in the dark comes to the light.

Note:

Some couples blame each other. One might say the other was or is insane, but if you spend any amount of time with each other you should see a red flag. Now, did you jump into bed immediately and focus on the moment? <u>After you fulfilled your desires / lust, you chose to marry her</u>. After she gave birth to your baby you concluded: "She's crazy and I want a divorce." If that were truly the case you should have recognized it early on and you certainly should have known before you told her to <u>strip.</u>

Some men make excuses to fulfill their desires. That is: Be with another woman. He has a wife; he is not satisfied. Mama-bow-hip is fine, illiterate and has no class but he wants to take her down. We call that doggish, but his wife does not have to take on the same trait (act like a she-dog). Listen, when a man hits the streets in search of other women, he will find some who are willing to allow him to <u>use them</u>. That does not mean that he <u>wants</u> them. He does his thing and moves on. The world looks-on and voices an opinion sometimes. Should a woman step-out on her husband, she will be noticed and labeled as if she were a slut, tramp and or a she-dog.

When a man consumes too much alcohol: Gets sloppy drunk or (inebriated) it shows because his actions change. His conversation is likely to change also. He might over-talk and find himself in what many call "hot water." Now, when a woman gets inebriated, starts to talk disrespectfully, she is labeled as a "drunkard," no-good or unfit mother if she has children. So, women, let us be on good behavior regardless of what the man-of-the-house does. There is a way to handle or deal with such situations!!!

Let's Recall
The Bible story of Jacob and Rachal
Laban, the uncle of Jacob deceived him. We remember Jacob worked seven years for Rachel whom he loved. Laban presented Leah, the oldest daughter to Jacob. Jacob slept with Leah and later realized he had been betrayed. It was dark and Leah may have worn a veil. Be careful what you do in the dark! Was Jacob inebriated with strong drinks? So, how did he handle the situation? Betrayal hurts, but Jacob worked seven more years for Rachel. Some may question his actions, but Jacob loved Rachel so the seven more years seems but a few days to him. Are there any Jacobs today?

Reality Set In
Years earlier Jacob had tricked his father, Isaac. He was old and his eyes were dim, so that he could not see (he was in darkness). Jacob deceived his father; took advantage of him in his old age. So, Laban tricked Jacob. We find in life what we put into it. Be careful to do unto other as you would them do unto you. Pay-back is a hard pill to swallow! Some say it's something else. Okay!

Listen Women: <u>Regroup</u>
If you are feeling down and out you might find solace after reading the book of Ruth. She was a woman of Moab, the great-grandmother of David and an ancestress of Jesus. Her husband passed away and she chose to go to Bethlehem with Naomi, her mother-in-law. Naomi's husband had passed away also. Ruth followed her heart and went with her mother-in law back to her homeland. She left the land where her husband had died; she began a new life. Sometimes; I did say sometimes change is good. Truth of the matter is: Sometimes one needs to leave the old life behind and start anew! Time and time again there will be reminders which will not cease to die. You can try leaving your past behind, but it continues to follow you. Some say, "Out of sight, out of mind." Even so, there will be reminders! Nevertheless, do not lose focus on your desired goal.

The Modest Wedding

Sometimes it is the best one and always the least expensive. Baby Jane and Slow Joe were high school lovers. They lived in the same poor neighborhood and attended the City Lane Missionary Baptist Church of Growing Town, USA. Both came from large families and Baby Jane's parents' motto was: *As for me and my house we will serve the Lord.* She considered her parents to be too strict. After all, she was twenty years old and still living with her parents. She was employed by a small law firm; her income was not sufficient to afford a decent apartment. I know that feeling!

Slow Joe was twenty-one years old; he lived in a tiny garage apartment. He worked as an auto technician which was referred to as a "grease monkey" by Baby Janes' father. Finally, Joe proposed to Baby Jane. She accepted his proposal because they were lovers and she asked herself, "Why not get married?" Little did she know, she was expecting a little one. Baby Jane would soon become a mother. She and Slow Joe went to the county court house and said their vows. She said they did not have time to plan a wedding or just a plain ceremony which they could not afford anyway.

When you make a vow to the Lord, be prompt in doing whatever it is you promised him, for the Lord demands that you promptly fulfill your vows; it is a sin if you do not.

Deuteronomy 24:21 TLB

The couple was blessed with six children (three girls and three boys). They were smart, intelligent and loved the Lord. All of them graduated from high school and furthered their education at universities. They received grants, scholarships, and loans. They were blessed with decent salaries and godly husbands and wives. Happy ending!

Notable Facts
Mr. Fairman Bright-Educator may have three wives during his lifetime. After death, all may be buried in the same section of the same cemetery in sites one, two, three, and four. It doesn't matter, he no

longer has a wife. In the resurrection neither one of them will be his wife. I recall, the Sadducees asked Jesus a question concerning the same. He said to them: For in the resurrection, they neither marry, nor are given in marriage… (Matt. 22:30a)

CHAPTER 19
A Mind-Blowing Experience

FACING ADVERSITY

All of us face numerous problems at one time or another. How we deal with them makes the difference. If a child has spiritual parents he should be in good hands when trouble arrives. An adolescent child who is transitioning from childhood into a young adult may hesitate before sharing his problems with his parents. Usually, he will seek answers from a non-family member. And parents sometimes need help. They should be able to speak with a qualified counsellor but, be sure to consult God.

In Retrospect...
No counsellor shared words of encouragement to Lilly and the younger children after the death of their mother and grandfather (two deaths within 24 hours). No one gave instructions or directions!

Lilly learned to rely upon God for strength. She and the younger children were left in the care of their oldest sister. Lilly did what she had to do. Working at a convalescent home was quite an experience. She said to herself: "If I can only finish my education, I will be in a better position." She felt like running away because the tasks were almost unbearable but, where do you run when you have no one or no hiding place to run to? Life taught her a real lesson.

Lilly read in God's Word:
Blessed be God, even the Father of our Lord Jesus Christ, the Father of mercies, and the <u>God of all comfort</u>; Who comforteth us in all our tribulation, <u>that we may be able to comfort them which are in any trouble, by the comfort wherewith we ourselves are comforted of God.</u>
2 Cor. 1: 3-4 KJV

<u>Now</u> she knows, you run to the rock that is higher than you are. That Rock is Jesus! When your heart feels heavy, your pain seems unbearable, you see through tear-stained eyes and your view is obscured, run to the Rock! Run child...

The Lord is my rock, and my fortress, and my deliver; My God, my strength, in whom I will trust; ...
Psalm 18:2a KJV

Some may ask, "Why share the story?"
My answer: It's one that shall never be forgotten! Mother said, "Don't forget about me." Until this day, I recall her speaking quietly. During that time of despair, I said to myself, "It will get better; brighter days are head." My consolation: There will be a reunion!

That time was a season of disappointments and dark days which left Lilly with no answers, but God took care of her. Many things were done by trial and error. I tell you, "Hard times will teach a sensible person to pray." I hope this is a lesson for someone who might be in a similar situation. Prayer is the answer! Today, I look back on those dark days as an eye-opener and a <u>period of hard lessons-learned.</u>

"Lilly"

"When it's <u>dark</u> in your life and you can't hear from God, keep calling him." Trouble was in Lilly's way; disappointment lingered and would not disappear for a spell. Just the thought was overwhelming. It could be liken to a terrible storm which arose suddenly. Why such misfortune? Lilly caught natural hell and suffered in silence. But God… She survived while resting on the wings of hope. Man will let you down, but trust God because He will not fail you, nor will He leave you! It is no wonder Reverend C. L. Franklin sang, "I will trust in the Lord until I die." I say ditto!

Today, I have relevant advice for all who have been disappointed in such a case as Lilly's, "WALK ON!" Do not put your trust in man, but trust God for everything. If you accept Him as your Lord and Savior you will not be disappointed; **<u>you will live FOREVER!</u>** **Amen**! One day there will be no more heartaches and no more pain. All the former things will have passed away.

The school of Hard Knocks was not easy to adjust to, neither was it easy to comprehend the lessons. However, Lilly moved on... not knowing what was <u>in store for her. She had no directions.</u>

Remembering now...
After the <u>death of Moses</u>, the Lord spoke to Joshua and gave him <u>directions.</u>

Have not I commanded thee? Be strong and of a good courage; be not afraid, neither be thou dismayed: for the Lord thy God is <u>with thee</u> whitherever thou goest (Joshua 1:9 KJV). Amen!

Biblical Characters
<u>Reminder:</u> Joseph did not know what was <u>in store for him</u> either. He was the eleventh son of Israel and a dreamer; his brothers were jealous of him. His father made him a coat of many colors. He had two dreams that made his brothers turn against him and plot to kill him. Joseph had done nothing wrong. Yet, his own brothers put him in a <u>dungeon</u>. They meant it for bad, but God meant it for his good. He went from a pit to prison; to a palace. Nevertheless, he helped his brothers during a famine. Many times, the one you misuse is the one who will come to your rescue. Be careful how you treat people!

Others...
Daniel, a servant of God was thrown into the <u>lion's den</u>. He was a man who prayed three times a day; he did nothing wrong. He refused to change for the sake of the king. Because he continued his routine (praying), he was cast into the lion's den. The king thought no one could rescue Daniel, but he apparently forgot or did not know that Daniel's God is Almighty. Daniel was delivered unharmed! The three Hebrew boys (Shadrach, Meshach, and Abednego) were bound and thrown into the midst of a burning fiery furnace because of their faithfulness to God. They refused to worship any other god, but the living God. King Nebuchadnezzar was furious and had the furnace heated seven times hotter than usual. The king was in for a Hugh surprise: God delivered the three Hebrew boys and they were not harmed. There is no secret what God can do! The point is one does not have to be guilty of wrong doing to be treated harshly. When God's hand is upon him, he will come out unscathed. I just want to

remind someone that God will work things out! He did it for others and he will do the same for you!

Lilly found a little duplex (another family occupied the other side of the house). Things were not as she wanted them to be, but at least she felt safe.

After a few months: An Impromptu Visit

It was late one Friday night; Lilly heard a knock at the door. To her surprise, two of her younger sisters and her niece stood there. They were trying to find shelter. They had overstayed the curfew which Big Sister had set. The young girls had gone to the recreation center for fun and games. Carolyn loved to dance! Rosemary was wearing the time-piece (watch) and she was supposed to let the other two know when it was time to leave the center. Unfortunately, her watch had stopped and she was unaware. When the lights were being turned off, they realized they were in trouble. They hurried home and knocked on the door. Big Sister answered, "Who is it?" They replied, "Let us in." Big Sister said in her commanding voice, "I don't know where y'all going, but you ain't coming in here." She meant business! The girls tried to explain, but Big Sister was not buying it. She said, "Get off my property." The girls went to the end of the driveway and sat down. Big Sister got her gun and threaten to fire it. The trio went to their auntie's house just a few streets away. They knocked on her door after midnight. She answered, asked a few questions and said, "If Big Sister did not let you into her house, then you cannot come into mine either." The girls were very disappointed! The trio had a serious problem. They were running from house to house like three little pigs. They were running out of options too. Finally, one said, "Let's go to Lilly's house." Bingo: They found shelter at house number three. When Lilly heard their voices, she immediately opened the door and invited them warmly, "Come on in." She didn't have the heart to deny them a place to spend one night. Lilly had only one twin size bed, but she gladly gave the girls blankets and a quilt to sleep on the floor. That was all they wanted: Shelter for one night. Lilly has a heart of Love. She understands that things happen in life. So, why make the girls spend the night outside? Big Sister could have found another way to punish the trio. The other sister didn't have to agree to let the girls wander outside after midnight also.

Just one thing troubled me: All of us make mistakes in life; both older sisters had disobeyed Mother's instructions. They were not punished for their actions. Therefore, they should have shown compassion for the trio. After all, we must do unto others as we would have them do unto us!

180-DEGREE TURN

Darkness still hovered over Lilly's life. Suddenly, there was a complete change. She had the experience of a life-time trying to manage all the expenses. Life was still very much complicated and her income was not adequate, but what else could she have done? She had no transportation and neither could she afford any. So, she could not get a second job; she struggled for a while. Assistance didn't come without a price and she was overwhelmed; taken advantage off. In such times one may easily become susceptible to physical and or, emotional harm.

Lilly's eyes were opened to see a picture which she had not seen before; she was encouraged to take a step in another direction. She was also enabled by one who was six years her senior. She thought that person might be reliable. Lilly made a mistake because she did not think things through. After a few days, she began to rethink her decision. All of a sudden it seemed as if she inadvertently staggered into what could be liken unto a cocoon. She was released to either **#1**: Face the danger of walking what can be likened to a tight rope or **#2**. Be caged and endure whatever storms which might come her way. She chose what she thought might be less dangerous, be <u>caged</u>. She recalled a poem to which she could relate. Even though her feet were not tied, yet she was locked-in. Her song: "Beams of Heaven."

I know Why the Caged Bird Sings

> ...a Bird that stalks down his narrow cage
> Can seldom see through his bars of rage
> His wings are clipped and his feet are tied
> So, he opens his throat to sing.
>
> The caged bird sings with a fearful trill
> Of things unknown but longed for still
> And his tune is heard on the distant hill for
> The caged bird sings for <u>freedom</u>...
>
> written by Maya Angelou

Lilly got married and gave birth to two children. God blessed them to build a nice home which they could afford and the girls were happy. Time passed and they did well in school, honor roll students, extracurricular activities, and they learned piano lessons from Mr. Walters. They participated in church activities, summer camp and also took swimming lessons at the Young Women's Christian Association (YWCA). They enjoyed vacationing in Hot Springs, Arkansas, Six Flags in Texas, and Disney World in Florida. Unlike their mom, they enjoyed their childhood and they did not know their mother's pain. That place was a "so-journ" or temporary place to dwell until the <u>storm</u> was over.

Moving Forward but, Facing Discrimination

In 1973, Lilly was employed by Confederate Memorial Medical Center. There were two canteens (places to purchase drinks, snacks and etc.), one for whites and one for people of color. Previously, people of color were not allowed to dine in the same area of the dining room as whites dined. The name, Confederate is a reminder of darkness, war, confusion and more. Robert E. Lee was a general in the Confederate army. The Confederate flag became a symbol of <u>racism.</u> It was believed to be claimed by <u>white supremacists</u>.

Time passed and Lilly did what she had to do. She saved small portions of her salary. She started-out with only $350.00 per month (she was paid twice per month on the 5th and 20th). She met the requirements for her position as a laboratory assistant II: College credits and a Civil Service Test Score. She was not paid justly. She chose to challenge the laboratory assistant III test and was very successful. She also successfully challenged the Clerk I and II examination. She was not compensated nor recognized for her efforts or accomplishments.

A few years later, Lilly noticed: Some high school students were hired to work during the summer. She requested employment for her girls but, human resource / personnel would not hire them. Lilly was told, "They can be volunteers." Lilly said, "No way." Slavery was said to have ended and she would not enslave her children. Discrimination still existed (modern day slavery).

Yesterdays' happenings are continuing...
A few years later to Lilly's surprise, a nurse's aide-turned clerk was brought into the lab. He was to supervise Lilly and other employees. He had no experience, only seniority. He was not required to challenge the exam. Guess who was told to train him? Lilly. **Surprise:** It was decided that no test was needed and neither was college credits to perform the duties. The job title was down-graded to compensate nurses' aides. That was a good deed for them, but Lilly and others who were hired on the basis of higher standards should have been allowed to kept the title which they earned and be transferred to the Central Laboratory. The first one promoted was the Union President who was formerly a nurse's aide. What an injustice! Human Resource played right into his hands. Lilly went to speak with someone in Human Resource to get answers, but that employee was not willing to research the problem. She did not want to be involved. God is not asleep and we reap what we sow. His word says: Do justly, love mercy and walk humbly with thy God. Just maybe, Lilly's God is not their god. She successfully challenged the Phlebotomy Certification Exam and received her license from Louisiana State Board of Medical Examiners. She continued to perform her duties.

We are our Brother's Keeper
We must reach-out to others, show concern and compassion when we recognize a need. It is our assignment to be of service to those who

need assistance. Sometimes one needs help with everyday task as well as medical and financial support. God will reward us for being attentive to the welfare of the disabled and those who are in situations which are beyond their control. We must show compassion!

But if someone who is <u>supposed to be a Christian</u> has money enough to live well, and sees a brother in need, and won't help him—how can God's love be within him?

I John 3:17TLB

An Example of Brotherly Love
Little Lilly remembered her great auntie who was a widow and had no living children. Aunt Matt lived alone; she had one living niece (her sister's child). She lived in another city and seldom visited. All of Aunt Matt's siblings had passed away. Her brother, Scarborough Salters passed away March 26, 1974 leaving her alone. He was Lilly's maternal grandmother's twin.

Lilly noticed that Aunt Matt was not able to walk steadily and that was a concern especially because she lived alone. That was a time of darkness and Lily was determined to help her aunt. She carried her to see Dr. Stewart D. Lee. After her visit with the doctor, Lilly carried her auntie home with her and she spent two weeks in her care. Her condition grew worse and she was hospitalized. The staff placed her in the last room on the 8th floor (State Hospital) and closed the door. Early on January 21, 1979, Lilly went to the hospital to see her auntie, she had aspirated and passed away at the age of 79years. The death angel had come and gone; the nursing staff was unaware.

Trying to Regroup
After taking care of financial business, Lilly turned her attention to dealing with the loss of her great auntie. Every life is precious and death leaves a void in one's life. But we know our God is a merciful God and He will give us peace that passes all understanding.

Continuing Her Duties...
Time passed and Lilly worked and did her best to care for her girls. She fashioned the majority of their clothes; did the same for herself.

She purchased Simplicity, Butterick, McCall and even Vogue Patterns. She did an excellent job. Lilly learned basic sewing from her mom who had a special talent. She was taught home-making (sewing) while in high school and she perfected the techniques. The girls were always neatly dressed.

As the Girls Matured

Lilly fashioned prom dresses for high-school, military ball and **wedding gowns** for each girl's **wedding. She also fashioned maid-of-honor,** bride maids and even flower girl dresses. She has a valuable gift! Lilly fashioned many garments for others as well. That was her extra job to earn a few more dollars. To God be the glory! Lilly purchased a second sewing machine in order to teach her girls to sew.

Kashundra's Wedding Ceremony witnessed
@ Chez Vous Motor Inn
Shreveport, LA 71108

*Cheryl's Wedding Day witnessed
@ Springtree Condominiums
Dallas, Texas 75243*

Other Challenges

During those years, there were numerous personal situations and new discoveries which arrested Lilly's attention, but she did not lose hope. The truth was uncovered and Lilly was overwhelmed to say the least. She cried many tears and things happened which she will never be able to comprehend. She had to take them to the Lord in prayer! He knows just what to do and when to do it. Amen! Lilly has certainly been through storms, but she is still standing by the grace of God.

"By God's Grace"

Remember to stay humble after you reach nobility or honor!

After many years of hard work, sacrifices and conversations with God, Lilly was able to build a new home. God blessed her to build one which <u>she could afford</u>; she was set free! Again, God is able to do what we need Him to do. Trust God because He never fails. Lilly can truly say: "Through many dangerous toils and snares I have already come; it was Grace that brought me..."

When God brings you out of a terrible or unfortunate situation, you MUST say, "Thank you Lord for Your grace and mercy." If there are any tears, they MUST be tears of joy. When the story is shared, it's to encourage others who faced the same or similar situations. You are saying, "God can do anything but fail." And no matter what the situation looks like, God can fix it! You no longer have to be a prisoner of your disgraceful or shameful past. You are never alone (there is always someone else who is struggling in life).

Deception or Betrayal

From My Experience:

I can attest to the fact that betrayal or deception hurts to the core or the innermost part which is the heart. After traveling down that rugged road, up and downhill; through many troubled times, I was compelled to makes changes. I made the wrong decision for the right reason. My intent was to correct a wrong which <u>someone else</u> deliberately caused by lying. After all was done I was left in yet another hurtful position.

I recalled Psalm 55:6:
"O, that I had wings like a dove! For then would I fly away and be at rest."

I chose to endure the pain for the sake of my children. Quickly, I recalled a song, **"His eye is on the Sparrow."**

Why should I feel discouraged; why should shadows come? Why should my heart feel lonely and lone for <u>heaven and home</u> when Jesus is my portion, a constant friend is he?...
Song by Whitney Houston

Now, I dare not take another chance and be hurt again. I can make it with God on my side. It has been said, "A woman needs a man and she cannot do without him." **That is far from the truth**. She might do <u>much better</u> without him, especially if he is not a godly man. If one is straddle the fence she does not need him either. Apparently, some have <u>head</u> knowledge only. They know what is right but, refuse to do the right thing. I learned my lesson well and I am speaking from experience. Thank God!

The Dawning of a New Day

The light was shining brightly. I could not, nor will I be ungrateful after all God has done for me and He is still keeping me! He was there for me when no one else was. He picked me up when I was down, <u>all the way down in "Sorrow Valley." I praise Him while I can.</u> Glory to God! He brought me out of sin and shame. My cup was filled and overflowed with love, joy and peace! When I was beaten down in life like a Palm Tree by strong winds God lifted me up again! Now, I feel like an evergreen tree that is planted by rivers of water. I shall flourish! God got me! I am in His hands and the devil in hell cannot pluck me out of His hands!!! G-l-o-r-y to the Lord God Almighty! What a wonderful change has taken place in my life. God did it; all to Him I owe!

In memory of SeDestini Fields
Glory to God (Precious and timely praise)

I praise God for the storms He brought me through...When family forsook me, (and they truly did) Jesus saw me through because He cares for me. Now I know that God can and will see me through whatever comes my may. He never fails; He promised to be with me even until the end of the world. He is God and He cannot lie. O' what assurance!!!! Hallelujah!!! Today, I walk alone physically, but I know God is the CONSTANT in my life. We have a relationship and I can depend on Him. Others turned on me, but God favored me and I am truly grateful! One song-writer said, "Sometimes you have to walk alone." I say, even when you walk alone physically, God's grace and mercy walk beside you." Keep the faith; walk on!

If you are on the mountain top today do not brag or be arrogant. You just might have to come down to the valley tomorrow or, even today. And on your way down you are subject to meet the same people whom you met on your way up to the mountain top!

By the way
I was Lilly. The name signifies purity and innocence. I was very young, shy and in need of directions when misfortune came my way. I had to play the hand which was dealt to me. Now I recall, "Is anything too hard for God?" NOTHING... Can you walk a mile in my shoes? It was nobody but Jesus who kept me; saw me **through** my valley experience. I Praise God; I thank Him!
Now I can say, "Look where He brought me from." It was God! He kept me in those dark and lonely days. When I had no money, He kept me! When I was hungry, God blessed me with food. I cannot help but lend a helping hand to the needy. I feel their pain.

I prayed to God with all my heart. I asked Him to work things out for me because I could not do it for myself. I was helpless, in a mercy situation and I knew not which way to go. What I did know was how to pray. Hard times, trials and tribulations taught me and molded my character in the process. I was broken, but I went by the Potter's house and today I am whole again. Jesus will fix it if you let him have his way. Trials comes to make us strong and today I am STRONG! I can give spiritual advice to the outcast and I surely know how to connect with God. He is the Constant in my life!

How I Forgave Others...
First, I acknowledged that I needed God's forgiveness. I went to Him in secret prayer; acknowledged/confessed my sins to God; repented

(turned away from sin to God). He already knew everything, he is all-knowing. We have not because we ask not.

Apostle Paul penned: *Be careful for nothing; but in everything by prayer and supplication with <u>thanksgiving</u> let your request be made known unto God. And the peace of God, which passeth all understanding, shall keep your hearts and minds through Christ Jesus.*

Philippians 4:6-7 KJV

I emptied my heart, poured-out <u>everything</u> sincerely. He knows the contents of every heart and out of it comes the issues of life. I admitted that I had issues/problems. I acknowledged that I was heart-broken and yet, I needed to forgive those who wronged me. <u>We are responsible for our actions.</u> After I asked God for forgiveness, I asked God for strength! Then I asked God to help me to forgive others and free me from bondage. <u>Today, I am free!</u> This is a true testimony! I passed the test which was beyond hard.

<u>Jesus, the Perfect One:</u>
He Set the Example

Remember, Jesus was perfect (He knew no sin). Yet, He was accused of making himself the Son of God. Actually, He was God in the flesh! He paid a price which <u>He did not owe</u>. He was beaten and a crown of thorns was placed on His head. He was <u>crucified for us</u>; His blood was <u>shed for us</u>. Without the shedding of blood there is <u>no remission of sin.</u> The blood of animals was not sufficient. God prepared a body (Jesus Christ). Jesus said from the cross, "Father, <u>Forgive them</u> for they know not what they do."

Luke 23:34 KJV

God healed my broken heart! <u>I am healed! I left all those who hurt me in the mighty hands of God.</u> I could do nothing else, but when I was needed, I <u>responded!</u> I did my very best for the sake of love and I have no regrets! God brought me <u>out of darkness into light.</u>

Jesus said, *"Let your <u>light so shine</u> before men, that <u>they</u> may see your good works, and glorify your Father which is in heaven."*

Matthew 5:16 KJV

Thinking of Others

My heart is warmed when I design an inspirational card of encouragement. I make it very personal for a student who is striving to reach a particular goal. I do not forget to share my resources either. Little becomes much when we put it in the Master's hand. Neither do I forget to share consoling scriptures with those who are grief-stricken, brokenhearted or under the burden of stress from disasters and the like. I know what God can and will do! Glory to God!

When I see one on the streets, I see myself as I was wondering how I was going to make it all alone. To God be the glory! He kept me... He said He would never leave me; He kept His promise. If you are in "Sorrow Valley," have a little talk with Jesus!!! I know He will bring you out. He did it for me and He has no respect of persons. That was years ago and I know He is the same today as He was yester-years; tomorrow He will not change. He said, "I am the Lord and I change not." Glory!! <u>My story is to encourage someone who might be struggling to survive.</u> I know that I am not the only one who has gone through stormy weather, days of gloom, hunger, and desperation. Now, I can tell...I am no longer ashamed!!! Glory to my God!

Call Jesus early in the morning before the break of day while it is still dark, while you cannot hear no one stirring. Ask Father God, Creator of all mankind, in the name of Jesus: Fill my cup (heart), let it overflow with love. He will do it.

CHAPTER 20
Church of Today

*Family @ Union Springs Missionary Baptist Church
Shreveport, LA 71106*

A Reminder:
*And the Lord said unto Noah, Come thou and <u>all thy house</u> into the <u>ark</u>; for thee have I seen **righteous** before me in this generation* (Genesis 7:1 KJV).

Noah's family went into the Ark for safety. He had fore-warned the people about the coming flood, but they refused to adhere to the declaration of destruction (it was going to rain). Who are the Noahs of this generation?

And if it seem evil unto you to serve the Lord, choose you this day whom you will serve; whether the gods which your fathers served that were on the other side of the flood, or the gods of the Amorites, in whose land ye dwell: but as for me and my house, we will serve the Lord (Joshua 24:15 KJV). Who are the Joshuas of today?

The church or sanctuary is the "Light House" of today and it is time to return to it (the house of prayer). We must praise and worship our God, the only wise God. We must fill our hearts with the Word of God and go out and share it with the lost; reclaim the backsliders. Thereby, our "lights" will shine brightly. Our job is not done until God says so.

Numerous Edifices

There are numerous church buildings all over the city. There is definitely no shortage of churches (edifices) to attend. Statistics: 440 structures/churches are in the Shreveport, Bossier City metro area. In some areas one church building is situated across the street from another. Although many have less than one hundred members.

Many preachers seem to think they should be pastors of their own flock. As soon as there is a disagreement some decide to organize their own church and maybe twenty-five members follow them. In such cases, <u>pastors cause division</u>. When there are eight or more church buildings within a mile radius; only about a hundred members or less per church, that's unnecessary. And yet, we say we love the Lord, but we have a problem with our sisters and brothers-in-Christ. So, how do we expect to bring lost souls out of <u>darkness</u> into God's marvelous <u>light</u>? How do we expect the unsaved to conform to what supposed to be our way of life? And how do we expect to re-claim back-sliders? In many cases, we drive them away from the church instead of drawing them to come to Christ! Amen somebody...

Woe be unto the pastors that destroy and scatter the sheep of my pasture! Saith the Lord.

Jeremiah 23:1 KJV

When the unsaved notice the Christian's ungodly behavior or when the married Christians keep company often <u>(not accompanied by their spouses</u>) with single members that is unacceptable. In such cases, the unsaved or lost do not want to hear what the Christians have to say. Their conduct is disgraceful, thereby, the Christians have no positive influence on the unsaved. The <u>unmarried preacher and deacon</u> must be mindful of their conduct as well. They get no pass; they will answer to God too. The public will be vocal, but it is the <u>conduct</u> which speaks volumes. Who can disagree?

No one should be offended if he is not guilty! After all, if one is guilty perhaps he should refer to Apostle Paul's writings and take heed.

I concur...
Never worry about who will be offended if you speak the TRUTH. Worry about who will be misled, deceived & destroyed if you don't.

Author Unknown

Apostle Paul pinned:
I advise you to obey <u>only</u> the Holy Spirit's instructions. He will tell you where <u>to go</u> and what to do, and then you will not always be doing the wrong things your evil nature wants you to (Galatians 5:16 TLB).

O' Come Let Us Worship the Lord...
Many do not care to fellowship with other people of God, some say they prefer to watch service via internet, television or Facebook. That is one way to hear the Word of God, especially for those who are homebound, in convalescent homes, hospitals or the like. However, the experience of worshiping in person is on another lever. It is not surprising that some do not attend church service when they don't have an offering to give. Many have said, "We were told, you have not worshiped until you give an offering." No one should feel that he or she cannot go to church (worship service) unless they have money. Sometimes one need to hear a word from the Lord <u>because he does not have money, food at home or because of health issues. We often say the church is the place to go to be healed.</u> We as Christians should not insult or belittle people. Everyone is not on the same financial level; church is or should be about more than paying money. Scripture says: Enter into His gates with thanksgiving and into His courts with praise.

God's word says: *Let us not neglect our church meetings, as some people do, but encourage and <u>warn each other</u>, especially now that the <u>day of his coming back again is drawing near</u>* (Hebrews 10:25). The scripture does not say assemble in the house of prayer only when you have money to give. Amen! Let's focus on saving souls and not on collecting money!!!!! In fact, we must put things in their perspective order.

It is understood that many things are <u>not written in the Bible</u>. Some things are done in the church today because someone decided to incorporate them into the church. Those are <u>man-made rules</u> which please the one who made the decisions or the originator. Some intimidate members by using scare tactics. Nevertheless, we must study God's word and ask to be enlightened by the Holy Spirit.

Some members work two jobs (minimal wages) and still do not have sufficient funds to cover all their responsibilities. It takes the income of both jobs to survive and some still need government assistance. We must take into consideration not everyone is educated. If one has not been there, he does not understand.

Example: It is like telling one to put on a coat when it is cold. If he does not own a coat, he cannot cloth himself with one.

Remember Jesus tells us in <u>Matthew 25</u> about clothing the naked. If we did it to the least (those who have little or have nothing) we did it unto him.

Warning:
I believe Apostle Paul would say, I beseech you to Listen:
All scripture is given by inspiration of God. We have been warned that Jesus Christ is coming back again. It behooves everyone to be ready because we know not the day nor the hour when He will appear. It is a fact that <u>He will appear!</u> Will you be ready?

Immediately after the tribulation (grievous trouble; severe trial or suffering) of those days shall the sun be darkened, and the moon shall not give her light, and the stars shall fall from heaven, and the powers of the heaven shall be shaken. And then shall appear the sign of the Son of man in heaven: and then shall all the tribes of the earth mourn, and they shall see the <u>Son of man coming in the clouds of heaven with power and great glory</u> (Matthews 24:29-30).

God's ambassadors are the salt of the earth; we know in years past our forefathers used salt to preserve meat. We, the people of God must share God's word with the unsaved (sinners) in order to lead them to Christ, who is the resurrection and the life. We hope that lives will be <u>preserved.</u> We must also reclaim the backsliders. Notice: Some of our children have gone their own way.

There is a way that seems right unto a man, but the end thereof is the way of death (Proverbs 14:12).

We must quickly help our children regroup; know they have choices, but God's way is the only way to heaven! We have a commandment from God to strive to reach those who are walking in <u>darkness.</u> Even though they have their physical sight, they are spiritually blind. Thus, it is our job to teach them and demonstrate righteousness by walking in the <u>light</u> (our lifestyle).

WE HAVE A COMMANDMENT TO EVANGELIZE

Evangelism is teaching the gospel (life of Jesus Christ) to the unsaved in hopes of leading the lost to Christ. Tell the old, old story! Thereby, we put our hands to the plow doing the work of God. Ambassadors must be alert, stand firmly and remind the unsaved that sin comes with an expense.

Night Club Visit
Many still seek entertainment in the night clubs for numerous reasons. The young at heart and some who are not so young say: It is a place to socialize, dance, have a drink, smoke and enjoy the company of friends. They listen to the music which is usually up-beat until the wee hours of the morning. Friday and Saturday nights are the norm to let their hair down and unwind... Some do not wait until the weekend, they show-up for what many call "happy hour." The disciplined Christian should be welcomed into the club, but for other reasons. He may be able to share the Word of God with the unsaved and introduce them to Jesus Christ. Inform them of a godly way to socialize; remind them that Jesus will return for the church (his bride). Death is inevitable and the two choice places to spend eternity are heaven or hell. The choice is ours. There are some Christians who frequent the night clubs for the same reason as the unsaved. We must come out from among the world for God's light to shine in us. Jesus has paid our sin debt in full. Today is the day of salvation. Inform the unsaved that all have sinned and fall short of the glory of God. <u>We must be careful to be good examples of Christ.</u>

Jesus said, *For God so loved the world, that he gave his only begotten Son, that whosoever believeth in him should not perish, but have everlasting life.*

John 3:16 KJV

Invite the unsaved person(s) to worship service: *O' come, let us worship and bow down: Let us kneel before the Lord our Maker. Today if ye will hear his voice, Harden not your heart...*

Psalm 95: 7b, 8a KJV

The born-again-baptized believer should not be found in the center of the night club except to bring someone out of darkness. We should be on a mission to share the Word of God with sinners, lead backsliders back to Christ and set an example for the unsaved. God created us for good works and for His glory. He speaks to the Holy Spirit; He speaks to us. God speaks through circumstances and He speaks to us through others also.

God's people must be a <u>light in darkness</u>. The night club is a place of darkness. When light shines, darkness disappears! The Christians (we) must walk in the light and not conform to the way of the world.

For you were once <u>darkness</u>, but now you are light in the Lord. Live as children of light.

(Ephesians 5:8)

Did you share God's word with some weary soul today? Did you help someone to clearly understand God's word, answer his questions and lead him from darkness to light? Did you bypass the stranger or ignore the backslider today? Tomorrow may be too late.

How do you know what is going to happen tomorrow? For the length of your lives is as uncertain as the morning fog----now you see it; soon it is gone.

James 14:4 TLB

Jesus said as the days of Noe were, so shall also the coming of the Son of man be. So, not all will be receptive to the

Word of God. It is ones' choice, but do not let it be too late.

ROLE PLAY HELPS THE BABE IN CHRIST

For Observation:
Evangelism ____Group 1, The Blaton Family
We must study the Word of God

It's Saturday, 1:30 pm.
Mrs. Jane Blaton (Mother): Children it's time for Bible Study.
Cloe (daughter): (Talking on the phone) "Girl I will call you later, you know Mom insist on having Bible Study Sessions."
Ben (son): "Mom I'm writing an essay for my English Class."
Mr. Tim Blaton: "Both of you, get in here NOW!"
Mrs. Blaton: (Prays to God for an understanding of His Word).

Cloe: Reads Ephesians 6: 1-3
Ben: Reads Ecclesiastes 12:1

Mr. Blaton: Explains the scriptures and asked: "Do you have any questions?"
The children answered: "No Sir."
Mr. Blaton stated: "Now, it's time for me to go to work so I can put food on the table, clothes on your backs and provide shelter for our family."

Mrs. Blaton: "Cloe did you press your dress which you will wear for Sunday morning service?"

Cloe: "No ma'am, but I will."

Mrs. Blaton: "Do it now, you will not iron on Sunday."

Cloe: (Gets the iron, ironing board, and her dress). She sings Amazing Grace as she presses her dress.

Mrs. Blaton looks at Cloe and remarks: "Sing Child, yes!." She waves her hands.
Mrs. Blaton: "Ben you need to clean the family car."
Ben: O' Boy! (Why waving his hands in disgust."
Mrs. Blaton looked around. "Did you say something?"
Ben: O' no ma'am, I'm just thinking out loud. He looked back at his mom as he hurried out the door.

Group 2
11:00 am Saturday morning (another group)
Sister Do-ALL and three members of the New Community Missionary Baptist Church arrived at the home of The Johnsons.'

Mrs. Do-All knocked on the door.
Mrs. Johnson: (Opened the door), Good Morning!!!

Mrs. Do-All: We are members of New Community Missionary Baptist Church. You have a nice home. By the way, we are seeking the lost (those who have not accepted Jesus as their Lord and Savior).
Mrs. Johnson:---"Hallelujah, I am saved and my family is too."
Mrs. Rally:-- "Praise God."

Mrs. Do-All:-- That's great! Now, do you and your family attend church regularly?
Mrs. Johnson: "Yes, we do. We are members of the House of Praise Missionary Baptist Church. Our Pastor is Reverend James All-Out Hummingbird Senior.
Mrs. Do-All: Well. Alright! Thank you and have a blessed day.

The group continued on their mission
They went to 2201 Dominos Hall Blvd. Mr. Watchmo Strayman and three of his buddies were playing cards (in the front yard). A stack of money was on the table and a Smith and Wesson was on the table beside Mr. Strayman.

Mrs. Do-All: Well Good morning! We are members of New Community Missionary Baptist Church. How you'll doing?

Watchmo Strayman: Don't you see, we doing mighty fine.
Mrs. Do-All: Ok, we-l-l. We are concerned about those who have not accepted Jesus Christ as their Lord and Savior (the lost).

Watchmo Strayman: I suggest you'll get lost because you disturbing the peace. I told you'll before and this the last time I'm gonna tell you. Get off my property. I'm filing a complaint against you'll. I'll see you in court; I'm gonna put a stop to this. The group left. They walked about ten yards and Mrs. Rally said, "Wait a minute, hold-up. Let's pray." They prayed and left feeling victorious, they did their job.

Many times, Christians come face to face with unsaved persons, or people of other beliefs. We must not try to force our beliefs upon anyone.

Any city or home that does not welcome you, shake off the dust of that place from your feet as you leave.
Matthews 10:14

OBEY GOD

Peter and the Apostles said, it is better to obey God than man. This was in reference to teaching in the temple after being put in prison. Although the high priest did not want them to preach about Jesus. However, they chose to obey God. God will always have a remnant that is willing to do His will. The pastors whom God called are to watch for the souls of God's people. They are to feed (the Word of God) to His sheep. Whatever is right, God will repay! We, the members pay pastors a salary although our resources are limited. I recall, Jesus asked Peter if he loved Him. *Peter answered, Lord, thou knowest all things; thou knowest that I love thee. Jesus saith unto him, "Feed my sheep."* God commanded pastors whom He called: Feed my sheep. Man cannot live by bread alone but by every word that precedes out of the mouth of God.

These twelve (disciples) Jesus sent forth, and commanded them, saying, Go not into the way of the Gentiles, and into any city of the

Samaritans enter ye not: But go rather to the lost sheep of the house of Israel. And as ye go, preach, saying, The kingdom of heaven is at hand. Heal the sick, cleanse the lepers, raise the dead, cast out devils: <u>freely ye have received, freely give</u> (Matthew 10:5-8).

Jesus <u>healed the sick</u>; he did not ask for money! In fact, the woman with the issue of blood had spent all that she had and was not better. He said to her, "Thy faith has made thee hold."

Jesus said, *Verily, verily, I say unto you, He that believeth on me, the works that I do shall he do also; and greater works than these shall he do; because I go unto my Father. And whatsoever ye shall ask in my name, that will I do, that the Father may be glorified in the Son.*
John 14:12-13 KJV

Pastors who do their work well should be paid well and should be highly appreciated, especially those who <u>work hard</u> at both preaching and teaching (I Timothy 5:17).

Pastors are <u>paid</u> a salary by the members of the church! <u>Many</u> are PAID WELL!!!!
There are some who teach well. However, some still choose to advocate for more money for themselves; it is done in several ways. That is a trait of prosperity preachers.
Those whom God called, He will equip and repay! All should <u>do what God said do</u>. All have a calling to fulfill; they must <u>serve</u> this present age! Do the master's will.

Listen: There was a marriage in Cana of Galilee and the mother of Jesus was there. Both Jesus and his disciples were there. When the wine ran out, the mother of Jesus said unto the servants, whatsoever he (Jesus) say to you, **do it**. Jesus said to them, *"Fill the water pots with water.* "They filled them up to the brim. They didn't question Jesus. He said to them, *"Draw out now, and take it to the master of the ceremony."* Jesus turned water into wine. The moral: <u>Just do what God said do! Leave the results to him.</u> A familiar saying: Do Not try to help God out!

The Philippians were supportive of Apostle Paul and he was thankful. Apparently, they believed it was the right thing to do and Paul gave them assurance. He knew that God would take care of their needs. He said so in his word.

The church will supply the pastors with a paper check, but Jesus will see that they receive their just reward! Be patient and trust God. Some staff members <u>may not</u> be on payroll; they may serve freely and God will reward them.

Choir members are expected to serve faithfully; use the gifts which God has given unto them in harmony with others. They are instrumental in setting the tone for the service, breaking the ice so to speak for the hearers of God's word. However, it is the members responsibility to enter God's house prepared to receive a message from God. Secondly, each one has the responsibility of living accordingly. Choir members serve this present age and God will repay them.

Paul pinned: *Speaking to yourselves in psalms and hymns and spiritual songs, <u>singing and making melody</u> in your heart to the Lord; Giving thanks always for all things unto God and the Father in the name of our Lord Jesus Christ;*

Ephesians 5: 19-20 KJV

Paul also penned: *Let the word of Christ dwell in you richly in all wisdom; teaching and admonishing one another in psalms and hymns and spiritual songs, <u>singing with grace in your hearts to the Lord.</u>*

Colossians 3:16 KJV

Ushers are expected to be on their post; serve faithfully. As they stand at the doors with smiling faces, they graciously greet the in-coming congregation. Part of their job is to assist or give instructions concerning available seats; they serve this present age. No one can pay and reward faithful workers like the Lord!

For a day in thy courts is better than a thousand. I had rather be a <u>doorkeeper</u> in the house of my God, than to dwell in the tents of wickedness.

Psalm 84:10 KJV

How many others will serve freely? <u>If you received freely, give freely, serve freely **sometimes** in some positions.</u> Do your best and God will reward you. I know this!

Apparently an impromptu moment...

One local pastor/teacher was programmed to bring a message at a specific hour at a church within the city. He arrived and said, "I have not been feeling well, but it is worth it to preach today!" He continued, "I have a child in college." He obviously did not want to miss the opportunity <u>to be paid</u>. O' what a shame. He should have kept that information to himself (between himself and God). He was there for the wrong reason. His priority was not to share the Word of God in anticipation of a soul being saved. Who can disagree? His statement may have been a turn-off for the babe-in-Christ. Apparently, preaching is "big business" for many when they accept multiple assignments. The door was open for speculation...

Solomon penned: *The eyes of man are never satisfied*. **Who can disagree?**

Isaiah, son of Amoz is often thought of as the greatest of the writing prophets. His name means "The Lord Saves." <u>He wrote about the failure of Israel's leaders.</u>

He penned,
Yea, they are <u>greedy dogs</u> which can never have enough, And they are shepherds that cannot understand: They all look to their own way, Every one <u>for his gain</u>, from his quarter.

The false leaders in Israel took advantage of God's people. Some of the leaders of today seem to be no different than those referenced by Isaiah. History does repeat itself; nothing is new under the sun! <u>Many are money-hungry!</u>

Today, many pastors boast about their lavish lifestyles. Some are well-known leaders and millionaires. **Some are not there yet, but it is their destination**. Some own jets, multiple vehicles, boats or maybe a yacht. They own large homes in gated communities while their members pay them large salaries. Some members struggle to make ends meet, live in apartments, trailer homes, or homes which need repairs. Some members have no transportation of their own. Many need much...They contribute a portion of their meager income to the church. Scripture said give large or small. God knows the heart of every man. We must do what we know is right and trust God to supply our needs!

Jesus taught his disciples and multitudes followed him; he did not have an extravagant two-story home to return to. But Jesus said, *"Foxes have dens and birds have nests, but I, the Messiah have no home of my own no place to lay my head"* (Matthew 8:20 TLB).

It is noteworthy to say the faithful pastor/teacher will receive a "Crown of Glory." Be thou faithful until death! God is your Rewarder. *And when the Chief Shepherd shall appear, ye shall receive a crown of Glory that fadeth not away* (I Peter 5:4).

It is also fair to say the church should do more than pay salaries, take care of the expenses of the church or do church work. Out-reach (ministry) is expected. We know expenses are required in everything! Members are not expected to pay dues today. God's word says give and we must do so according to how we are blessed.
We are aware that to whom much is given, much is required. Pastors use this statement to encourage those who earn large salaries to give more.

We must teach our children to give, but if the parent does not give to the child, he will have nothing to give to the church. We also know the poor we will always have. Who is qualified to receive a benevolent offering?

Let's Hear From God:

I knew you before you were formed within your mother's womb; before you were born, I sanctified you and appointed you as my spokesman to the world.

Jeremiah 1:5 TLB

Jeremiah, one of the major prophets made it clear that <u>God had plans for his life</u>. He did not choose to be God's spokesman, but was set aside to speak to the people on God's behalf. He warned them of their wickedness and disobedience. Israel had forsaken God by worshiping idol gods. Jeremiah warned Israel of coming disaster and he made an appeal to the nation to turn back to God.

Not every preacher is a pastor. Some might be called to mentor others. Many pastor/preachers say, "I am not a man like any other man." **I understand the statement.** Some have told the church this, but the world (unsaved) is watching and they draw their own conclusion. They see **some pastor/preachers** doing what they do. Notice I said, "some." They see them going and coming from the same places which they frequent, hotels, casinos, liquor stores and etc. The unsaved one knows if he should not be there but, he does not expect to see the man of God there too. He hears them talk like he talks. Man has a free will! God will deal with them in His own time! He is a forgiving God, but there are consequences for our actions. God has an all-seeing eye. We know God <u>did not call every man to feed his sheep</u>. <u>That sets the called ones apart!</u> They may be found in unusual places, let's hope their reason is justified; only God knows. Those who are called are expected to live morally right. How can one give instructions to others if he does not walk worthy himself. **Yes, we give account to God!**
Just as I wrote that information, a **minister** sent me a message: *Only God is able to solve man's greatest problem: which is <u>sin</u>* (Micah 7:18). I could only reply: Amen!

You are a corrector of the foolish, a teacher of the childish, having in the Law the embodiment of knowledge and truth----Well then, you who teach others, do you not teach yourself? While you teach against stealing, do you steal (take what does not really belong to you)?

Romans 2: 20-21 The Amplified Bible

Apostle Paul penned:
All things are lawful for me, but all things are not expedient (practical)*: all things are lawful for me, but all things edify* (improve morally) *not.*

1 Cor. 10:23 KJV

Man has a free will to do as he pleases, but if entering the casinos and gambling causes a brother to do the same, it is not practical. We must not be stumbling blocks to others! Someone is always watching and may want to emulate us. Therefore, we must carefully choose our pathways.

"I therefore, a prisoner for the Lord, urge you to walk in a manner worthy of the calling to which you have been called, with all humility and gentleness, with patience, bearing with one another in love, eager to maintain the unity of the Spirit in the bond of peace."

Ephesians 4:1

When I was a babe in Christ there were times when I wondered if leaders/pastors were saying what many professionals have said. "Do as I say and not as I do." Wisdom taught me God has an all-seeing eye and he that keepeth Israel neither slumbers nor sleeps. So, He will make corrections in His own time.

Apostle Paul wrote to the Corinthians:
Wherefore come out from among them (the worldly) *and be ye separate, saith the Lord, and touch not the unclean thing; and I will receive you,*

II Cor. 6:17 KJV

Since we have accepted Jesus Christ as our Lord and Savior, we MUST strive to set good examples. We must <u>not plan</u> sinful activities, wallow in sin and act as if God does not see us! Satan is a deceiver and a liar too. Let us not become servants of his. Even when we do our best, we will fall short, but God knows our hearts and He is a forgiving God. He will also <u>make a way of escape</u> and we must stand for righteousness! Right living makes righteous! Do we want to live right?

Pastors are not GOD! Those whom He called are his messengers. They are imperfect and they make mistakes. The church belongs to God, Jesus is the head of the church and the pastor is the under-shepherd. God called pastors to feed His sheep the Word of God; and He speaks to others who trust, praise and worship Him in spirit and in truth too. We must know our place. *"In the last days, God says, I will pour out my Spirit on all people. Your sons and daughters will prophesy, your young men will see visions, your old men will dream dreams."* Acts 2:17 NIV

Minister Gerald R. Scott, Sr.
Grandson of Reverend Curtis F. Roberson, Sr.

The Call From God

Apostle Paul wrote the letters of Ephesians, Philippians, Colossians and Philemon while he was a prisoner in Rome. He pointed out that in the present there will be great conflict because our battle is with the forces of evil. Because we are members of Christ's body (the church) we have power to withstand.

Some have special abilities

And he gave some, apostles; and some, prophets; and some, evangelists and some, pastors and teachers; For the perfecting of the saints for the work of the ministry, for the edifying of the body of Christ: (Ephesians 4: 11-12 KJV).

Apostles are any of the 12 disciples <u>chosen</u> by Jesus Christ. **This means they walked with Jesus.** They were sent out to preach the gospel and made up of Christ's <u>12 original disciples and Paul</u>. It is my understanding that these men were chosen to set up the foundation of the church. It (the foundation) was laid in the first century. The Apostles played a part in establishing the church.

A Disciple is a student, one who learns from a teacher. An Apostle was sent to deliver those teachings; all disciples are NOT Apostles. Please hear this.

Prophets: There were Old Testament Prophets (major and minor). The Prophets proclaimed a <u>message</u> from the Lord <u>to the early church</u> (for the laying of the foundation) Ephesians 2:19-20. The foundation has been laid. Years ago, God spoke in many different ways to our fathers **through the prophets, in visions, dreams, ...**

From the Old Testament
*...the armies of the kings of **Moab, Ammon, and of the Meunites** declared war on <u>Jehoshaphat and the people of Judah.</u>*
II Chronicles 20:1 TLB

<u>The son of Asa; king of Judah</u>

*...**Jehoshaphat** stood and said, Hear me, O **Judah, and ye inhabitants of Jerusalem**; Believe in the LORD your God, so shall ye be established (have success) believe his prophets, so shall ye prosper <u>(everything will be all right)</u>.*
II Chronicles 20:20

They were <u>all right</u> because the armies began fighting each other. King Jehoshaphat and his people went out to plunder the bodies and came away loaded with money, garments, and jewels stripped from the corpses. <u>Study God's word for yourself!</u>

<u>Note this:</u>
*The law and the prophets were **until John**: since that time the kingdom of God is preached, and every man presseth into it.*
Luke 16:16 KJV
<u>Until John the Baptist</u> began to preach, the laws of Moses and the

*messages of the prophets **were your guides**. But John introduced the Good News that the Kingdom of God would come soon. And now eager multitudes are pressing in* (Luke 16:16 TLB).

RELEVANT NOTICE:
But now in these days he has spoken to us through his **Son**... (Hebrews 1: 1-2 TLB). God speaks to us through His word! Let us hear God! He tells us what to expect; we know there are false prophets! Believe not every spirit, but try the spirits whether they are of God.

All scripture is given by inspiration of God, and is profitable for doctrine, for reproof, for correction, for instruction in righteousness.
2 Timothy 3:16 KJV

We have what we need! If one cannot read, he can pray and God will reveal His word to him. Amen somebody! Today with new technology one can pick up his/her cellular phone and have the word read to him/her. Even pronunciation of words and names are made possible! Additional news: Practically everyone of age has an iPad or computer now days. **I am aware that there is always someone who can shed light on any subject.** The Holy Spirit is the Master Teacher. I didn't ask if anyone agrees. There are also many different interpretations of the "Word." We have the King James (study Bible), the Living Bible, Amplified Bible and others.

All Christians
Christians should be held to a higher standard. We should not dress nor live like the world. I am not proclaiming that members are on the same level as Pastors. We know that pastors and elders represent Our Lord and Savior, Jesus Christ to the congregation. They represent the church to the world or the unsaved. All who teach God's word should live accordingly. **All** who confess Jesus Christ should strive to live morally right. We should not tell others how to live when our lifestyle is raggedy; disgraceful. If something is wrong for the members it is also wrong for the leaders. No one gets a pass! We as Christians should be living better lives than we were when we were in the world. Who can disagree? We should have grown-up after studying God's word. We say God has called us out of darkness into His marvelous

<u>light</u>! We must let our <u>lights</u> shine, strive to lead the unsaved to Christ (reach the masses).

Let us Detour for a Moment

Some years ago, a member of a local church said to me: "There are so many preachers out there, maybe God told some to pray and they thought he said preach!" O' well...Solomon said: In all thy getting, get an understanding. If you find this to be humorous laughter is said to be good for the soul.

In this day and time, many are <u>selfish</u> and seem to be <u>unconcerned</u> about <u>the needs of the poor</u>. They are self-centered and they preach prosperity, name it and claim it. It's basically about money! We love to say, "Money answers all things." It is the **love** of money that brings about many problems; many are **<u>money hungry</u>** and sin is the root of all evil. Amen! Some will say anything to encourage people to give money to put into their pockets. We must be wise, study God's word and rely on the Holy Spirit for guidance. How can anyone heap to himself all that he can grasp and not consider the poor? <u>Jesus said, the poor we will always have</u>. He that giveth to the poor lendeth to the Lord. The church should help the poor! **<u>We must give</u>** in order to have funds available to help the poor. Jesus is coming back for the Church, his bride.

Know Your Responsibility

Every Christian is responsible for sharing God's word with the unsaved. We must strive to reach the masses. Jesus said, "And I, if I be lifted up from the earth, will draw all men unto me." I can say when we as Christians share God's word with those who are in darkness we can lead them to the light which is Jesus. They must be willing to make the change. Jesus is the light of the world; we must <u>lift-up His name</u>. We must share the old, old story! It will not change!

We Should Help Others

I contribute cheerfully and regularly to the support of <u>the ministry and the expenses of the church.</u> I make an annual donation to "The American Red cross," a humanitarian organization.

American Red Cross of North Louisiana

Donation Processing Center
P.O. Box 208, Houston, TX 77001-0208

Today, we must remember Clara Barton, American Red Cross Founder. Many people are helped after natural disasters.

I also support "Saint Jude Children's Research Hospital."

ST JUDE CHILDREN'S RESEARCH HOSPITAL
P.O. BOX 50
MEMPHIS, TN 38108-9929

Children are treated for cancer and other life-threatening diseases; their parents are helped as well. They are relieved of the financial stress, but they still need our help; our prayers. There are times when others need help as well; I do not turn a blind eye nor a deaf ear. We as Christians should be Christ-like. It is not always about money. Some need a word of encouragement or a piece of clothing; many need instructions in righteousness; we know that some are hungry. Prayer always works, but we should share...There are many organizations to choose from if we truly want to be supportive.

We must be attentive

Jesus said, *"For I was a hungred, and ye gave me meat: I was thirsty, and ye gave me drink: I was a stranger, and ye took me in: Naked, and ye clothed me: I was sick, and ye visited me: I was in prison, and ye came unto me."*

Matt. 25: 35-36 KJV

...*Verily I say unto you, inasmuch as ye have done it unto one of the least of* these *my brethren, ye have done it unto me* (Matt. 25:40b KJV). And forget not to show love to strangers: for thereby some have entertained angels unawares...We give to those who already have much; to those who are in our inner circle. Why? We want to fit-in or appear to be financially able to do whatever is expected of us. Some of us want to be the so-called elite group. This includes sororities, fraternities and the like and some of us apparently do not want to disappoint the one who is in charge. If the leader says, "Let us give to Dr. Longstreet Joe Batman in Johannesburg, Africa," we will do our best, but charity begins at home. Sometimes we see the need, but ignore it. Man can be selfish!

A Good Example

Consider the rich man whose barns were full to overflowing. He did not have room for more. He decided to tear down his barns and build bigger ones. He said then he would have room enough. He said to himself, you have enough stored away for many years to come. Now take it easy! He was selfish by thinking only of himself and did not consider the fact that he did not have control of his own life. But God said to him, Fool! Tonight, you die. Then who will get it all? (Luke 12:18-20). Some have used the same thought pattern and went to their graves leaving their abundant possessions behind. Of course, we brought nothing into this world and we will take nothing when we leave. So, why not share with someone in need? Why be greedy? In fact, <u>allow others to have or possess something too</u>. Allow others a chance to take a break from the many man-made obligations.

Sometimes we have much more than we need (multiple this and that). We will never use all we have acquired, accomplished, compiled. But we do not seem to be satisfied (our forefathers called this **long-eyed**).

CHAPTER 21
Giving According to God's Word

BE FAITHFUL

II Corinthians 9:7 (TLB) *Everyone must make up his own mind as to <u>how much he should give</u>. Don't force anyone to give more than he really wants to, for <u>cheerful givers are the ones God prizes.</u>*

I understand this to mean: Decide how much you want to give. The scripture does not say you <u>must</u> give a specific amount of money. Be mindful: God is pleased with those of us who give <u>willingly</u>. It is clear to me; we should not assess anyone to give. I recognize: Some will

say that is a matter of opinion. But what about one whose income is $200,000 annually and another's income is $20,000 annually? Both are assessed to give $1,000. That is not equal sacrifice.
Paul penned,
For I mean not that other men be eased, and ye be burdened:
II Cor. 8:13 KJV

It may very well be a burden on the one whose income is less. One can easily give a lot when he or she has a lot to give from. Remember what Jesus said concerning the widow who gave two mites!

Paul is clearly saying: God does not want anyone to be troubled because his resources are too small to meet the expectations of those who are in a better financial category. Who are they to set standards for others to follow?
Here Apostle Paul reassures the Corinthians that he means what he writes in his letters. The Corinthian church had been infiltrated by false teachers who were challenging Paul's authority as an Apostle.

You might not hear me, but please hear Jesus. He did not say pressure the people nor coerce them. Let's hear what he said:

Luke 6:38 (TLB) *For if you give, you will get! Your gift will return to you in full and overflowing measure, pressed down, shaken together to make room for more, and running over. Whatever measure you use to give----large or small---will be used to measure what is given back to you.* Be obedient!

Yes give, it's an act of obedience. Make your decision! Jesus did not say give 10%. If you choose to give 30%, that's your choice. I heard the Lord; I give faithfully. I am a witness that He will and does keep His word. You might not trust me but trust Jesus! You will be glad that you did. Give from your heart. God will bless you abundantly.

II Corinthians 8:12-13 (TLB) *If you are really eager to give, then it isn't important how much you have to give. God wants you to give what you have, not what you haven't.* One's attitude plays a very important role concerning giving. God owns everything and He needs nothing! Whatever we are, God made us and whatever we have God gave us. Praise God! We must remember who our source is and be good stewards. We do not need anyone to rule with an iron fist nor, try to coerce anyone into giving. Sometimes one's reason for asking may be wrong!!! Where is his compassion for people?

KNOW GOD'S WORD BY STUDYING

We need to study the Word of God, hear his word and everyone should be <u>convinced and convicted by the Word of God.</u>

We cannot <u>repay</u> the Lord; we should do our best to support those who are in need. I also know that Jesus said, "The poor you will always have with you" (Matthew 26:11). Solomon, the son of David and Bathsheba penned: <u>*He that hath pity upon the poor lendeth to the Lord*</u> (Proverb 19:17a).

Relevant Note: The word **"testament"** in the expression New Testament refers to a <u>new covenant.</u> Christians believe it **completes or fulfils the Mosaic covenant.** The <u>old covenant</u> was made by Yahweh with the people of Israel on Mount Sinai through Moses. The Old Testament includes prophecy which has been fulfilled. **Christ fulfilled the law and died for our sins**. We believe and confess that Jesus Christ is the Son of God. Thereby we are sons of God. Think about the term **"testator"** which refers to a person who <u>has died</u> and left a will. Christ died for mankind. Amen! It is my belief that the old preachers understood the previous record. In my studying, I have not read any scripture in the New Testament which states that the New Testament Church (God's People) are required or commanded to pay tithes. We are told to <u>GIVE!</u> However, I began to <u>pay tithes</u> after listening to Pastor Flannigan **and I do so until this day**. I <u>give</u> because Jesus said give (**large or small**) in Luke 6:38 and I am blessed! <u>Follow your heart and give according to what you have.</u> Give the way you want to be blessed! I give faithfully and regularly; my bills are paid in a timely manner, no late fees! God is my "Provider." I praise Him!!! I also realize we are told to give for two reasons. (1.)

God blesses a cheerful giver, be obedient. (2.) We support the Church and the Ministry (we pay salaries)!

Listen to This for What it is Worth

Should one make up his mind to increase his giving he should not be expected to suddenly give 10%. That should be between the giver and God. Furthermore, a growing process might be necessary. If one usually gives $50.00 per month, he may give more the next month and continue giving an increased amount until the desired total is reached. That's sensible unless one's monthly income will allow a big sudden change in financial obligations. Yes, we trust God!

The Widow's Mite

We remember the widow who put two pennies into the collection. Some who were rich put in large amounts. Jesus said, *"That poor widow has given more than all those rich men put together! For they gave a little of their extra fat, while she gave up her last penny"* (Mark 12:41-44). She gave what she had! So, don't be intimidated when you don't have much to give.

My understanding is every time one helps a person in need, he plants a seed. That seed is planted in good ground. We reap what we sow! Our harvest is based upon what we planted. We are not obligated to give to those who are greedy. There are plenty neighbors in need of one thing or another. Needs are not always financial. We, the people of God should want to help some needy soul as we travel day by day. We do want our names to be written with the blessed.

Jesus spoke a parable: *...The seed is the word of God.* (Luke 8:11 KJV).

But that on the good ground are they, which in an honest and good heart, having heard the word, keep it, and bring forth fruit with patience (Luke 8:13 KJV).

I look at this way: Share God's word with the unsaved and hope to bring someone to Christ. Jesus did say the harvest is plentiful, laborers are few and we do know he that winneth souls is wise! Apostle Paul reminds us that the fruit of the Spirit is love, joy, peace, longsuffering, gentleness, faith, meekness, and temperance. We must be careful to show love to our fellowman; be patient with the unlearned. We acknowledge that the Word of God should be preached continuously. We, the people of God must ask Him to condition our hearts; take out the stony hearts and give us hearts of flesh. Ask God to give us a receptive heart to His word and strengthen us to make application in our lives.

From The **Law** Books
Old Testament

Exodus 34:26a (KJV) *The first of the first fruits of thy land thou shalt bring unto the house of the Lord thy God.*

Fruit of thy land is not money. It is what has been grown from the grown as a crop.

Leviticus 27:30 (TLB) *A tenth of the produce of the land, whether grain or fruit, is the Lord's, and is holy.*

We are under grace, yet I found these scriptures to be very interesting and informative: *You must tithe all of your crops every year. Bring this tithe **to eat** before the Lord your God at the place he shall choose as his sanctuary; this applies to your **tithes of grain, new wine, olive oil**, and the firstborn of your **flocks and herds**. The purpose of tithing is to teach you always to put God first in your lives (when I give, I put God first!) If the place the Lord chooses for his sanctuary is too far away that it isn't convenient to carry your tithes to that place, then you may **sell the tithe portion** of your crops and herds and take the **money** to the Lord's sanctuary. When you arrive, **use the money to buy** an ox, a sheep, some wine, or some strong drink, to feast there before the Lord your God, and to rejoice with your household.*
Deuteronomy 14: 22-26 TLB

*Don't forget to share your income with the Levites in your community, for they have no property or crops as you do. Every third year you are to use your **entire tithe for local welfare programs**:* (Deuteronomy 14: 27-28 TLB)

Pastors/ministers or teachers ... We know this is not done today! We are not under the law, **but under grace**. When we lay aside a portion of our earnings according to how we are blessed, we honor the Lord by supporting the Church and the ministry. We put God first.

In my research

Annually, a tenth of all Israelite produce was to be taken to the city of the central sanctuary for distribution to the Levites. Every third year the tithe was gathered in the towns and stored for distribution to the Levites and the less fortunate: aliens, fatherless and widows.

The writer (Moses) of the five law books did not say what those did who did not grow crops. Those books are also called the Torah. It means the same as Pentateuch. We do know that the earth brought forth vegetation, plants yielding seed according to their own kinds, and trees bearing fruit in which is their seed, each according to its kind.

According to the book of Deuteronomy 8:7-9. *The Lord God brought the people into a good land, a land of brooks of water, of fountains and depths that spring out of valleys and hills. A land of wheat, and barley, and vines and fig trees, and pomegranates; a land of oil olive, and honey. A land where **food is plentiful and nothing is lacking.***

Tithing was under the law.
Many quickly refer to Malachi, the last book of the Old Testament. The prophet was sent as a **messenger to Israel.** The basic problem that Malachi discussed concerned the corruption of the priest, the neglect of God's Temple and personal sins.

The priest offered polluted bread upon the alter and they brought animals which were torn, and lame and sick. Their offerings were not acceptable. **The people** had gone away from the ordinances and had not kept them.

Malachi 3:7 ----*Return unto me, and I will return unto you, saith the Lord of host.* V.10 *Bring ye all the tithes into the storehouse, That there may be meat in mine house, And prove me now herewith, said the Lord of hosts, If I will not open you the windows of heaven, And pour you out a blessing, that there shall not be room enough to receive it.* **The people were still under the law; Christ had not come in the flesh!**

ALSO NOTICE:
Storehouse:
Joseph built grain storehouses in Egypt to get ready for the years of famine. Had the priest brought the tithe into the storehouse, there would have been enough food for <u>his house</u>. **The food was for <u>Levites</u> who were on duty in the Jewish Temple.** The tribe of Levi descended from Levi, the third son of Jacob and Leah (Jacob had twelve son). **Moses was of the tribe of Levi.** God delivered the Law to him on Mount Sinai.

<u>The Levites were made priests.</u> There were many priests and they did not continue by reason of death. When the temple was destroyed in AD 70 <u>tithing ended</u>. **<u>This was decades after the crucifixion of Jesus.</u>**

Eye-Opener
Malachi 3: 11 Your <u>crops</u> will be large, for I will guard them from insects and plagues. Your <u>grapes</u> won't shrivel away before they ripen, says the Lord of hosts. Grapes were a crop (not money) which was grown from the grown.

The 10 Commandments are laws handed down to Moses by God on Mount Sinai. The Mosaic law lays down both moral and social responsibilities. They are the unchanging, eternal laws of God.

1. You shall have no other gods before me.
2. You shalt not make unto thee any graven images.
3. You shalt not take the name of the Lord thy God in vain.
4. Remember the Sabbath day and keep it Holy.
5. Honor your father and mother
6. You shalt not kill
7. You shalt not commit adultery
8. You shalt not steal
9. You shalt not bear false witness against your neighbor
10. You shalt not covet.

The Great Commandment:

One of the Pharisees which was a lawyer asked Jesus a question. "Master, which is the great commandment in the law?" Jesus said unto him, *Thou shalt love the Lord thy God with all thy heart, and with all thy soul, and with all thy mind. This is the first and great commandment. And the second is like unto it, Thou shalt love thy neighbor as thyself. On these two commandments hang all the law and the prophets.*

Matthew 22: 37-40 KJV

Know This

Hebrews 10:5-6 ...*Christ said, as he came into the world, "O God, the blood of bulls and goats cannot satisfy you, <u>so you have made ready this body of mine for me to lay as a sacrifice</u> upon your alter. You were not satisfied with animal sacrifices, slain and burnt before you as offerings for sin.*

Remember: <u>God sent his Son, made of a woman, made under the law, to redeem them that were **under the law...**</u> Christ was born while the <u>law was still in effect.</u> It was in place to lead followers to Christ. Since Christ has come and fulfilled the promise, **the law is no longer needed**. **Hebrews 7:5** says, And verily they that are of the <u>sons of Levi</u> who receive the office of the <u>priesthood</u> have a <u>commandment</u>

to take <u>tithes</u> of the people according to the <u>law</u>, that is, of their brethren, though they come out of the <u>loins of Abraham:</u>

<u>Now</u>
The church is under the new covenant established by the death and resurrection of Jesus Christ. Jesus is NOT of the tribe of Levi; order of Aaron. He is of the tribe of Judah; (the Lion of the tribe of Judah) after the order of <u>Melchizedek</u>. He had no known mother or father, no beginning and no end.

When the priesthood changed there was also a change of the law<u>.</u> <u>Christ is our High Priest Forever Amen!</u>

Before Christ was crucified...
Matthew 23:23 *Woe unto you, scribes and Pharisees, <u>hypocrites</u>! For you pay tithe of <u>mint and anise and cumin</u>, (those are plants) and have omitted the weightier matters of the law, judgement, mercy, and faith: these ought ye to have done, and not to leave the other undone.*

The word, woe was used by Christ; it represents His righteous anger! <u>Here</u> Christ pointed out the most important concerns of the law which were **judgement, mercy and faith**. The people were tithing of what was grown <u>from the ground</u> (from their gardens). That was alright because they were still under the law, but they ignored judgement, mercy and faith. That's why he called them hypocrites. Mint is any <u>plant</u> of the mint family. <u>Anise</u> is a herbaceous plant, <u>cumin</u> is a small, apiaceous plant (seed like fruit). Christ **did not** say bring 10% of your money to the sanctuary. Neither did He say how much to give in Luke 6:38.

CHAPTER 22
Serving During Challenging Times

ANTICIPATING THE WINTER SEASON (OF LIFE)

We should be comfortable and relaxed. Yet, many of us continue to labor as if our lives depend on it. We take on responsibilities to hopefully maintain and secure comfort. As soon as we think everything is under control the cost of living escalates. We also strive to be somewhat prepared for challenges which sometimes interrupt our lives unexpectedly. Our forefathers said, "If it's not one thing, it's another." Nevertheless, they worked hard from sun up to sun down. They had little, they were treated harshly yet, they were obedient to slave masters and prayed hard. When they hummed a tune, it was usually a prayer included. Today, we ask, "Hear our prayer O' Lord."

Cheryl Cuningham, RN-ADN, LVN, ORT, USNC
Dallas Regional Health Care
Great Granddaughter of <u>Willie Clarkson</u>

Cheryl is a Shreveport, Louisiana native. She graduated from Woodlawn High School with honors and participated in the choir and on the "Flag-line" in 1986. She joined the United States Navy Reserve; trained in Pensacola, Florida. She was transferred to Great Lakes, Illinois for Hospital Corps School and graduation. Cheryl, US Naval Corpsman relocated to Dallas, Texas. There she successfully completed the requirements for the Surgical Technology Program at El Centro College. She was activated to serve her country in San Diego, CA. during Operation Desert Storm.

Upon returning to Shreveport, Louisiana, Cheryl successfully completed the requirements for Licensed Practical Nurse at Louisiana Technical College. She challenged the exam and received her license for the states of Louisiana and Texas. She worked for Progressive Care in Shreveport and later returned to Dallas, TX; began her journey in the medical field at Dallas Regional Hospital. Simultaneously, she furthered her nursing education via Excelsior University of New York and earned an Associate Degree in Nursing (ADN). God blessed her to successfully challenge the National Council Licensure

Examination (NCLEX). She has a husband, two children and one grandchild. She is very active in her field and also works with Home-Health Patients. We thank God for every blessing!

Cheryl and family are members of Gospel Tabernacle Missionary Baptist Church. She sings with the choir.

Kashundra L. Lynch, MBA, BS-CIS
Director of Child Nutrition in Caddo Parish
Great Granddaughter of <u>Willie Clarkson</u>

Kashundra is a servant for God and mankind. She enjoys singing with the choir at Paradise Missionary Baptist Church. She serves in several capacities: Assistant Sunday School teacher (occasionally), Vacation Bible School Worker and she assist workers with the "Feeding Program." She worked with the "Drill Team" for several years. She has a passion for people which she refers to as "Christian Affliction." She often says: "I am following in the footsteps of my mom." Kaye plays the piano during her leisure time.

Kashundra graduated with honors from Woodlawn High School where she participated in extracurricular activities including Reserve

Officers' Training Corps (ROTC), choir and majorette. She earned a Bachelor of Science Degree in Computer Information Systems from Grambling State University. She is employed by Caddo Parish School Board and has served 20 years. She formerly held positions of State Grant Bookkeeper and Finance Budget Supervisor. Kaye previously worked for a business firm approximately ten years which preceded foreclosure. While employed, she used her skills and acquired knowledge which helped land her in a better position. Kaye continued her education; earned her Master's in Business Administration from the University of Phenix. She is currently the Director of Child Nutrition for 64 Caddo Parish Public Schools. To God be the glory for the things He has done!

Hardships

Often, we strive to do our very best, yet <u>trouble</u> finds its way into our dwelling places, our jobs and even into the church. It does not discriminate. Some of us work and give 100%, assist others as needs dictate, be fair with our resources and the list goes on. Sometimes it seems as though we cannot catch a break from the many obligations, trials and whatever. Suddenly, it seemed as if my memory bank opened up. It was then that I recalled:

In the world ye shall have tribulation: but be of good cheer; I have overcome the world.

John 16:33KJV

Then I encouraged myself and said boldly: I am an overcomer! Even though we notice some <u>do not</u> attend church anywhere. They may party until the wee hours of the night; the drum-beat or the music goes on and on. Yes, we have many rights and privileges. Perhaps some say: "I will eat, drink and be merry for tomorrow we die." It's one's choice to do as he or she pleases and I sometimes wonder when do some work or what is their profession? They seem to have plenty of everything.

My next thought: Psalm 73: 2-3
<u>Psalm of Asaph</u>, a prophetically gifted Levite (member of the Hebrew tribe).
But as for me, my feet were almost gone; My steps had well-nigh

slipped. For I was envious at the <u>foolish</u>, When I saw the prosperity of the <u>wicked</u>.

At that time, I said to myself: It's right to do right. For right living makes righteous; gives us right standing with God. I also recalled: The wise teaching of Solomon (a black man).

------the wicked shall fall by his own wickedness. But righteousness will deliver from death. That's pure consolation!

CHAPTER 23
History Made in the USA

THE LIGHT OF DAY

Our forefathers, the black man was commanded to "enter through the back door, sit at the back of the bus; stand at the end of the line." They worked to make changes; we must be proactive and not react violently. Rosa Parks, Dr. Martin Luther King, Jr. and others fought for civil rights. We know God is not asleep and He will make corrections in His own time. In the meantime, we must awake; be vigilant. We must do what we can for ourselves and God will do the rest.

After more than a century, we are still considered to be second-class citizens. We must work the hardest, be **exceptionally smart** and be well educated and prepared to be considered for some positions. God's word is very encouraging!

And the Lord shall make thee the head, and not the tail; and thou shalt be above only, and thou shall not be beneath;...
Deuteronomy 28: 13a

In this scripture, Moses warned the people to obey all the commandments of the Lord. He informed them that God would transform them into the greatest nation in the world. Obedience to God is the key. Today, we must put our trust in God and obey His will if we expect him to bless us. What God bless no man can curse!

Scores of African Americans are blessed with great talents

The first television sitcom to portray black people was **Amos 'n' Andy**.
Sidney Poitier was Hollywood's first black global megastar.
In 1963, Cicely Tyson was the first African American star of a television drama.
In 1970, James Earl Jones was the first Black man to be nominated for an Oscar.

Mary Jackson, Katherine Johnson & Dorothy Vaughn
I am reminded: In the movie, "Hidden Figures" those three black women were electronic computer programmers. It was their brilliant work that sent the first American into orbit in 1962. Those women are historical icons. They were brilliant African-American women who worked at NASA (National Aeronautics Space Administration). Even though they were needed to do the job, they were discriminated against (an injustice). God used them to prove to the world their value. Sometimes he uses ordinary people to make a point. Let us not overlook those who man considers to be insignificant.

NATIONAL NEWS
Dr. Ben Carson from Detroit, Michigan
In 1987, Dr. Carson, neurosurgeon received world recognition after he performed the first successful separation of twins joined at the back of the head. He perfected what is currently the standard medical procedure for separating conjoined twins.

General Colin L. Powell
Powell was an American politician, diplomat and decorated United States Army Officer who served as the 65th United States Secretary of state from 2001 to 2005. He was the first African-American to hold the position and he was instrumental in shaping America while serving this country under several Republican Administrations.

Condoleezza Rice

Condoleezza is an American diplomat, civil servant and professor who is the current director of the Hoover Institute at Stanford University. She served as the 66th United States Secretary of state from 2005 to 2009. She also served as national security advisor from 2001 to 2005.

Barack Hussein Obama & Michelle Robinson-Obama

Barack was the first African-American president of the United States. He was born in Honolulu, HI; became the 44th president in 2009. He is an American politician, author and retired attorney. He attended Harvard Law school. Barack received the Grammy Award in 2007 and Nobel Prize in 2009. Michelle, his wife was educated at Princeton University and Harvard University. She is a woman of integrity and author of a book.

Kamala Devin Harris

In 2021, Kamala became the <u>first female vice president of the United States of America</u>. History was made; she is the highest-female officer and also the first African American/Asian American to hold this office. We applaud her! God willed it so and we pray that God will direct her mind, thoughts and actions.

National News Report:
Ketanji Brown-Jackson

2022 Historic Rise

Mrs. Jackson, an African American Attorney who served as a federal judge on the United States Court of appeals for the District of Columbia Circuit since 2021 was confirmed to the Supreme Court. When God says "YES," No man can say "NO."

For centuries, the Black man was at the bottom of the list for top positions. Now the last has become first. Look at God work...**There are many more who have paved the way for this generation.**

Sacrifices were made to bring about "change."

*The Voting Rights Act of 1965
Was Signed into Law by:
President Lyndon B. Johnson*

Caddo Parish Voting for Election of Officers 2008

Mrs. Ella, Carolyn Rhymes, Mattie Wilson and two other workers
Commissioners at Southern Hills School

Mrs. Bobbie Ellis, Mattie Wilson and one other worker
Commissioners at Sunset Acres School

Community Service

Some of us work as **commissioners** during parish election of officers and for major elections. Even though we work voluntarily for long hours, it's necessary. Many have died that we may have a right to speak or participate during such times. The **Voting Rights Act** outlawed the discriminatory voting practices. Before the law was signed, there was a prerequisite to vote and literacy tests. Today, we must cast our vote; work for necessary change! I performed the duties of a commissioner for fifteen years and what an experience it was!

Some of us have worked as **numerators** during census count which takes place every ten years. It has advantages also: Parishes/states receive finances based on the population. The count is ordered by the constitution and conducted by the United States Census Bureau. It's certainly an experience! I worked in the year 2010.

Our Christian Duties

There are times when we should avail ourselves to be of service to those who are <u>home-bound, hospitalized, in convalescent homes and even imprisoned.</u> They need to hear a word from the Lord and be encouraged also. Some residents don't seem to have family to visit with them, to show concern for their well-being. Surely, that is depressing to say the least. I have observed, shared God's word (one-on-one) and prayed with many. It was a joy! Glory to God! We often say the prayers of the righteous availeth much. And so, we must go where there is a true need; share with those who are not physically able to worship in the house of prayer. Many are not capable of caring for themselves and some just need assistance. Therefore, we decide to house our loved ones in facilities which are designed to do what we cannot do. That is because many couples work full time jobs and some have children who need constant care as well.

Home-care

There comes a time when children should take responsibility for caring for their parents. The role is reversed. We are accustomed to things being the other way around however, as we age time brings about changes. It is a fact that our elders said, "Once a man and twice a child." When a child is born, he or she is taken care of by the parents.

This includes all the child needs for survival and protection. When the child becomes an adult, he or she chooses which route to travel. Even when one chooses to relocate in a distant city, he should remember Mom and Dad. When there are as many as four siblings, sometimes only one will take the responsibility of looking after their parents. We must remember that God's word says, *"Honor thy mother and father that thy days may be long on the earth."* That's a commandment with promise. We must be careful to remember we reap what we sow. When we honor our parents, we respect, obey, and give them <u>appropriate attention as needed.</u> This includes care which is required when the adult has gone back to a <u>child-like stage</u>. They may or may not remember to do certain things to care for themselves.

I applaud those family members who retire, or hire qualified health-care workers to assist their love ones at home. This gives the patients the pleasure of dwelling in their familiar surroundings. It also makes it easier for those who are responsible for their parent's care. They know what's happening daily without waiting to hear from those in charge at health-care facilities. Sometimes health-care workers are overwhelmed with heavy workloads. They must focus on providing the best possible care for their patients; remembering lives are at stake. Therefore, they don't always inform family or return phone calls in a timely manner. That is, unless something is an urgent matter and requires immediate attention. Those of us who work or have worked in healthcare facilities are familiar with the process and we understand.

CHAPTER 24
Sickness and Medical Care

Dorita Grigsby, Jacqueline Hall, Miyoki Williams, Mattie Wilson & La Donna Smith

In any profession, team work is important. The phlebotomists are the backbone of the laboratory. Clinical Laboratory Scientists cannot perform their duties until an acceptable blood sample has been collected and transported to the lab in a timely manner. Physicians await results in order to confirm diagnosis in many cases. Phlebotomists deserve respect!

UPS AND DOWNS

*Man, that is born of a woman is of a few days, and full of **trouble*** (Job 14:1).

Trouble comes into the lives of all: The rich have money, but it cannot buy happiness. It will pay medical bills but it cannot buy health; purchase material things and still not bring joy. Children of the rich may have all their hearts desire, yet they find themselves in trouble with the law. Parents bail them out of trouble and they commit murder and sometimes commit suicide. Trouble does not discriminate. The poor knows hard times, identifies with sickness and diseases, struggles to obtain and keep health insurance. Some have no health insurance nor life insurance. The poor makes the hard decisions: Pay the rent or the mortgage, purchase food and pay a portion of the monthly expenses (rob Peter to pay Paul). Some of the utilities may be disconnected. Sometimes all the bills are paid and one or two appliances play-out or malfunction and need to be replaced. The mortgage gets paid off and the roof needs to be replaced. Child #1 needs money to pay for college education, clothes, shoes, and he/she needs transportation. The couple has only one old car and it needs repairs. The poor knows to call on God who is our Source. God has brought us through slavery and He will never leave nor forsake his own. Stay close to our Maker!

If old man Trouble has not made his way to your house, don't count him out. He is still in route. Obtain Mother Wisdom and keep as many dollars as you can because you need them. You need the coins also; they are not spare change. Don't splurge every chance you get. Enjoy something because you deserve it, just be cautious.

Physician's Diagnosis

Many are blessed to live long lives and have minor medical concerns. Some patients are diagnosed with serious or life-threatening diseases. Sometimes life becomes complicated after physician's diagnosis (medical problems). Prescriptions are filled and directions are followed, yet other problems arise: Medications have many side effects. We are told, "The benefits outweigh the risk." We are aware that medications help to a certain extent; most do not solve the issue. Patients need a cure and not merely a temporary fix, or one which is needed for the duration of life. Physicians write prescriptions and Big Pharma makes huge profits, but patients are still suffering.

We must be proactive in solving health issues:

Monosodium glutamate (MSG) is a **flavor enhancer**. It has been alleged that it is often added to restaurant foods, canned vegetables, soups and deli meats. Fresh vegetables should be our first choice, but today we do not know how they are grown. Equal and splendor should be avoided! MSG is said to be linked with obesity, metabolic disorders and has detrimental effects on the reproductive organs. That is not good! We must avail ourselves to antioxidants, a substance that protects cells from the damage caused by free radicals (unstable molecules made by the process of oxidation during normal metabolism). Antioxidants include vitamin C and E to name a few. Antioxidants support disease prevention and aid in brain function. Some foods are: Broccoli, spinach, carrots and potatoes and all are high in antioxidants. Cabbage, asparagus, avocados, radish and lettuce are included. Information was provided in part by qualified medical personnel.

Patsy W., RDN

In Grandmother's day, most people lived on farms in the country. They were able to plant gardens of vegetables. They also raised hogs, cattle and poultry. Thereby, they did not consume over fertilized veggies. Neither did they have to contend with poultry which was grown by unnatural methods which are used to speed-up the process. We were not aware of the many health problems which man has today. Medical care was not easy to obtain due to the fact that the nearest physician was approximately twelve miles away. Most families did not own transportation either. They relied upon the few who owned a car, or the Landowner or Overseer provided transportation when necessary.

Today's Changes

Those who care for the sick may be forced to make changes which alter their educational plans. Not only educational plans may be altered but there may be a complete life-style change. In many cases it is hard to adjust to change. That is, most times it comes when one had no idea there was a health issue. They didn't see it coming or some say they were blind-sided. If there were an inkling of a problem, one could not imagine the severity of such.

During my tenure working in the health care field, I witnessed many cases of various diseases. I saw first-hand how patients suffered through pain, seizures, surgery, memory-loss, the death of loved-ones and so much more. Many times, after patients are diagnosed, they are admitted into the hospital immediately. It is important to explain the "Patients' Bill of Rights." Many elderly patients do not understand medical terms and they need a patients' advocate. They may have traveled many miles in search of much-needed assistance. The family members were not prepared for a hospital stay. Some facilities have rooms to accommodate families but many do not. This has been a burden for families which live in distant cities. A few patients may have family nearby. Sometimes they are not very hospitable. We as people of God must be mindful how we treat others. We do not know when we may be in a similar situation. The same people whom we treat coldly, just might be the ones whom we meet when we are in need. Do we want them to turn and walk away?

Not all sickness is until death. God is still in the miracle working business. So, don't give-up, but keep hope alive! God has shown us that He is the Healer and He has no respect of person. If you don't have money, but you have Jesus, you have everything you need. He makes the final decision. Trust God because He knows best.

Chapter 25
Sickness and Death

Miraculous Improvement

God is still working miracles!
In the year 2004 (approximately), one of my younger sisters was hospitalized. The physicians seemed to be baffled. She was so very ill, but she told me, "I have coins (change) which I have saved, give them to my church." She continued, "I don't need them where I'm going." She also said, "You be good." I looked at her and I prayed. I didn't allow her statements to bother me. I know in whom I trust and I did not lose hope. Sister got better and she was discharged from the hospital. Praise God!

Sometime later she was hospitalized again. After a few days, her health improved and she was discharged after a very traumatic experience. We know God is able and faithful! He stepped in and did what no other could do. We praised God! Sister lived about <u>5 more years.</u> I am reminded of Hezekiah, who was sick until death. He turned his face to the wall and prayed to God. Fifteen more years were added to his life.

Dealing with Death

From My Experiences
We know that all living will die unless they are here when the Lord comes back. However, death leaves a void or an empty space in our lives which no one else can fill. Reality is: All have an appointment with death which we cannot cancel. Age has nothing to do with it; words and good deeds are inadequate, but we give words of encouragement. We must regroup; it is a good thing to go into the house of the Lord and praise Him as David did after the death of his child. We can release our frustrations and trust God to heal the hole in our hearts.

One who has dealt with the loss of a child, sister or mother can encourage another who is dealing with the death of the same. We knows first-hand what someone else is dealing with; we understands their pain. However, every time the death angel takes one away, it is a different experience. We also reflect on past experiences.

Perhaps we may view the loss of a love one in a positive way. All wounds will be healed as time passes and memories are forever. This thought is for peace-sake:

The Gardener, The Giver of Life
He plants a variety of flowers for His glory. He owns the garden. When the flowers spring forth, grace the earth with beauty and charm, they bring joy and happiness. Be reminded, they are only for a season. Therefore, the Gardner needs no permission to choose, pluck and arrange a colorful bouquet or a gorgeous family spray. <u>Some</u> flowers have earned a place in The New Jerusalem.

Everlasting Flower Display
Representation:
    Mother = White Magnolia for Stability
    Father = Blue Morning Glory for Love
    Grandmother = White Calla Lily for Rebirth
    Grandfather = Gladiolus of orange; lavender for Strength

Sister = Baby breath (white) for Purity and Hope
Brother = Fern (green) for New Life
Auntie = Pansies (yellow; purple) for Remembrance
Uncle = Fern (green) for New Life
Cousins, Nieces and Nephews = Colorful Tulips for Deep Love

The display is in the presence of The Lord God Almighty. It will not be removed!

Mattie P. Wilson, Author

I witnessed many patients transition during my tenure in the healthcare field. I gave words of encouragement, explained scriptures, prayed and stood by the bedside of many. I tried to console family members because I had been where they were. I gave directions based on the Word of God.

I entered rooms in healthcare facilities and discovered patients had expired and apparently the staff was not aware. The worst situation: A patient had expired, a family member was sitting by the bedside but, was unaware that her love one was gone. I checked the patient, told the family member, "I will be back shortly." I notified the charge nurse, "Will you come with me to room #XX immediately and check the patient?" I did my job professionally. It was not my duty to inform the family member of the patient's death.

On March 05, 2009

My sister was still dealing with serious medical problems. <u>I stood by her bedside and prayed</u>. Time passed and I was beginning to feel tired. I expected my two older sisters (who lived within the city) would come to the hospital and at least sit in the waiting room, but they did not. One cousin had compassion and she showed <u>love and concern</u>. She reported to the hospital to be with me. I said to myself, "I am now stronger and wiser." I recalled a scripture to re-assure myself.

Jesus said, "And lo, I am with you always, even unto the end of the world."

Matthew 28:20

This is my commandment, that ye <u>love</u> one another, even as I have loved you.

John 15:12 TLB

Just two of us (my cousin and I) sat in the waiting room and suddenly the nurse asked for my sister's son. She had tried to contact him by phone but was unable to reach him. He was aware of the situation and he knew I was there. I went back to my sister's room and shared final words with her. I stood there until the end. Love kept me at her bedside. She was 54 years old and no longer in pain because my Lord and Savior took the sting out of death. So, death does not hurt! <u>I closed her eyes</u> and I said, "Lord, it's me and You." He gave me the strength to stand the test without wavering. I did not shed one tear because I had done all that I possibly could. I said, "All is well; what a journey!" So, when you feel all alone, just remember: God is there too. You are really not alone, although family may fail you. My family failed me also!

A question was asked: For what is your life?
It is even a vapor that appears for a little time and then vanishes away.

James 4: 14 KJV

A positive note: New "baby breath" has been added to the family spray.

As I reflect on that night, I am reminded Mary, the mother of Jesus stood at the foot of the cross when Jesus was crucified. <u>She was there! O' what love!</u> John was there; he proclaimed, "Jesus is the Lamb of God." Others remained near Jesus at the foot of the cross on Calvary and there were numerous women. Where was Peter, the rock? He was one who associated closely with Jesus. Was not this a time when he should have been there also? That is what people do when they care about a love one who is about to transition (they support each other). There is strength in numbers; they lean on each other.

September 2013, One Friday evening my younger daughter rushed her dad to Veterans Administration Hospital. The next morning (Saturday), he was transported to Louisiana State University Health Sciences Center. I stood by his side and shared words of encouragement. Manuel passed away on Labor Day, Monday, September 02, 2013 at the age of 88 years.

He was blessed to live beyond four-score years. He labored from childhood throughout the majority of his adult life. For many years, he worked two jobs. He volunteered to serve in the United States Army; spent a number of years there. He received: American Theater Ribbon and World War II Victory Medals. He also served with the 464th Aviation Squadron in San Francisco, California and in Guam. The highest grade held was Corporal. Manuel was honorably discharged after an injury.

He was a dutiful Usher at Paradise Missionary Baptist Church. He came off the battlefield and the spiritual war was over also. He laid down his weapons of warfare; he studied war no more... Another flower, "Blue Morning Glory" has been added to the family spray representing love for his children.

A prayer of Moses, a man of God:
Teach us to number our days and recognize how few they are; help us to spend them as we should.
Psalm 90:15 TLB

My Advice to all

Pray daily because death knocks on the doors of all families and enters in. We know not the day nor the hour when a loved one will depart. We must stay close to Jesus. If we draw nigh to Him, he will draw nigh to us. Keep a close relationship with the Lord. He will see you through any situation. Sometimes the Lord gives us a warning but, be not dismayed whatever betides you. God will take care of you. Death is inevitable, be strong! It is not easy to do but keep praying. I prayed and prayed to the Lord and He heard my cries. Sometimes the death of a love one seems like yesterday. Sometimes it seems like today but keep praying. "Pray on my child."

To everything there is a season, and a time to every purpose under the heaven: A time to be born, and a time to die...
Ecclesiastes 3:1-2a

It behooves us to *Pray without ceasing* (1 Thessalonians 5:17 KJV).

David, A Man After God's Own Heart
How did he deal with death?
David committed adultery with Uriah's wife, Bathsheba and had Uriah killed! A child was conceived and the Lord made Bathsheba's baby deathly sick according to II Samuel 12:15 TLB. David begged the Lord to spare the child, and went without food and lay all night before the Lord on the bare earth (he fasted). Then, on the seventh day, the baby died. David got up off the ground, washed himself, brushed his hair, changed his clothes, and went into the Tabernacle and worshiped the Lord. Then he returned to the palace and ate. V22-23, *And he said, While the child was yet alive, I fasted and wept: for I said, Who can tell whether God will be gracious to me, that the child may live? But now he is dead, wherefore should I fast? Can I bring him back again? I shall go to him, but he shall not return to me.* David said, so no need to fast after the child died.

Job, God's Servant
How did he deal with death?
Job lived in the land of Uz. He was a good man who feared God. His seven sons and three daughters were dining at the oldest brother's house, tragedy struck. A mighty wind swept in from the desert and engulfed the house so that the roof fell in on them and all were dead. Job was stricken with grief. He fell down upon the ground before God. *"I came naked from my mother's womb,"* he said, *"and I shall have nothing when I die. The Lord gave me everything I had, and they were his to take away. Blessed be the name of the Lord."*

Job lost everything he had, his animals, farmhands, sheep and camels. Satan went out from the presence of the Lord and struck Job with a terrible case of boils from head to foot. In all this Job said nothing wrong. At last Job spoke, and cursed the day of his birth. After all that happened; all the things his wife and friends said, the Lord gave him twice as much as before. God also gave him seven more sons and three more daughters. God blessed him... (from the book of Job).

Fear thou not; for I am with thee: Be not dismayed; for I am thy God. I will strengthen thee; yea, I will help thee; Yea, I will uphold thee with the right hand of my righteousness.

Isaiah 41:10 KJV

Isaiah wrote about the comfort of God's people in chapter 40. Today, I find comfort in God's Word.

Sacrifice (Family First)

In December 2013, I received a phone call late one evening. I was informed that another one of my younger sisters was ill. She presented to an emergency room in Dallas, Texas. It was alleged that one of the medical staff administered medication and she coded; was placed on a ventilator in Surgical Intensive Care. I resigned from my job and God gave me and my daughter safe passage to Dallas. Days later my sister who was ill said to me, "I had an outer-body experience in the ER. I heard Sister's voice." Remember, that sister transitioned in 2009. This sister continued, "I felt myself get up off the stretcher in ER and Sister said to me, "Gal what you doing, get back up there (on the stretcher)." It was not her time to transition. What an experience! I felt my legs tremble; I was suddenly surprised, <u>a moment of weakness.</u> I was told perhaps God dispatched an angel who appeared to my sister and spoke to her in a familiar voice. My sister who was hospitalized is still here by the grace of God although she has experienced many rough times. God has kept her; He is still keeping her. We praise God!

Another Unexpected Trip

I was hired to work on an <u>evening shift</u> as a Security Operator for Caddo Parish Schools. I had only been with the company a few weeks. During my training, my grandson was in Dallas, Texas. He presented to an emergency room with abdominal pain and was admitted for emergency surgery. His mother was by his side; she informed me of his sudden need for medical care. After I was called twice and told her son was asking for me, I could no longer focus on the task at hand. Again, I resigned from my job and hurried home to pack a bag. It was about 6:30pm. That time I was all alone and again I said, Lord it is me and You on the interstate late in the afternoon (a <u>second sacrifice</u> because of family). I made it safely. I recalled: Jesus commanded us to love one another! What sacrifices have you made for the sake of others?

CHAPTER 26
Nurses Support Group

Cheryl C. Wilson *is standing on the second row, 2nd from the left*

FOURTH SEASON OF LIFE: WINTER

During this season: Most senior citizens are retired and receiving an income based on the amount paid on their last job (retirement plan). Some are physically able to work a part-time job should they choose to do so. It's a time when retirees take vacations regularly, visit family and friends or sight-see. They have choices! Some baby-sit for their children, take a class for enjoyment and etcetera. This is well earned. During this season some face sickness and diseases; some retirees care for sick family members. Life happens and everything is in God's hands. He rules and super-rules.

Daily Routine
Routines vary from one patient to another.

- Some patients are transported to therapy sessions once or twice per week
- Most are on multiple medications which are to be administered daily
- Many patients need assistance to take care of their personal hygiene which includes shampooing their hair
- Some are not able to feed themselves; some patients have feeding tubes
- Many patients need assistance with insulin dosage/injections
- Vital signs must be monitored and a log need to be kept
- Bed linens must be changed as needs dictate
- It is important to assist patients who use walkers/wheelchairs
- Some patients are bed-ridden and have bedsores (pressure wounds)

All of the above duties must be performed by responsible and qualified care-giver (s). Patients require much attention and there is little or no room for errors, which may be life threatening. Some patients suffer from dementia and may or may not be able to communicate well at all times. They become confused and do not know the difference between day and night (Sundowners).

It is very important that caregivers be able to perform cardiopulmonary resuscitation (CPR). Sometimes a patient's life depends on it. All emergency phone numbers and names of some immediate family members must be kept in a precise location. In some cases, patients and their power-of-attorney have a signed form:

Do Not Resuscitate (DNR) on file. When caregivers perform their duties to the best of their abilities they should not fret. People in general will be critical, but remember you will reap good benefits in due time. "We find in life what we put into it." God is a JUST GOD!

Read/Pray Daily to Maintain Strength
When the schedule is relaxed it is very helpful to the patient and the care-giver to read the Word of God. It is good for the mental state of mind. The patient might have a special Bible verse he or she wants to hear. Prayer is always in order. It is also helpful to maintain a positive attitude.

Remember Jeremiah 17:14 *Heal me, O lord, and I shall be healed; save me and I shall be saved; for thou art my praise.*

The care-giver needs to be encouraged also. Remember and be assured: The battle is not yours, it's the Lord's. Cast all your cares upon him…

On a good day, some patients might be able to complete word search or puzzles to relax the mind. Some are able to watch television, listen to spiritual singing or gospel messages via radio. All of these can be very helpful or inspiring. It all depends on what the patient is capable of doing.

When the Patient Becomes Depressed

It is not uncommon for patients to become depressed. They become weak, weary, worn and tired. Some have no desire to continue living. Many long to transition to the other side where there is no more pain nor sorrow. Sometimes they refuse to accept the prepared meal. At this time, the physician might suggest that the family be informed: Patient needs to be tube fed (nutrition administered via the gastrointestinal tract). In most cases, one who has power of attorney will agree with the physician's assessment of the patient's condition.

Some patients might begin to reflect on how long they worked for the Lord; how faithful they have been. At such time, one might recall the prayer of Hezekiah. He turned his face to the wall and prayed unto the Lord, saying, I beseech thee, O Lord, remember how I have walked before thee in truth and with a perfect heart, and have done that which is good in thy sight. <u>The Lord heard his prayer and added fifteen years to Hezekiah's life.</u> Jesus Christ is the source of all mercies and one who comforts and strengthens us when hardships and trials prevail.

The Psalmist says: *Be of good courage, and he shall strengthen your heart, all ye that hope in the Lord* (Psalm 31:24).

Hospice Care

Sometimes patients are released from the hospital to be cared for in convalescent/nursing homes. Some are placed in Grace Homes. Many choose to return to their residence. They prefer to spend their last days in their own home. At this time, the physician has previously informed the patient and family that nothing else can be done medically (it's out of their hands). Hospice takes over to give palliative care (pain management or comfort-care). Many patients live years beyond the time-line which the physician has stated. Only God has the final say.

CHAPTER 27
Perilous Times
God is Speaking

CORONAVIRUS DISEASE

<u>The year 2020</u> brought an illness (Covid-19) which no one could have imagined, not in their wildest dreams. Physicians and scientists alike were appalled. This virus does not discriminate. Many young people and the elderly have been stricken and many have succumbed to Covid-19. It has claimed over 3.3 million lives. Although a vaccine has been approved by the FDA (Food and Drug Administration), many refuse to be vaccinated. Because some were stubborn and listened to false or incorrect advice, their lives have been cut short. Their bodies are now resting in a grave somewhere. Their families are hurting and mourning the loss all because those persons would not hear nor be receptive to sound advice. They were selfish and had no concern for themselves nor for their families. Scores of healthcare workers and people of numerous occupations have risked their lives to save others. Many become ill and put healthcare workers and others at risk. Some nurses and physicians honored their positions, did their jobs and lost their lives. However, we are grateful to God for the many citizens who made an informed decision to be vaccinated. We are now aware of a booster shot especially for those who have severe

underlying medical conditions. We have been informed that Covid-19 has variants also.

Despite all that has happened and continue to happen many are still hard-hearted, disrespectful, hateful and overlook the poor. Not only were there lives lost from Covid-19, but other forms of disaster reck havoc in the world as well. God is still in control and He has gotten the attention of the universe. He is saying: **I am that I am!** He is still saying to us what He said to Moses.

There were plagues in the Bible Days and people were afraid then just as they are today. They entered their homes and shut the doors. Covid-19 has caused many to make life-style changes.

The year 2021...

A Sign of the Times: A perceived attack of the devil; war was waged by one who is believed to be the Antichrist. Who is he?

*Little children, it is the last time: and as ye have heard that antichrist shall come, even now are there **many antichrist**; whereby we know that it is the last time* (I John 2:18 KJV). **Note:** John viewed the whole period beginning with Christ's first coming as the last days. Never in my life-time have I seen so much hatred, and unrest (agitation in a group of people, public demonstrations). This is spiritual warfare (fighting against the work of evil forces).

America Must Awake to "Righteousness"
Unusual Occurrences Wreak Havoc

Take Heed...News Reports:
Other Disasters In 2021

Wildfires raged and destroyed acres of land on the West Coast. Many lost not only their life-time possessions, but some lost their precious lives. Some of the wealthiest people in America were affected. There was no discrimination. Professional Firefighters tried unsuccessfully to extinguish the fires; some lost their lives in the line of duty.

Storms/Tornados

The East Coast was hit hard by a historic storm, Ida which killed several dozen residents. Apparently, Ida was like no other in years of history. She brought high levels of rain which caused flooding. Some residents were drowned and swept away. We can only imagine the pain which survivors feel. The loss of possessions is one thing, but the loss of lives is Hugh! We cannot put a price on human lives.

In the South

Hurricane Ida left much destruction in Southern Louisiana. Much rain left high levels of flooding in a number of cities and towns. Most were left with no power which posed another problem for the residents. Many fled the city to find shelter. The intense hurricane caused a number of deaths which were also reported.

Haiti Earthquake

Early one morning in August, the news broke: An earthquake hit the Caribbean nation of Haiti. Buildings were destroyed, thousands of people were injured and many did not survive. Many or most residents were believed to live in poverty and we can only imagine the devastation. I understand that many fled the country in search of a better life. They lost what little they had in Haiti. Upon coming to America, I noticed the news: Men were on horses whipping them as though they were not even humans. That's unacceptable; God will deal with all who are responsible for such disturbing behavior. He will also deal with whomever was in a position to put a stop to the inhumane behavior. We reap what we sow! God's eye is in every place.

In spite of all that is happening America is still blessed. Therefore, we should lift our hands in praise to our God. He is our Protector, our Guide; His mercies are new every morning. Every day is a day of thanksgiving. O' give thanks unto the Lord and bless His name. **To the unsaved**: Remember, today is the day of salvation.

Today: Hardships

These are perilous times which God's word said would come. Many have turned a deaf ear and will not hear no one. Man has gone his own way, but there is a way that seems right unto man but the end thereof are the ways of death. Sin and every evil act has been, and is being committed. Many people in general have no respect for God nor for the lives of each other.

God sent a messenger to Israel because of the sins of the people and the conduct of the priests. This is a warning: Get our houses in order! Our forefathers warned: Get right Church! God has called us out of darkness into His marvelous light. We cannot walk in tune with the drumbeat of the world. Neither can we serve two masters, either we will love one and hate the other. God's eye is in every place; he beholds the evil and the good. He's omnipresent and there is a day of reckoning! In that great day, will you be able to stand?

Have We Forgotten Sodom and Gomorrah?

Again, God brought judgment upon the people.

The men of Sodom were wicked and sinners before the Lord exceedingly. And the cry of Sodom and Gomorrah was great and their sin was very grievous according to the book of Genesis.

Abraham, Father of the faithful asked a question of the Lord, *"Wilt thou also destroy the righteous with the wicked?"* And God said, *"Then, for the sake of ten, I won't destroy it* (the city*)."* That evening two angels came to the entrance of the city of Sodom. Lot invited them to come to his home as guests. After the meal, the men of the city, Sodomites young and old from all over the city surrounded the house and shouted to Lot, "Bring out those men to us so we can rape them." Lot stepped outside the door to talk to them. *"Please, fellows," he begged, "don't do such a wicked thing. Look I have two virgin daughters, and I'll surrender them to you to do as you wish. But leave these men alone, for they are under my protection."*

At dawn the next morning the angels became urgent. *"Hurry," they said to Lot, "take your wife and your two daughters who are here and get out while you can, or you will be caught in the destruction of the city." "Flee for your lives,"* the angels told him. *"And don't look back."* The Lord rained down fire and flaming tar from heaven upon Sodom and Gomorrah and utterly destroyed them along with the other cities and villages of the plain, **eliminating all life, people, plants, and animals alike**. But Lot's wife looked back as she was following along behind him, and became a pillar of salt.

Today, we call to remembrance what happened prior to **the flood**. The people had become wicked and they broke God's heart. Therefore, God said he was sorry he had made man and he **destroyed them with a flood**. Noah and his family were spared. We are aware of the power of God and we MUST awake to righteousness and seek the Lord with our whole heart! God is speaking!

Glorious, Victorious Future For Prepared People

CHAPTER 28
When All is Well

CONFESSION OF SINS TO GOD

One acknowledges or confesses that he/she has sinned.
It is written, every tongue shall confess to God

Romans 14:11

For if you tell others with your own mouth that Jesus Christ is your Lord, and believe in your own heart that God has raised him (Jesus) from the dead, you will be saved. For it is by believing in his heart that a man becomes right with God; and with his mouth he tells others of his faith, confirming his salvation.

Romans 10:9-10

Baptism
Mark 16:16a (KJV):
He that believeth and is baptized shall be saved; ...

Peter clearly stated to everyone in Israel that God has made Jesus who was crucified to be Lord, the Messiah. They were moved deeply and they said to him and to the other apostles, "Brothers, what should we do?"

And Peter replied, *"Each one of you must turn from sin, return to God, and be baptized in the name of **Jesus Christ** for the forgiveness of your sins; then you also shall receive this gift, the Holy Spirit."*
Acts 2: 38 TLB

Water baptism is an initiatory, symbolic ordinance. It is an <u>outward</u> manifestation of an <u>inward work.</u> The believer is raised in newness of life. He identifies with the death, burial and resurrection of Jesus Christ.

Jesus said to his disciples, "I have been given all authority in heaven and earth. Therefore, go and make disciples in all the nations, baptizing them into the <u>name of the Father and of the Son and of the Holy Spirit."</u>
Matthew28: 18-19 TLB

One of the thieves on the cross <u>express doubt</u> that Jesus is the Son of God. He said, *"<u>If thou be Christ, save thyself and us.</u>"* The other thief acknowledged his wrong and recognized Christ, who is the Savior; <u>Light of the world</u>. He knew that was his last chance to be transformed from **darkness to light**; he did so just in the nick of time.

And he said unto Jesus, *"Lord, remember me when thou comest into thy kingdom."* And Jesus said unto him, *Verily I say unto thee, To day shalt thou be with me in <u>Paradise.</u>*
Luke 23:42-43

Note: but, beloved, be not ignorant of this one thing, that one day is with the Lord as a thousand years, and a thousand years as one day (2 Peter 3:8).

Scripture did not state the thief was baptized. <u>In other words</u>, should one confess Christ but does not get baptized, <u>he is still saved.</u>

Church Membership
Unite with a local church and study God's word that you may grow thereby. Fellowship with other born-again baptized believers and do not neglect to assemble with the church (God's people). If one is unable to make it to the house of pray, he can praise and worship God anywhere. God is omnipresent. Always praise and worship God, pray

daily and ask God for guidance. Use your gift (s) for the Lord.

Some of us have multiple talents, but don't expect to sing like another. Just be yourself. Don't expect to teach like another. His style may not fit your ability. When you pray, be yourself and keep in mind, you are talking to God. Don't pray selfishly, remember others and ask God to intervene in their lives as well. By all means, please pray for those who have not accepted Jesus as their Lord and Savior.

Note: Some prayers should be prayed in private. We must talk with Jesus before we do whatever job we are called upon to perform.

It is every born-again-believer's duty to reach out to those who have not accepted Jesus as their Lord and Savior. God created us for good works and for His glory. We must study God's word and rely on the Holy Spirit to bring to our remembrance what we have studied. We must also ask God to condition the hearts of those whom we may contact: Take out the stony hearts and give them hearts of flesh. Despite danger which may be lurking in any area, remember God said, *"I am with you always, even to the end of the world."* Let each of us strive to reach at least one as often as we have opportunity. We will not win everyone, but remember Christ came unto his own and his own received Him not. Do not be discouraged, but continue to plant the seed. The seed is the Word of God.

I planted the seed, Apollos watered it, but God gave the increase.
I Cor. 3:6-7

When we plant the seed perhaps someone else will provide additional teaching.

When the unbeliever is receptive to the Word of God; confesses his belief in Jesus, it means God gave the increase. It was not man, but the Lord God Almighty!

Not all will be receptive to the Word of God. Today is the day of salvation...

We do not know what our lives will be like tomorrow. *For you (we) are just a vapor that appears for a little while, and then vanishes away* (James 4:14).

Final Decisions (Burial)

Some have pre-arrangements in place. Others may have written instructions for a close or trusted family member to carry-out when necessary. It is important to also have a <u>trusted, knowledgeable non-family person to help in such times</u>. That person should be able to think more clearly. In any case, this plan should relieve the family from unnecessary stress. Let's be realistic: We make preparation to live; we must also make preparation to die.

THE FIFTH SEASON: ON THE OTHER SIDE OF THROUGH

After soul and body separates, after the days of our lives are cut off, we fly away!

From Earth to Glory

Cleveland Clarkson
Rashonda J. Powell
Mamie W. George
Henry Lee Anderson
Joyce Franklin-Spates
Willie Mae Wardell-Carter
Willie Wardell, Jr.

GLORY ROAD
"None can walk up there but the pure in heart"

Ministers / Pastors: The Church needs to hear this from the pulpits! After death, when the **Christian** is no longer living in his earthly house (tent), he is present with the Lord. The **unsaved** goes immediately to a place called Hades.

I am reminded: Some say they celebrate the birthdays of their love ones who have gone on. They say, "Happy Heavenly Birthday" on that special day. Actually, when soul and body separates, no one ages as they did while in the flesh. The Spirit, that part of man which is not physical goes to be with the Lord. Who can communicate with Spirits? The body returns to the dust from whence it came. So, our love ones <u>cease to grow old</u>; birthdays mean, we get older each year. Some don't seem to look at it that way. Many have said they return to the gravesites of their love ones and talk to them. **We must face reality! However, I understand remembering our loved ones. I never forget my beloved mother.**

> *But the dead know nothing, they don't even have their memories.*
> Ecclesiastes 9: 5 TLB

Hear this:
James C. Moore pinned a beautiful song: *Where we will **never grow old**. It's a beautiful home of the soul; built by Jesus on high.* Presently, we live in (the body) tents which are temporary dwelling places.
Apostle Paul pinned:
> *For we know that if our earthly house of this tabernacle were dissolved, we have a building of God, a house not made with hand, eternal in the heavens.*

"In my Father's house are many mansions."
That's the house which Mr. Moore referenced. It's on a far-away strand. We might say the third heaven (wherever The Lord is).
That is where the <u>Christians</u> will be until the resurrection. Christ will

bring them with him and they will connect with new bodies and the dead **in Christ** will rise first. They will not go to heaven until after the judgement.

I call to remembrance also:
By faith Enoch was translated that he should not see death; and was not found, because God had translated him: for before his translation he had this testimony, that he pleased God.
Hebrews 11:5 KJV

Enoch was the son of Cain and the father of Methuselah whose life span was 969 years, the longest-lived human.

Relevant Information

The **breath** symbolizes life. When man has breath in his body, he is a <u>living **soul**.</u> Adam was not a <u>living soul</u> until God breathed into his nostrils the breath of life (from Genesis 2:7).

Soul: Your inner-life in relation to your experiences such as your mind, heart, will and imagination. Your thoughts, desires, passions and dreams are included.

<u>Soul and body separate at death</u>. The spirit is the part of man that is not physical. The **spirit** returns to God who gave it (from Ecclesiastes 12:7).

Spirit: Speaks of inner-life in relation to God such as: Your faith, hope, love, character and perseverance.

Precious in the sight of the Lord is the death of his saints.
Psalm 116:15

Apostle Paul penned in his Second Epistle to the Corinthians:
We (**Christians**) *are confident, I say, and willing rather to be absent from the body, and present with the Lord* (II Cor. 5:8 KJV).

Another version of the scripture:

And we are not afraid, but are quite content to die, for then we will be at home with the Lord (II Cor. 5:8 TLB).

The body: *The dust returns to the earth as it was* (Ecclesiastes 12:7) We know that on the day of Resurrection the **soul** will be returned to a new body and people will stand before God for judgement. Those who have believed him (Christians) will be rewarded with Heaven (resurrection of the just).

When Change has Come
So, when this corruptible shall have put on incorruption, and this mortal shall have put on immortality, then shall be brought to pass the saying that is written, Death is swallowed up in victory (I Cor. 16:54 KJV).

There will be two Resurrections:
    1. The Just/The Righteous
    2. The Unjust/Unrighteous

The dead in Christ shall rise first then we which are alive shall be caught up together with them <u>in the clouds,</u> to meet the Lord <u>in the air;</u> and so, shall we ever be with the Lord. Amen!

Annie Clarkson-Turner, Daughter of Willie Clarkson
July 19, 1922—March 16, 1965

Mother was the daughter of Willie and Dollie Salters-Clarkson. She accepted Jesus as her Lord and Savior and served faithfully as an Usher at Mount Olive Baptist Church, Grand Bayou, LA (Highway1). At the time of her departure, she was only 42 years old. Our hearts were broken, but we know that she was prepared to make the transition. I will see her in the rapture!!!

She was known as a gifted fashion designer (without the use of a pattern). She was also a beautician by trade.

...for now, they shall rest from all their toils and trials; for their good deeds follow them to heaven (Revelation 14:13b TLB)

Most bodies are buried in graves and I recall Job said, *"And though after my skin worms destroy this body, yet in my flesh shall I see God"* (Job 19: 26 KJV).

Scripture tells us Job was a perfect and upright man. He is with the Lord and Christ will bring him with Him when He comes back. Job will connect with a **new body** and he will be raised an immortal soul (he will live forever with the Lord). No one can live forever without accepting Jesus Christ as Lord and Savior.

Some choose to have their bodies cremated and their ashes placed in an Urn or sprinkled at sea. Some may choose to have their Urn placed at the foot of a love one's grave. Make no mistake. The river waters will still be flowing, waves will be dashing. The sea, ocean and the like will give up the dead that is in them. There will be no hiding place. God's eye is in every place; no matter how wide, long or deep the burial place. The mountains will be brought low; everything will be and is in God's view. Amen!

Abington, LA: Cemetery was previously maintained by family members before it was demolished/ruined or destroyed by the land owner. It was located directly behind New Star Missionary Baptist Church.

In November 2022, I visited the site / area where my mother, her parents and other relatives and neighbors are buried. I was astonished to say the least. I was unable to identify the cemetery because the land owner had demolished the church building, possibly destroyed the headstones (they could not be seen). It was disheartening to observe only an overgrown area. The little shot-gun houses which once lined the country road had been demolished also. A number of thoughts crossed my mind, but I know when Jesus returns, all those who died in Christ will get up. They will rise from the dead. It will not matter

how man disrupted or disturbed the burial ground.
Some people have no <u>respect for the living and they definitely have no concern for the dead. In New Jerusalem, there will be nothing but</u> **PEACE!**

On the Island of Patmos:

John, the Revelator had a **vision** and he penned, *And he **(God)** shewed me a pure river of water of life, clear as crystal, proceeding out of the throne of God and the Lamb. In the midst of the street of it, and on either side of the river, **was there the tree of life,** which bare twelve manner of fruits, and yielded her fruit every month: and the leaves of the tree were for the healing of the nations.*

"Healing of the Nations," There will be no sickness, there will be perpetual blessings of the new heaven and earth. The tree of life will perpetually sustain the physical life of humanity.

Now: we know there will be no sickness there because there will be no evil, nor sin. This is so great, it grabbed my attention; arrested my little thoughts because it must be a glorious sight (the Holy City, the New Jerusalem). It's beyond my imagination! I want to see Jesus; I shall behold his face!

Don't you want to go there? Prepare today! There will be nothing but peace.

CHAPTER 29
Rapture/Judgement

The Rapture
Two men will be working together in the fields, and one will be taken, the other left. Two women will be going about their household tasks; one will be taken, the other left. So, be prepared, for you don't know what day your Lord is coming.

Matthew 24:40-42 TLB

Accept Christ today, tomorrow may be too late! You don't want to be left behind!

Therefore, prepare to meet King Jesus! He is on his way back for the Church, His bride. Eyes have not seen nor ears heard what the Lord has in store for those who love Him.

Tribulation Period

Tribulation means a cause of great trouble or suffering. It will take place immediately following the Rapture. The tribulation period will last seven years. There will be some with earthly bodies who lived through the tribulation period. And God will allow people to accept Jesus or reject Him.

The Devil is Bound

The Millennial Reign
During this time, Satan will NOT have influence over the inhabitants of the earth.

There will be one thousand years of peace and harmony.

John wrote,
...I saw an angel come down from heaven with the key to the bottomless pit and a heavy chain in his hand. He seized the Dragon---that old Serpent, the devil, Satan--and bound him in chains for 1,000 years, and threw him into the bottomless pit, which he then shut and locked, so that he could not fool the nations any more until the thousand years were finished.

John continued,
And I saw the souls of those who had been beheaded for their testimony about Jesus, for proclaiming the word of God, and who had not worshiped the Creature or his statue... They had come to life again (glorified bodies) and now they reigned with Christ for a thousand years. The Church will be included. *The rest of the dead did not come back to life until the thousand years had ended. This is the First Resurrection.*

"Peace in the Valley"

Inanimate group displaying peace and harmony

The wolf also shall dwell with the lamb, and the leopard shall lie down with the kid, and the calf and the young lion and the fatling together, and a child shall lead them.

Isaiah 11:6 KJV

Paradise will be restored; there will be peace, no more sickness or pain. There will be no more sorrow. That's a perfect day! What a day of rejoicing that will be!

The second coming of Jesus

...and they shall see the Son of man coming in the clouds of heaven with power and great glory (Matt. 24:30).

Millennium means a thousand years. During the Millennial the Savior will reign personally on the earth. The government will be under the administration of the Savior and His righteous Saints. The earth will be renewed, transfigured and receive its paradisiacal glory (Isaiah 65:17). He will be called: Wonderful Counselor, Mighty God, Everlasting Father, and Prince of Peace. In that day, the Lord will give his people rest from sorrow and fear from **slavery and chains.** God's people will express their gratitude for deliverance from **darkness to light**. The Church will be unified and Christ will reign forever and ever.

For behold I create new heavens and a new earth: And the former shall not be remembered, nor come into mind (KJV). *Be glad; rejoice forever in my creation. Look! I will recreate Jerusalem as a place of happiness, and her people shall be a joy! And I* will *rejoice in Jerusalem, and in my people, and the voice of weeping and crying shall not be heard there any more* (Isaiah 65:18-19 AMP). The violence of both man and beast will cease during the millennium.

Paradise will be restored; there will be peace, no more sickness or pain. There will be no more sorrow.

The Loosing of Satan

When the thousand years end, Satan will be let out of his prison. He will go out to deceive the nations which are in the four quarters of the earth.

And the devil that deceived them was cast into the lake of fire and brimstone, where the beast and the false prophet are, and shall be tormented day and night for ever and ever (Revelation 20:10 KJV).

The Great White Throne Judgement

John the Revelator pinned:
And I saw the dead, small and great, stand before God; and the books were opened: and another book was opened, which is the book of life: and the dead were judged out of those things which were written in the books, according to their works. And the sea gave up the dead which were in it; <u>and death and hell</u> delivered up the dead which were in them: and they were judged every man according to their works. And <u>death and hell</u> were cast into the lake of fire. This is the second death

Rev. 20:12-14 KJV

Some have said, "I wouldn't mind dying, if dying was all." So, no, dying is not all. After death comes the judgement. All will spend eternity in either heaven or hell. Everyone will be judged according to his works. Make no mistake! John penned: *But the cowardly, the unbelieving, the vile, the murderers, the sexually immoral, those who practice magic arts, the idolaters and all liars—they will be consigned to the fiery lake of burning sulfur. This is the second death. I will give unto every one of you according to your works.*

Revelation 2:23b KJV

Judgement

And he shall set the sheep on his right hand, but the goats on the left. Then shall the King say unto them on his right hand, Come, ye blessed of my Father, inherit the kingdom prepared for you from the Foundation of the world:

Matthew 25:33-34 KJV

Those who successfully endure temptation will receive a <u>crown of life</u>. Faithful preachers and teachers will receive a <u>crown of glory</u>. After the judgement of the saints, the marriage supper consummates the marriage of Jesus and His bride (the church). I believe there will be a <u>great celebration</u>. The Heavenly Choir (Angelic Voices) will sing praises unto our God. Glory! Glory! Hallelujah!

Announcement:

Now is the time to audition, all sopranos, altos, tenors, bass, and contraltos.
The call is for: <u>Who-so-ever will!</u>

Your long white robe will fit you well and your shoes will be the perfect size. You will not be denied. Remember God has no respect of persons. I believe among the group will be some of the greatest known gospel singers: Mahalia Jackson who was known to belt-out, "Soon I will be done with the Trouble of the World; How I Got Over." Aretha Franklin left many in awe after hearing "Amazing Grace." They will lift their voices in praise unto Our God (the Great Celebration).

To get a glimpse and imagine the glorious time, watch the "Reunion Choir" of Fellowship Missionary Baptist Church, Rev. Clay Evans (youtube.com)

Song: Leaning on the everlasting arms
O' what a time when we all get together; when we see Jesus!!!Hallelujah!!!

Souls A' fire: A beautiful religious group from Oral Roberts University visited Paradise Baptist Church, 1706 Hollywood Avenue in Shreveport, LA in the late seventies.
Make a joyful noise unto the Lord, all the earth: make a loud noise, and rejoice, and sing praise.

Psalm 98:4 KJV

John the Revelator wrote:
144,000 of all the tribes of the children of Israel were sealed in their foreheads.

***After this I beheld, and lo, a great multitude, which no man could number, <u>of all nations, and kindreds, and people, and tongues,</u> stood before the throne, and before the Lamb, clothed with white robes, and palms in their hands.* Victory!**

"Victory is mine" Amen! Let the church say Amen!

A Beautiful; Safe Place to Dwell Forever
There will be no robbers, thieves, and no other acts of violence. The

streets are paved with pure gold. There are twelve pearly gates (each gate is a pearl) to the city, and at the gates twelve angels, and names written thereon, which are the names of the twelve tribes of the children of Israel. And no one needs a code to enter. The gates will automatically swing open and you can walk on in!!! Jesus will welcome you home!!! Home at last! You will be free!!!

John, the Revelator wrote:
And the city had no need of the sun, neither of the moon, to shine in it: for the glory of God did lighten it, and the Lamb is the light thereof.

He continued to write:
And the gates of it shall not be shut at all by day; for there shall be no night there.

Can you picture the city? Don't you want to go there? <u>SIGN-UP TODAY</u>! Get on board the Glory Train.

CHAPTER 30
Joint Heirs With Christ

*The Spirit Himself testifies together with our own spirit, assuring us that we are children of <u>God</u>. And if we are His children, then <u>**we are His heirs**</u> also: heirs of God and fellow heirs with Christ sharing His inheritance with Him; only we must share His suffering if we are to share His glory.*

Romans 8: 16-17 TAB

Bonnie Rose Hall and Lamar Anthony Hall, Son
Mrs. Bonnnie Rose Hall was a former public-school teacher. She taught in Red River and Caddo Parishes before her death.
Remembering Lamar (Former Classmate)

Lamar attended **Springville High School in Coushatta, LA**. He graduated in 1963 from Notre Dame High School in Shreveport, LA. He continued his education and graduated from Xavier University of Louisiana in 1967 and received his medical degree. He also graduated from the University of Michigan Medical School in Ann Harbor, Michigan in 1976. Lamar returned to Shreveport to complete his internship; his next plan was to enter into private practice in Evansville, Indiana. According to his mom, Dr. Hall served as medical director of the Memorial Healthcare Center; always provided samples and services without bias. He will be remembered as a compassionate physician who served people regardless of ethnicity, income level, or ability to pay. Dr. Lamar Anthony Hall, Sr. was born on January 3, 1947. He entered into eternal rest on April 2, 2012 at his residence in Evansville, Indiana. He was a native of Shreveport, LA. He now lives in the hearts of those whom he touched.

Other Joint Heirs with Christ

Joyce C. Spates

Charlene Y. Cobbs

Bessie L. Turner

Rosetta C. Jackson

Rev. Charles Washington

Rev. Murphy Giles

Rosie L. Giles

Rev. Charlie Henry

Willie Wardell, Jr.

Willie M. Wardell - Carter

John Jiles

Larry Morris

Deborah Brown

Napoleon Jones, Jr.

Aunt Clemetine Turner

Jim Turner

Mattie M. Turner

These have come out of great tribulation, washed their robes, and made them white in the blood of the Lamb (Jesus Christ). Amen! They prepared for a glorious future with Jesus Christ, Our Lord and Savior. Praise God!

Mattie P. Wilson, LTA, CPT, (IAPS)
Retired Phlebotomy Supervisor

Mattie, a compassionate leader with strong interpersonal skills rendered professional service at Louisiana State University Health Sciences Center, WK Pierremont, Quest Diagnostics, Cigna and several other Centers. She also served her parish as Commissioner for Elections and Census Enumerator in 2010

I performed many therapeutic phlebotomy procedures for patients who presented to the donor room. The procedure reduces blood volume, viscosity and exogenous iron that results in such disease as polycythemia and hemosiderosis. Other duties included phlebotomy procedures, blood gases, blood cultures, tuberculosis skin test, glucose tolerance testing, specimen processing, in-services. The LDX machine was utilized, capillary sticks were performed. Other duties were: data entry, check patient's vital signs, customer service and much more including phlebotomy supervisory duties.

To God be the Glory!

www.ingramcontent.com/pod-product-compliance
Lightning Source LLC
LaVergne TN
LVHW021233080526
838199LV00088B/4338